CENTER FOR TEACHING EFFECTIVENESS
111 Pearson Hall
University of Delaware
Newark, DE 19716-1106

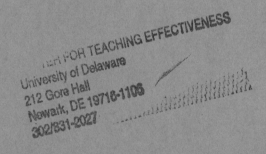

Successful
Training Strategies

CENTER FOR TEACHING EFFECTIVENESS
111 Pearson Hall
University of Delaware
Newark, DE 19716-1106

*Jill Casner-Lotto
and Associates*

Preface by Jerome M. Rosow

Successful Training Strategies

Twenty-Six Innovative
Corporate Models

A Work in America Institute Publication

 Jossey-Bass Publishers
San Francisco • London • 1988

SUCCESSFUL TRAINING STRATEGIES
Twenty-Six Innovative Corporate Models
by Jill Casner-Lotto and Associates

Library of Congress Cataloging-in-Publication Data

Casner-Lotto, Jill.
    Successful training strategies.

    (The Jossey-Bass management series)
    "A Work in America Institute publication."
    Includes bibliographies and index.
    1. Employees, Training of. 2. Labor Supply—
Effect of technological innovations on. I. Title.
II. Series.
HF5549.5.T7C2987   1988   658.3'1243   88-42781
ISBN 1-55542-101-6 (alk. paper)

Manufactured in the United States of America

The paper in this book meets the guidelines for
permanence and durability of the Committee on
Production Guidelines for Book Longevity of the
Council on Library Resources.

JACKET DESIGN BY WILLI BAUM

FIRST EDITION

Code 8831

The Jossey-Bass Management Series

Published in association with
Work in America Institute

Contents

Preface

New technology and the new processes that accompany it are being felt throughout the American economy, requiring vast changes in every aspect of enterprise. The ability to make these changes, however, depends upon an organization's proficiency in training employees to respond effectively to the new and evolving demands of the workplace.

The creative application of new technology depends on the understanding, skills, and knowledge of the user. In the final analysis, the users are the employees and the managers. Their ability to achieve creative applications of the new technology translates directly into improved quality, lower costs, faster return on investment, higher productivity, and the long-term growth and survival of the organizations they work for. The best way of ensuring these results is through a policy of training that provides continuous learning for all employees, throughout the organization.

The purpose of this volume is to bring the state of the art in training and on-the-job learning to public attention and to disseminate this knowledge to a wide audience of corporate and union decision makers. It contains detailed descriptions of how leading-edge companies in the United States have reshaped their training strategies to respond to worldwide competitive forces and to rapidly changing technology and organizational systems. The twenty-six case studies are the product of a three-year research program (1985 to 1987) conducted by Work in America Institute, with the assistance of a National Advisory

Committee of twenty-three prominent Americans, representing labor, management, academia, and the field of human resource development and training. Valuable insights and leads were provided by the committee, and its discussions of research papers commissioned by the Institute led to many of the study's conclusions.

This book is a companion to the policy report entitled *Training—The Competitive Edge: Introducing New Technology into the Workplace* (Jossey-Bass, 1988) and, as such, provides in-depth accounts of the practical experiences on which many of the report's findings and recommendations are based. Ideally, the two books should be used together as a guide to the formulation of corporate training policies and programs.

Innovative programs and useful approaches in both the private and public sectors are offered primarily to employers and unions involved in the design of corporate training strategies. Training for new technology, as discussed here, will be of special concern to various individuals in the workplace: managers, technical specialists, employees, training professionals and consultants, equipment manufacturers and vendors—anyone directly involved in the planning, implementation, and use of new technology.

In its examination of the problems faced by employers and unions when introducing new technology, the Institute has singled out issues it believes to be the most critical—and often the most troublesome. The cases are organized into five different parts, each of which focuses on a specific issue: coordinating training and corporate strategies, continuous learning and employee involvement as a response to change, encouraging manufacturer-user cooperation, the cost-effective design and delivery of training, and linking continuous learning and employment security practices.

Overview of the Contents

The book begins with an introduction, which describes the topic and highlights the cases treated in each chapter. Part One examines how the alignment of training strategy with corporate goals has resulted in new approaches to the budgeting, implementation, and evaluation of training. In addition, the mechanisms that support the linkage between corporate strategies and training strategies are described. The case studies analyze experiences at Travelers Corporation, New England Telephone, Motorola, Corning Glass Works, American Transtech, and Gilroy Foods, Inc.

Part Two demonstrates how a new mode of "continuous learning" is emerging in some leading-edge companies and how continuous-learning strategies have equipped these organizations to cope with change. Companies described in the cases include General Electric's Aerospace Electronic Systems Department; General Foods; the S. B. Thomas English muffin plant in Schaumburg, Illinois; and Pacific Bell/Communications Workers of America.

Part Three highlights companies that have made significant gains in the application of new technological systems through imaginative manufacturer-user partnerships—a rarity in today's corporate environment. Firms described in the cases include Control Data Corporation; General Motors' plant in Linden, New Jersey; Goodyear Tire and Rubber; Ford Motor Company's plant in Sharonville, Ohio; Caterpillar Inc.; and Miller Brewing Company.

In Part Four several innovative approaches that have improved the cost-effectiveness of training are examined. Organizations described in the case studies, which focus on design and delivery systems, include IBM; Manpower, Inc.; Travenol Laboratories, Inc.; General Motors' Automotive Service Educational Program; and the National Technological University.

The final section, Part Five, demonstrates how continuous learning practices combined with employment security enhance the quality of learning throughout the organization and strengthen the firm's competitiveness. Corporations whose policies illustrate the continuous learning–employment security connection include Xerox; General Motors' Packard Electric Division; General Electric's Fort Wayne, Indiana, facility; Pacific Northwest Bell; and Hewlett-Packard.

More and more companies are addressing the problems

of training for new technology. Relatively few, however, have devised solutions. The practices and programs described here are among the most progressive and innovative training approaches and have come to the Institute's attention only after a long and persistent search. It is our hope that the progress and successes of the companies that have agreed to share their hard-won achievements will both encourage and challenge the readers of this book to undertake similar efforts. We are proud to place this research in the public domain for broad imitation and application and to serve as a basis for further innovation.

Acknowledgments

This study was made possible by the vision, financial support, and continuing confidence provided by the U.S. Postal Service. The Institute also thanks the General Electric Foundation, whose generous grant assisted us in preparing and disseminating this volume.

Work in America Institute wishes to express its thanks and appreciation to the countless individuals—both company and union representatives and educators—who provided extensive information in interviews and written materials. Their assistance and cooperation proved invaluable in the preparation of these case reports. We wish also to thank the authors of the various cases, including both training consultants and professional business writers, who interviewed the principals in various programs and conducted site visits of plants and offices in pursuit of accurate information.

Jill Casner-Lotto, research editor for policy studies and editor of this book, tracked down and evaluated the cases presented here, recruited writers, and directed the writing of the cases. She has herself researched and written many of the cases in the book as well as acted as its editor. Robert Zager, vice-president for policy studies, was responsible for the overall direction of the three-year policy study of which this book is an integral part, and he worked closely with the editor in coordinating the policy report with the casebook. The Institute is proud of their tireless efforts in bringing these significant case studies to the attention of the American public and thanks them for their valuable contributions. The Institute also wishes to thank the following members of the staff, without whose editorial and production efforts the five interim reports and the final policy report and casebook could never have materialized: Frances T. Harte, communications and marketing director; Carol Nardi, executive assistant to the president; and Beatrice Walfish, former editorial director. Virginia Lentini, assistant to the vice-president for policy studies, and the library staff were also helpful in bringing this project to fruition.

Scarsdale, New York Jerome M. Rosow
August 1988 President
  Work in America Institute

The Authors

Jill Casner-Lotto is research editor for policy studies at Work in America Institute, where she manages the research, on-site investigations, and writing of case reports in connection with the Institute's national policy studies. Formerly an editor of the Institute's monthly newsletter, *Work in America* (formerly *World of Work Report*), she has written extensively for Institute publications and others on such topics as managing new technology, productivity innovations, job training, labor-management cooperation, and other human resource issues.

Casner-Lotto received her B.A. degree from Johns Hopkins University and her M.A. degree from the Medill School of Journalism at Northwestern University. She served as a news and feature writer for Cornell University and also produced public affairs films. At St. John's University she coordinated the research and production of nationally televised educational programs. She also worked as a documentary producer for public television in Phoenix, Arizona.

Claudia Feurey is vice-president and director of information for the Committee for Economic Development, a private, nonprofit research organization of top business leaders, based in New York City.

Jocelyn F. Gutchess is currently an economic analyst and employment and training consultant, based in Washington, D.C., who writes frequently on labor relations and the management of human resources. She has served as consultant with the Organisation for Economic Cooperation and Development (OECD) in Paris and has held various positions with the U.S. Department of Labor.

Sandra Kessler Hamburg is deputy director of information for the Committee for Economic Development.

Kathleen C. Hemmens is a New York–based free-lance writer and consultant specializing in social policy and employment and training issues. She has served as executive assistant to the Under Secretary of Labor and as senior associate for the National Institute for Work and Learning in Washington, D.C.

John V. Hickey is editor of *Work in America,* a monthly publication of Work in America Institute, which specializes in such topics as quality of working life, productivity improvement, and the management of human resources. He has also edited and written extensively for other business publications.

Jeanne Leonardi is program manager for Xerox Corporation's Critical Skills Training Program.

Richard Morano is manager of technical education and human resources research at the Xerox Corporation. He is a visiting professor of organizational behavior at Cornell University and an adjunct faculty member at Rochester Institute of Technology, teaching training and development courses.

F. K. Plous, Jr., is a Chicago-based business writer specializing in workplace issues, transportation, and urban affairs.

Nancy Rubin is a New York–based writer specializing in psychology, education, and careers. She is the author of two books and contributes to *The New York Times, Business Week's Careers,* and other national publications.

Russell W. Scalpone is a consulting psychologist with the firm of Medina & Thompson, Inc., in Chicago. He assists clients in operational improvement, manufacturing organization development, management assessment, and the design and implementation of human resource selection and training systems.

Joan L. Sickler is manager of Work in America Institute's Productivity Forum, a membership organization including some of America's leading corporations, unions, and government agencies. She has written for Institute publications and others on labor-management issues, training for new technology, and productivity innovations.

Peter S. Smith is a New York–based free-lance journalist who writes frequently on business, management, and economic issues. He is also the publisher and editor of several business publications.

Leslie Stackel is a New York–based writer with a special interest in the changing workplace and the quality of working life. She is a frequent contributor to *Work in America*, as well as to other employment-related publications.

Successful Training Strategies

Introduction:
How Leading Companies
Are Reshaping
Their Training Strategies

Despite the massive influx of new technology into both factories and offices—and the billions of dollars spent each year on training and education—there is scant evidence to suggest that managers and employees have acquired all the skills and knowledge required to successfully apply and adapt the technology to the changing needs of the workplace. The promise of spectacular productivity growth as a result of new computers and electronic technology in the service sector has failed to materialize. And while productivity in the reinvigorated manufacturing sector is now up to a 2.7 percent annual average growth rate, many manufacturing industries still have a long way to go toward optimizing their investments in new technology.

Increasingly, however, among the most forward-looking U.S. firms, training for new technology is moving to the top of the corporate agenda. Under intense pressures to compete, improve quality, and lower costs, these companies have come to regard training as a function that is central to the firm's operations and as vital an investment as the new technology itself. Indeed, in a growing number of cases, companies are finding that only the most innovative applications of new technology will deliver the promised gains in productivity and efficiency.

1

A formidable array of economic, social, and political forces has heightened the need for new, more dynamic training strategies that are closely aligned with the strategic goals of the corporation and that increase its responsiveness to change. In response to that need, Work in America Institute launched a three-year national policy study in 1985, "Training for New Technology," which examined organizations that had adopted successful training strategies. The study identified five major forces affecting corporations and their implications for training:

1. *Increased global and domestic competition* is leading to a greater need for competitive strategies, which often include training as an essential element.
2. *Rapid changes in technology* result in changes in operations, products, and processes; job design; work flow; and skill requirements. These changes, in turn, create an acute need for people with specialized technical skills.
3. *Widespread mergers, acquisitions, and divestitures,* which realign corporate structures and functions but not necessarily the ability of people to carry them out, require long-term training plans linked to decisions on the business future.
4. *A better-educated work force,* which values self-development and personal growth, has brought about enormous learning needs plus a growing desire for participation at work. Employees' ability to contribute to the organization depends on adequate levels of training.
5. *Occupational obsolescence and the emergence of new occupations*— resulting from the changing nature of the economy, the shift from manufacturing to service industries, and the impact of research, development, and new technology—require flexible training policies to prevent increased turnover and lower productivity.

Leading-edge companies that have reshaped their training strategies in response to competition and changing technology have found that training is not simply a matter of learning how to operate the technology. To be effective, training in new technology must equip employees and managers with broader knowledge, which enables them to plan for the effective utilization of new technology, integrate it into the work process, maintain it, improve it, and, when necessary, replace it and start over. Broader knowledge can also lead to the discovery of other profitable applications of the technology, as well as to the possibility of technological advances that can help employers develop new products or processes. Increasingly, companies are beginning to address these training needs through a variety of innovative approaches and programs. As illustrated by the cases in this book, the results can be rewarding. More creative applications of new technology, faster implementation, improved quality and productivity, more cost-effective training, and enhanced quality of learning are among the specific benefits cited.

The twenty-six case studies presented here explore the experiences of employers and unions that have devised highly imaginative solutions to the problems of training for new technology. Among the most exciting cases are those in which the employers and unions cooperated in training programs to increase the firm's flexibility and responsiveness to change in ways that would be unachievable if each side worked on its own. Partnerships with community colleges and government agencies, also described here, have further enhanced the quality of the training.

Research for this casebook was conducted in conjunction with Work in America Institute's policy study on "Training for New Technology," which has culminated in the publication of a comprehensive policy report and this companion volume. The published report, *Training—The Competitive Edge: Introducing New Technology into the Workplace,* examines in detail the key issues faced by employers and unions when implementing state-of-the-art training programs and presents a series of practical recommendations directed primarily toward employers and unions. In many instances, these recommendations are based on the actual experiences of companies, as described in this volume.

Information used in the preparation of these cases was obtained through on-site visits and interviews with company and union representatives; in several cases, the author was an actual participant in the company's training program. The authors include both training consultants and professional writers who specialize in business and human resource issues.

The intent here is not to cover every aspect of training for new technology, but to explore in depth only the most important issues faced by employers and unions—and those most difficult to solve. Five critical issues have been identified by Work in America Institute, each of which is discussed in a separate section and illustrated by the actual experiences of leading companies:

1. coordinating training strategy and corporate strategy
2. implementing continuous-learning and employee-involvement strategies as an effective response to change
3. encouraging manufacturer-user cooperation as a means of stimulating more creative and profitable applications of new technology
4. improving the cost-effectiveness and quality of training for new technology
5. linking continuous learning with employment security practices

It should be remembered that *training,* as discussed here, encompasses much more than formal classroom or seminar instruction organized by the training department. Training also refers to a variety of less formal but equally valuable—and sometimes more valuable—means of learning: role modeling, coaching, rotational assignments, on-the-job training, self-instruction, and so on. *New technology* applies not only to high-tech computers and robots, but to a host of other technological advances in electronics, pneumatics, hydraulics, and other fields, as well as social and managerial technologies, such as advanced problem solving and quality-control methods—all of which require intensive training.

Most of the cases are drawn from the manufacturing sector, since these companies have faced the most difficult competitive challenges in global and domestic markets to date. But several services are also represented—the most progressive service organizations, which have begun to realize that their ability to compete depends on a work force well equipped with the latest technological skills and know-how. However, the issues related to training for new technology currently being addressed by the leading-edge companies are of concern to any U.S. company that wants to stay ahead in an increasingly competitive and turbulent economy. For no matter what the products or services provided—high-tech and low-tech alike—a company's competitiveness and training strategies are intricately linked.

Aligning Training Strategy with Corporate Goals

Organizations that have successfully linked training strategies to the corporate strategy of the firm find that the quality of training improves and the results more closely support corporate goals. Traditionally, training activities have been organized and carried out by professional trainers in the corporate or site training department who possess little or no knowledge of the corporation's overall business strategy. Not surprisingly, training programs tend to be unrelated to the needs of the business and are often reduced or eliminated during periods of economic stress. However, in certain major companies, where training assumes a more central, strategic role and training strategies are driven by the needs of the business, critical decisions about how much to spend on training and the cost-effectiveness of training programs are reached in response to business requirements as outlined in the corporate strategic plan. The cases presented here cover three issues related to the linkage of corporate and training strategies: budgeting, evaluation, and mechanisms of linkage.

Coordinating training and corporate strategies makes it possible to approach training budgets in a new way and helps to clarify budget options. At the Travelers Corporation, top management committed extensive funds for an expanded computer literacy program, a state-of-the-art training center, and a management redevelopment program, after corporate training officials demonstrated that the company's strategic goals would be unattainable without timely, cost-effective training.

The experiences of several companies illustrate the accurate evaluation of training in terms of its fulfillment of corporate strategy. At Travelers, the cost-effectiveness of training programs is determined before implementation. If a genuine training problem is recognized, the training department determines the needs, sets training objectives, and then prepares a detailed proposal—including development and operational cost estimates and the size of the trainee population—which translates into estimated cost per student. The trainers and client department jointly determine if the training is worth the estimated cost and then jointly evaluate the results after the training is performed.

One of the few companies that have developed highly advanced methods of costing and evaluating their training is New England Telephone. The company's evaluation department regularly compiles statistical indicators to measure costs, volume, and efficiency of training operations; produces course evaluation questionnaires for trainees and their immediate supervisors; and issues guidelines for evaluating vendor courses and services.

Several major companies have established mechanisms that help ensure the accurate exchange of information between the corporate strategic planners and training officials, which, in turn, reinforces the linkage between corporate strategy and training. At Motorola, for example, involvement of the chief executive officer (CEO) in the formulation of technical training policies has helped align training strategy with corporate goals to improve product quality and inventory productivity. At Travelers, the corporate strategy planning group includes the vice-president for administration, to whom the training function reports. Involvement of the CEO and a top-level management team at Corning Glass Works has also helped to coordinate a companywide campaign to improve quality with a massive quality education effort.

At American Transtech, the linkage between corporate strategy and training has been facilitated by a highly successful participatory style of management and a team-based training approach, while at Gilroy Foods, Inc., the processes used in determining training objectives and course curricula and in evaluating the training results have helped to reinforce companywide objectives to boost quality, lower costs, and promote increased career opportunities for hourly workers.

Continuous Learning for All Employees

In today's corporate environment, the success of the business is directly tied to its ability to manage change. Constant change in technology, products, markets, jobs, and competition has necessitated a new approach toward training—*continuous learning*—which is fundamentally different from conventional training.

The goal of continuous learning is to encourage everyone in the organization—employees, line managers, supervisors, and technical personnel—to become actively and continuously involved in expanding their skills. Specifically, continuous learning methods differ from more traditional types of training in the following ways: learning becomes an everyday part of the job rather than being confined to the classroom; employees learn skills of others in their work unit as well as those related to their own jobs and also understand how their work unit relates to the rest of the business; and employees teach, and learn from, one another.

While no one company to date has completely adopted the continuous learning model, several important employers have put into practice one or more components. For example, continuous learning characteristics are often featured in employee involvement programs that encourage interactive teaching and learning among various levels of employees. The case studies examine the various mechanisms companies have used to promote continuous learning and a participative approach to training.

At General Electric's Aerospace Electronic Systems Department, the successful completion of continuous-education courses for engineers is tied to the company's performance appraisal process, as well as to career advancement. But perhaps the most unique aspect of General Electric's Continuing Engineering Education Program is an advisory council of engineers, technical managers, and marketing representatives who ensure that the course curriculum meets business needs and reflects the latest trends in various technological fields.

General Foods is cited for its train-the-trainer programs, which have involved teams of hourly employees, line managers, and technical experts in the design and delivery of training courses. The company also uses other approaches to continuous learning, such as a corporatewide network to share training resources and ideas as well as annual "technology roundtables" for manufacturing managers. The involvement of employees and managers in the planning, design, and implementation of training programs is considered to be a major determinant of success.

Employee involvement in the learning process is especially pervasive among semiautonomous work teams, as illustrated by the S. B. Thomas English muffin plant in Schaumburg, Illinois. Here the line between training and work has disappeared: Team members train one another as a routine part of their job and rotate through other managerial duties as well. The concept of continuous learning is further strengthened by the plant's pay-for-knowledge reward system.

Union involvement in corporate training programs is not widespread. But in the few instances in which unions have become equal partners with management in the training process, the quality and scope of training are enhanced, as illustrated by the Pacific Bell–Communications Workers of America case. Labor and management sponsor both job-specific training and generic training to equip employees with knowledge that applies broadly to telecommunications in order to give them a head start in this highly competitive job market.

Manufacturer-User Training Partnerships

The relationship between the manufacturers and users of new technology presents a host of opportunities for learning on both sides. From the initial contracting to the design, building and testing, implementation, and training for new technological systems, a genuine learning partnership can lead to applications and innovations that far exceed the expectations of either user or manufacturer/vendor. Unfortunately, few users and manufacturers take advantage of the opportunities that exist. More commonly, the manufacturer-user relationship ends when the equipment is purchased.

Several cases are highlighted in which manufacturer/user cooperation at various stages of the relationship results in benefits for both parties: for users, more uptime and faster, more flexible, more creative applications; and for manufacturers, increased customer satisfaction, improvement in design and performance of products, and ideas for marketable new hardware and software. One company described here, Control Data Corporation, has begun to transform the manufacturer-user relationship. Control Data's Training and Education Group (TEG), which develops and markets a series of computer-based training courses used by manufacturing industries, has devised two highly effective vehicles to seek detailed information on customer needs and modify its products accordingly: (1) a training advisory board, which includes representatives from major Control Data customers, and (2) visits to customers' work sites by TEG consultants, many of whom have technical backgrounds.

Both the General Motors plant in Linden, New Jersey, and Goodyear Tire and Rubber exemplify a proactive approach on the part of the user in obtaining a training commitment as a condition of the product sale and in initiating jointly developed and implemented training strategies with the suppliers of new technology.

Ford Motor Company's truck transmission plant at Sharonville, Ohio, demonstrates the informal, yet valuable, learning experiences that can be provided inexpensively during the course of the manufacturer-user relationship. Members of a joint employee-management training team at the Sharonville plant, which has undergone a major technological changeover, interacted regularly with vendors during the initial contracting, design, and building/testing phases of the new technology.

Two final examples of innovative user-vendor relationships involving multivendor computer-integrated systems are described: Caterpillar Inc. and Miller Brewing. In both cases, the users turned for training to third-party specialists who were not major hardware or software suppliers to the integrated systems but who had specific training skills in integrated systems and were willing to adapt the training to meet the user's needs.

Designing and Delivering Training Cost-Effectively

Driven by the pressures to compete, some leading U.S. companies are putting more and more of their resources into the design and delivery of high-quality, cost-effective training for new technology. Several innovative approaches that have enhanced cost-effectiveness are described.

A "systems approach" to training, pioneered by IBM, organizes the educational process into discrete, manageable steps and has resulted in improved decision making and training delivery. The company has cut training costs significantly through the use of work-site training systems, such as computer-based training and other self-study methods.

Two additional cases illustrate similar systems-based programs that have aided in design and delivery of more cost-effective training: Manpower, Inc.'s computerized SKILL-WARE system, used to train temporary word-processing operators for its client companies, and Travenol Laboratories, Inc.'s training program for maintenance supervisors implemented at one of its high-tech manufacturing facilities.

Training partnerships with community colleges are proving to be another cost-effective approach to training, particularly when colleges respond to industry's needs through increased flexibility and high-quality design of training programs. Community colleges that have been most responsive to industry needs have created training consortia, in which many colleges join with one or more employers to mount large-scale training programs. One example is General Motors' Automotive Service Educational Program, in which thirty-nine community colleges have formed a nationwide network with the firm to train its technicians.

Finally, National Technological University's attempt to bring graduate-level engineering courses to the work site via satellite communications and live interactive television represents a particularly exciting—yet affordable—response to the threat of obsolescence in the engineering profession. Nearly 1,000 engineers and scientists at major high-tech companies are linked to faculty members at leading engineering colleges and universities.

Combining Continuous
Learning and Employment Security

Employers that are committed to the continuous upgrading and training of their employees and to providing some degree of employment security (as opposed to the guarantee of a specific job) have found that these two practices, in combination, represent a powerful strategy for improving the competitiveness and long-term growth of the firm.

Although many in the business world assume that employment security is an impractical, costly policy that reduces the ability of the company to respond quickly to change and increased competition, organizations that have practiced it find otherwise. Employment security fosters increased motivation to learn among employees and can actually help the company adjust to change and stay ahead in a highly competitive, changing economy.

The cases presented here demonstrate how continuous learning and employment security policies interrelate and strengthen each other.

Three aspects of employment security in which continuous learning and training are important elements are explored in the cases: the cost-effectiveness of retraining for new technology as against hiring already-trained recruits; managing the redeployment of employees from old to new jobs; and enhancing the success rate of retrainees by bringing them into contact with the new work unit as early as possible.

The Xerox Corporation's Critical Skills Training Program retrains specialists to fill completely different professional positions in the organization—something few employers do. Xerox found that retraining was cost-effective when weighed against the steep costs of layoff and/or relocation. Beyond the financial advantages, however, company officials point out the hidden benefits that come from a commitment to employment stability that do not show up in a cost-benefit analysis: higher productivity, stored know-how and experience, increased loyalty to the company, and a climate that encourages flexibility and creativity.

Three cases are examples of the redeployment of employees from redundant jobs to new jobs that require retraining.

At General Motors' Packard Electric Division, a joint union-management employment security initiative has led to the successful introduction of, and training for, new technology, as well as improved productivity, lower absenteeism, and higher morale. General Electric transformed an aging industrial plant in Fort Wayne, Indiana, into a high-tech site and staffed it with the company's own displaced employees. Another example is Pacific Northwest Bell's computerized system, which has been particularly useful in redeploying managers to high-growth fields within the company by notifying them whenever there is a job vacancy that matches their skills, work and education background, and relocation preference.

To achieve the highest possible success rate in retraining, employers should ensure that trainees understand early in the training process the nature of the jobs they will be occupying and the work environment in which the jobs exist. Hewlett-Packard's program that retrains surplus production employees to fill high-demand office jobs incorporates several procedures that familiarize trainees with their new work units.

The chapters that follow reflect the five themes outlined in this introduction and illustrate them with firsthand accounts of the training programs and approaches of major companies, unions, and institutions of learning.

PART ONE

ALIGNING TRAINING STRATEGY WITH CORPORATE GOALS

More and more frequently today, training activities are becoming an integral part of the corporation's strategic plans. Often, the training programs address key business needs—as defined by the corporate strategy—and provide the skills required to meet those needs. As demonstrated by the cases presented in this part, when training is viewed—and treated—as a strategically important function directly related to overall corporate strategy, training results are more likely to support the broad objectives of the firm. The rewards for the corporation can be immeasurable.

For example, coordinating these two strategies enables the organization to cope more effectively with the rapid changes in technology, jobs, products, and business conditions that have become an everyday part of the corporate way of life. Linkage results in a more dynamic approach, which anticipates the future training needs of the employer, the employee, and the employee's manager and meets them in a proactive rather than defensive manner.

Another advantage of the coordination of training and corporate strategies is that it provides a more objective basis on which to budget training, estimate costs and benefits, and evaluate results. Decisions about how much to spend on training are made in the context of the overall business plan and are

13

guided by the requirements of that plan. Investment in training is elevated to the same status as research and development, equipment maintenance, or capital investment in new technology.

Companies that have successfully aligned training strategy with corporate business strategy also find that the organization can respond more quickly and efficiently to corporate decisions. When the providers of training are involved in the formulation of corporate strategy, strategists know what skills are available or what skills may be required to implement their plans and meet goals on time. Sometimes, that knowledge may lead corporate decision makers to change course. In essence, training serves a dual function: both to influence strategy and to carry it out.

Three issues relating to the linkage between corporate and training strategies were examined in the study "Training for New Technology": budgeting of training funds, evaluation of training programs, and mechanisms for the accurate exchange of information between corporate and training strategists.

Budgeting

One of the cases presented here, the Travelers Corporation, illustrates how key decisions concerning the budgeting of training funds were made possible by linking corporate and training strategies. Training has played a central role in the Travelers Corporation's process of changing from an old-line insurance company to a more diversified financial services company. In a series of detailed presentations to top management, the training and development divison demonstrated that the company's goals of rapid automation and high technology would be impossible to achieve without the necessary knowledge and skills. As a result, the training division received the commitment of top management for the funds needed to carry out the required programs: a new state-of-the-art training center, a custom-designed computer-literacy program, and a management redevelopment program.

Evaluation

If the primary purpose of training is to carry out corporate strategy, it is particularly important to evaluate the effectiveness of training in relation to corporate strategy. Some measures of evaluation are: how well the training is received and actually applied on the job; the particular skills or techniques learned; the degree to which training has changed the job behavior of employees and improved the performance of the work unit; and how well the training achieved its skill objectives in terms of corporate strategy. But none of these measures can be accurately assessed without the input of those for whom the training is intended: the trainees and, most important, their immediate supervisors and higher-level managers. Ideally, needs analysis, objective setting, and evaluation of training should be jointly carried out by managers and the training department. When such responsibilities are shared—and when the training department clearly communicates corporate strategy to managers—training efforts are better integrated into operations and planning and reflect both corporate priorities and the needs of employees and their managers. The Travelers case illustrates some of the potentials.

Another company that has developed an innovative approach to the evaluation of training is the New England Telephone Company (NET). NET's comprehensive evaluation system has assured high-quality training services at reasonable cost, according to company officials. The company's advanced methods of costing and evaluating its training programs, while predating the Bell System divestiture, have become increasingly imperative in light of the company's drive to improve efficiency and quality.

Mechanisms for Linkage

To ensure that training is successfully linked to corporate strategy, some of the most forward-looking companies have established mechanisms for both conveying the corporate business strategy to the trainers and trainees and making sure that the formulation of strategy is based upon accurate information about the availability of skills needed to carry out the strategy. Motorola, for example, has an executive advisory board that directs all training policies carried out by the Motorola Training and Education Center (MTEC), based at the company's headquarters in Schaumburg, Illinois. The CEO's involvement as the chair of that board ensures the close coordination of training policies with corporate goals and increases the likelihood of long-term financial commitments necessary for strategic training. Additional guidance comes from five advisory councils representing the five major functions of the company. These councils help to identify training needs and priorities and translate the executive board's general directives into specific training policies.

Corning Glass Works' "Total Quality" campaign also illustrates the support and involvement of the CEO and a top-level management team as the necessary link aligning the company's strategy to improve quality throughout the organization with a massive education effort designed to reach all 28,000 worldwide employees. The Department of Education and Training was responsible for disseminating the business strategy throughout the organization and implementing the programs necessary to carry out the strategy.

At American Transtech, the participatory work style and team-based training approach enhanced organizational resources and flexibility and facilitated corporate strategy. This company, a wholly owned subsidiary of AT&T, was formed in 1983 to handle stock transfers for AT&T's 3.2 million accounts. The company was faced with a formidable productivity challenge when divestiture increased the number of accounts to 22 million. Having successfully achieved that goal—and far surpassed productivity levels achieved by AT&T's old Stock and Bond Division—the company has now begun to diversify into shareowner services outside the Bell System, focusing on financial and direct marketing services.

At Gilroy Foods, Inc., a leading producer of high-quality

dehydrated onions, garlic, and capsicum, advances in both production and quality-control technologies necessitated a more
structured and focused approach to the technical training of
maintenance workers and quality-control technicians. This case
study examines the way carefully selected training objectives
and methods of training design supported companywide goals
to improve quality, reduce costs, and enhance career opportunities for hourly workers.

1

The Travelers Corporation: Expanding Computer Literacy in the Organization

John V. Hickey

The Travelers Corporation has an ambitious and easily stated strategic objective: In a fast-changing and increasingly competitive marketplace, it intends to become the preeminent financial services company.

Management recognizes that it cannot hope to achieve this goal without the full participation of the training function:

- Employees at all levels must be trained to make the best use of the data-processing technology that is transforming the financial services industry—a technology that is available to competitors as well as Travelers.
- Managers must be ready to manage an organization transformed by technology.
- New financial service products require state-of-the-art electronic data processing, which, in turn, requires cost-effective, timely training.

Training has assumed a central role in the change process by allying its objectives closely with the broader objectives of the company. It has developed training programs that meet the needs of the changing organization—and make maximum use of technology for quality and cost effectiveness.

Moreover, training has not merely responded to initiatives from top management, but has taken initiatives of its own. It has made management aware that certain strategic directions are possible only if training plays a major role. It has shaped top management's thinking.

A Changing Organization

Based in Hartford, Connecticut, Travelers has long been known as a major insurance company. It has evolved considerably, however, from its traditional business. It is now a broader-based financial services organization—in which, however, insurance operations of various kinds are still vital. Of 1986 revenues totaling $16.0 billion, $12.2 billion came from premiums. The remaining $3.8 billion represented investment income on $52 billion worth of assets managed for itself and others.

The Travelers Corporation is essentially a wholesaler of insurance and other financial services. It is a leading provider of group life, health, and casualty property insurance to large companies, for which it also manages pension and profit-sharing plans. The company also provides—largely through independent agents—life, health, and casualty property insurance and annuities to more than four million individual customers.

Of the company's 32,000 employees, some 12,000 work in the Hartford area. The rest are at approximately 250 locations in the United States and a few small offices abroad.

The completely nonunion work force is overwhelmingly white collar. It includes clerical employees, such as raters, claims processors, and secretaries; professional employees, such as account analysts, data-processing specialists, accountants, and trainers; and managers, who are responsible at different levels for all these activities.

The task and the strategic role of training can best be understood against the background of the company's business environment and the organization's response. Competition in the company's markets has intensified greatly in recent years. Consumers give a lower priority to traditional life insurance, and they look for other options in financial security. In response to changing social factors and employee demand, companies are redesigning their benefits packages. Both trends have created insurance products that are more complex to sell and to administer. Concurrently, insurance and other financial services are now available through increasingly varied nontraditional outlets such as banks, brokerage houses, and retail stores.

These trends pose a competitive challenge. The company has found, in particular, that many of its independent agents have a hard time meeting their new competition effectively. So it made the strengthening of the agencies' position an important goal of the major reorganization announced in February 1985.

In the past, the company organized its insurance operations by type of product. Separate departments existed for group insurance; for individual life and health insurance and financial services; and for casualty/property insurance (further divided into commercial and personal lines). Departments operated quite independently and communications with one another were minimal—even though, in many cases, they shared field-office facilities.

The reorganization abandons the product-based structure and aligns operations with specific markets. The company now consists of five major groups:

1. *National Accounts* services large and medium-sized corporate customers directly with group insurance, casualty/property insurance, and pension and profit-sharing management.
2. *Agency Marketing* serves the varied insurance needs of individuals and smaller businesses through agents.
3. *Business Diversification* is responsible for mass-marketing activities and development of new businesses.
4. The *Investment Group* encompasses a number of investment-oriented departments and subsidiaries.
5. *Finance* provides staff support in financial matters and manages the company's extensive data-processing operations.

The new structure is designed to give the customer a single source for varied insurance and financial services, whether dealing with Travelers directly or through an agent.

The Current Training Function

As the business environment and organization structure have changed, so have training needs—and the role and resources of the training function.

In the past, each product-based department maintained its own training capabilities. These training units operated with great independence and limited external communication. In addition, some staff functions had their own training units.

Even before the recent corporate reorganization, management recognized that future training needs would increasingly cut across product-line boundaries. Both automation and the evolving single-source marketing concept would require more training that was applicable throughout the company. The training function is now evolving to fill this need.

In 1983 the company established a Corporate Training and Development Division within its Personnel Administration Department. Headed by Robert S. Fenn, national director of training, the division is responsible for coordinating training activities throughout the corporation. It provides all management development as well as training that crosses product or departmental lines. Office automation training is an important part of its responsibility.

The Corporate Training and Development Division has not generally become involved in product or sales training for a specific product or department. Under the market-based organization, the need for specific product-oriented training will change, as will the role of the separate training units that serve the product departments. At present, their role is in transition.

According to Fenn, Travelers now has about 130 full-time training employees. Training expenditures for the whole company are about $16 million a year.

Fenn estimates that as many as 25,000 employees have at least some kind of training contact each year. One recent calculation indicated there had been nearly 62,000 contacts during the year. In other words, nearly every employee was exposed to some kind of training, and many had between two and three contacts.

Fenn concedes that these figures provide only a rough index of training activity, and especially of its intensity. A training contact may range from fifteen minutes of self-paced instruction at a computer terminal to attendance at the Harvard Advanced Management Program. As the company turns more and more to self-paced (usually meaning computer-based) instruction, tracking both the number and length of contacts will become more difficult.

Travelers uses a variety of training methods and resources, including classroom lecture courses; workshops; self-administered instruction via computer or home study; courses offered by professional and management associations, colleges, and universities; and the whole gamut of available audio and video materials.

Travelers uses outside resources in addition to its own, but the use pattern of these resources is changing in some respects. The company uses some training packages developed and sold by outside vendors. In a few cases—for example, reading programs—the training is actually delivered by the vendors. More often, however, such programs are acquired on license from the vendors and are delivered by the Travelers Corporation's own trainers. More and more frequently, though, Travelers is developing its own training.

According to Fenn, the company does not have a large training development staff and therefore often uses outside consultants in the development phase.

In the future, Fenn expects, most of the training programs will be developed by the company itself, with or without outside consultants' help. Terrance Goyer, assistant director of training, adds a qualification: As the expected shift from classroom to self-administered training continues, the company hopes to find major components of training in vendors' catalogues. At that point, says Goyer, training's job increasingly will be to find the right pieces and adapt and combine them to suit Travelers' particular needs. Currently, however, Fenn and Goyer feel that few well-designed self-administered programs are available from vendors.

The physical facilities for training have just been expanded. As the result of several studies of changing training needs, Travelers built a new training center close to its home offices in Hartford.

Figures cited in these studies provide insights into the changing mix of training methods at Travelers. In 1982, one study found that 1,532 field personnel and 811 agents came to Hartford for training and spent an average of five days. On each of about 220 days when training was conducted, about 50 people were in Hartford to participate.

The study concluded that in the future it might well be possible to deliver much of the needed training to field locations electronically—and much more cost-effectively. The study concluded, however, that the growing volume of training needs would demand a substantial increase in facilities at the home office. Student days were projected to increase from 6,428 in 1982 to 20,988 at some point between 1985 and 1993.

One important training objective was to move away from the classroom and toward self-administered training. Accomplishing this change would require a substantial increase in self-study carrels. The study calculated that the 1982 load of student days would require 29 such carrels. At the time of the study, not nearly that many were available. Trainees in self-study programs were forced to share carrels or, in some cases, to study at their work sites. Both situations undercut training effectiveness.

The projected load of student days for 1985–1993 was calculated to require 95 carrels, a requirement that was central to the design of the Hartford training center. The completed training center now contains a total of 45 study carrels in rooms that are convertible to classrooms, but the number of carrels can easily be expanded.

Other facilities at the center include 16 classrooms, with a capacity of 20 to 35 students each; 14 breakout rooms accommodating 8 to 10; an amphitheater seating more than 150; a teleconferencing room; and satellite broadcast reception capabilities. These instruction facilities are supplemented by office space for 130 training staff and a variety of support and recreation facilities.

The Long-Range Training Strategy

The training function at Travelers has been pursuing two overriding and related strategic goals:

- *To expand computer literacy* (a goal that has been partially completed)—defined by Goyer as "a reasonable appreciation of the potential value of automation to the job."
- *To change and expand management development* so as to foster the changes of style and behavior required by the changing technology of work. Fenn describes the basic style required by the new technology as "allowing people to make more decisions with the more complete information now available to them; leading more than controlling; motivating and giving freedom."

A subsidiary but nonetheless important strategy is the automation of the training process itself. Fenn notes: "Automation is a corporate strategy, and training helps everyone else to automate. But training also backs the corporate strategy by automating itself. In fact, the extent to which we achieve this is a good intermediate measure of training's effectiveness."

Finally, training has taken upon itself to reinforce subtly, through all training materials, important corporate goals—even those that may not be central to a particular training program. To this end, several themes are woven into all training materials: creativity/innovation; productivity; customer service; low cost; fairness; and affirmative action.

The Travelers Computer Literacy Program. In recent years, the company has purchased about 12,000 IBM personal computers (PCs). Eventually they will total 15,000 or more—in the home office, field offices, and independent agencies.

By late 1983, hundreds of employees had access to PCs, but it was obvious that the new tools were substantially underused. The company engaged two consulting firms—Cavri Systems and VASA HRD—to help in developing a program to expand computer use.

A survey of representative employees from home and field offices found that, while employees were not afraid of the PCs, they did have some concerns that were holding them back from using them for their work. Some employees feared loss of their jobs. Some feared they would look foolish while learning about the computers. Many expressed concern about the time they would be away from their jobs for computer training.

The survey findings pointed to several implications.

- Most employees felt that personal computing was an inevitable development and would affect them sooner or later.
- They wanted to know how the PCs could help in their own jobs before they would invest the time in learning.
- Training would have to be available at employees' convenience.
- The computer would have to be consistently relevant to the individual employee's type of job, tasks to be performed, and present knowledge.
- Training should allow trainees to experiment and make mistakes, and should leave them with reasonable expectations about ease of use and learning.

Designed in response to these criteria, the Travelers Computer Literacy Program emphasizes teaching only what an employee needs for his or her specific job tasks. It has the following characteristics:

- *Self-study* reduces training time. It makes instruction available at the student's convenience and at any location, and it maintains consistent quality of instruction.
- *Student-tailored* instruction uses diagnostic testing to identify and prescribe the segments of the program that are appropriate to each individual. It lets the students review segments as they wish, leave a segment at any time, depart from the recommended sequence, and explore segments that have not been prescribed.
- *Interactive* instruction encourages trial and error, and it ensures active student participation in the training process.

- *Computer-managed* instruction provides necessary guidance no matter how far off course a student may stray. It allows restart at a point of departure if a session has been interrupted. Finally, it ensures that the student finishes prescribed segments before completion is certified.
- *Media* of instruction can be selected for the effects they produce. Interactive video visually brings the student into the emotional issues of PC use. It also provides transitions between segments and makes the program engaging. Computer-generated screens, with audio over, are used for information-transfer segments, and computer-based training for job- and task-related examples and exercises. Finally, a workbook supports the computer-based training segments and serves as a reference after training.

Travelers began student testing of the program in October 1984. By the end of 1986, almost 5,000 employees had been through it. Reactions have been consistently favorable. Asked to rate various aspects of the program on a scale of one to five, test students gave the following assessments:

- Preference for the program over classroom training, 4.1.
- Satisfaction with pacing and ability to work independently and move around, without getting lost, 4.2–4.6.
- Adequacy of content and effectiveness of instruction, 4.1–4.6, with most responses close to 4.5.
- Increased awareness of the PC's usefulness on the job, 4.3, although Goyer says that a solid answer to this question requires further on-the-job use of the skills learned.
- "Would you recommend this program to others?" drew a 4.5.

Although the students' responses were overwhelmingly favorable, some expressed a few reservations. Some found the course content too basic in some respects—but conceded that the ability to pick and choose segments made the experience worthwhile. Some found the accompanying workbook unnecessarily detailed. Some said they wanted more opportunity to practice and experiment with their new skills.

Management and trainers also voiced some reservations. Trainers have questioned the cost-effectiveness of this kind of training. Goyer agrees that development is costly and is probably not justified in companies without large trainee populations—which Travelers emphatically has. Some trainers also questioned whether Travelers could offer effective follow-up training for specific applications. Goyer and Fenn feel that it has been difficult to find existing software suitable—either as is or with adaptation—to Travelers' needs. They note that the company cannot develop all its training materials itself. They also express the hope that recent signs of improvement in vendors' microcomputer-based training software reflect a genuine trend.

Many senior executives and middle managers tend to take only the overview segments of the training program. Even this exposure, however, has apparently increased recognition of management issues linked to the spread of computing. Managers generally agree that the computer literacy program will speed up the impact of change on the organization, and that since the change is vital to the company's success, they will learn to manage and control the new environment.

The Challenge to Management Development. To meet its second major training priority, Travelers is now formulating a much-expanded management development program. As a preliminary step, the Corporate Training and Development Division undertook a study of some 300 management jobs to get a clear picture of the competencies required by managerial jobs. The survey asked about job requirements and how they were expected to change over the next decade. This question was asked not only of the present job holders but also of their superiors at the next higher level of management.

The new program will consist of twenty-seven separate courses or seminars. Fifteen will be self-study, eight will be classroom, and four will be computer-based simulations. The first ten will be introduced in 1987, the remainder in 1988.

One important requirement will be the reeducation of management to understand its new role. As automation makes more information available at lower organizational levels, Fenn explains, more decisions once reserved to management can be made without them. Many managers see this as a threat to their power—and they resist. Management development can help to lessen the resistance by educating managers in new ways to manage.

Automation also expands the range of a manager's concerns. The technology influences the way services are delivered to the customer and, inevitably, the way they are marketed. Thus, a manager's concerns are no longer confined to a single function but extend from "back-office" operations directly to the customer.

Furthermore, marketing full financial services requires a lot more product tailoring than marketing insurance alone. Whereas in the past a manager was expected to be an expert on a specific product—for example, life insurance—now the demand is for a manager who understands a broader picture, although perhaps not in the same depth as before. Instead of being a technical expert, he or she must know how to sort out the customer's needs and bring in those technical experts who can fill them.

Concurrently with design of the management development program, the company is developing executive and management-level work stations that integrate various computerized information systems to help managers work more effectively.

According to Fenn and Goyer, some of the same techniques used for computer literacy will be used for management development. For example, the program might offer computer-based diagnostic tests that would assess managers' skills and knowledge and then prescribe appropriate courses of study.

Cost Controls for Training. Travelers does not undertake any training program without an idea of its cost-effectiveness. "This is an absolute requirement in any kind of automation training," says Goyer. "Anyone who does it any other way, or takes it as an article of faith that doing it will result in a better world, is crazy. Even in the 'softer' areas, like management development, you should still quantify. You may eventually say, 'the cost is too high, but we'll do it anyway.' But you should determine cost-effectiveness in advance."

The estimating process begins with a front-end analysis, whose first question is, "Are we really dealing with a problem that will be solved by training?" In many cases, the answer is no. For example, a supervisor might say that claims processors lack adequate keyboard skills and need training to increase their productivity. But in some cases, the problem lies with design of either the documents from which processors are inputting data or the computer screens. In other cases, there may be an observable link between high employee turnover and the lack of certain kinds of training. Trainers might then determine that providing or increasing training would reduce turnover without any direct impact on productivity. The training would be a reward for employees. It would make them feel better and would improve their resumes. It would not be a solution to a true training problem, however, but a solution to a morale problem. In either of these cases, Goyer concedes, it may be important politically for training to develop the requested course. But wherever possible, training should try to say no.

If a genuine training problem is recognized, the training function—working with the line department—determines the need and the appropriate training objectives. It then prepares a detailed proposal, including estimates of both the expected trainee population and the development and operational costs—and, therefore, the estimated cost per student. Whether the training is worth the estimated cost is then decided jointly by the trainers and the client department.

If a training program's costs start to exceed the estimates, two solutions are available. Approval can be sought to continue the project, despite the overruns, and to obtain additional funding. Or in some cases, funds already appropriated for other training activities can be shifted, if advisable.

Evaluating Training Programs. The Corporate Training and Development Division defines its responsibility—and its main criterion of success—this way: to bring trainees to a point where they can do something they could not do before training, or where they can do it more effectively. Fenn and Goyer feel, however, that even if this goal is achieved and measured at the end of a training course, the environment back on the job can make or break the ultimate effectiveness of training.

"I don't think training can be held responsible," says Fenn, "for making sure that change takes place on the job and is maintained there. The best we can do," he continues, "is to work closely with the client department to identify exactly what the job requires—and then make sure we design training that meets those requirements.

"We can design the training to increase the odds that what is learned is carried back to the job and used there. For example, we can include in the training many examples and exercises based directly on the job itself. And when a training course is spread out over time, we can assign trainees projects that they can practice at their work sites between training sessions."

Travelers does not, in general, develop training programs on a pilot-project basis, in which the program is tested systematically on a limited population before being extended to greater numbers. Goyer comments: "With the possible exception of supervisory training, we are essentially stepping into a void. So, unless we have developed two separate training programs—which we haven't the time or the resources to do—we have to trust our own best judgment as to approach, content, objectives, theme, and so on."

While no segment of a training program is isolated to serve as a pilot project, the program as a whole is tested along the way to determine if it appears to be meeting objectives. For example, the company has, from the start, monitored trainees' reactions to the Computer Literacy Program to determine if it was achieving one very basic objective—to make employees feel more comfortable with the PC and aware of its potential uses in their work.

Aligning Training Strategy with Corporate Strategy

Senior executives are deeply involved in planning the company's strategic objectives and in developing support for their implementation.

The role of the company's chairman and CEO, Edward

H. Budd, has been mainly to determine what kinds of changes would take place. According to Fenn and Goyer, the success of the company's change effort has been due, in large part, to Budd's ability to give direction to change while motivating other senior managers to carry the ball in day-to-day implementation.

Budd makes basic change decisions—including those with training implications—with a small group of executive vice-presidents and other top managers. In cases where the group does not fully agree on the advisability of change, or on its nature or speed, Budd makes the final decision and takes personal responsibility for it. He announces the change and shows his commitment to it through publicity in the company's various information media—newsletters, videotapes, and so on. Such was the case, for example, in building support for the Computer Literacy Program and for the new training center.

Although the CEO is deeply and publicly committed to these changes, he entrusts a small number of executives with the responsibility and accountability for making the changes happen. He gives them wide latitude in implementing the strategies that he has led them in setting.

Training Implications. The senior executive group responsible for planning includes the executive to whom the Corporate Training and Development Division reports—Harold E. Johnson, senior vice-president for personnel administration. Therefore, corporate strategies reflect training implications or, more broadly, human resources implications. The link is made explicit in a videotape for employees, "Strategy for the 90s." Among the tape's themes are several that imply or specifically mention a training impact:

- Customer service as a competitive device depends on training employees to serve customers' needs across the full line of the company's insurance and financial services.
- Automation, the driving force behind cost-effectiveness, is an indispensable component of financial-services delivery.
- Low cost and high quality are achievable only by fullest use of technological and human resources.

- Training and development—and opportunities for individual growth—will receive greater emphasis as jobs change in response to technology, customer demands, and political and legislative changes.
- Effective, efficient distribution through independent agents and other channels will require training to improve both the competence of these channels and the responsiveness of the internal organizations serving them.

The Importance of Thinking Strategically. According to Fenn, training can meet a challenge like that faced at Travelers only if it perceives itself to be a strategically important function—and gets others to do the same. He concedes that thinking this way can be hard. In many cases, Fenn says, trainers are not used to being asked for their input into strategic decisions. And one of the most common failures of training, he says, is not taking the time to demonstrate to top management and the company as a whole that training and the future of the company are intimately connected.

Training at Travelers used to be completely decentralized. When Fenn joined the company with the task of revitalizing the training function, he found almost immediately that few of the hundreds of people he surveyed saw the link between training and corporate strategy. In a series of presentations to management, Fenn demonstrated that there was such a link. He says, "We pointed out that if we wanted to have a strategy of rapid automation and high technology, the training function would have to be up front, leading the way and able to provide the necessary skills and knowledge." As a result of the presentations, says Fenn, management approved funds for the new training center, a budget for the development of computer-based training, and a number of other needed changes.

Fenn insists that a corporate training function with a strategic viewpoint must be centralized to deliver programs that reflect the culture and philosophies of the corporation. At the same time, training specific to a line organization should be decentralized to better respond to the immediate daily operational needs. There must, however, be close coordination between the corporate and line training functions for efficiency and cost-effectiveness. Although training at Travelers is still evolving, he says, "Now that we have reorganized our training function, finished our training center, and are implementing our management development continuum, we are on the way to beginning to make a contribution to the corporation's strategic objectives."

2

Keeping Track of Training Quality and Costs: New England Telephone

Jill Casner-Lotto

Despite the increased emphasis many employers give to training today, their efforts to track the costs and value of that training remain relatively meager. But this is not so at New England Telephone (NET). With a training department that offers over 1,000 courses, employs close to 300 trainers, and operates on a $15 million yearly budget, NET's rationale for spending time and money on the evaluation of training is simple: It may be more expensive not to evaluate it.

As stated in the *New England Telephone Training Evaluation Plan* (1984), a document containing more than twenty exercises and instructions on how to assess training: "Without evaluation, faulty instruction may go uncorrected . . . costs of training can be wasted. Undetected job performance deficiencies can result in lost productivity, errors and work defects, and unnecessary on-the-job training."

Indeed, a major reason for the success of NET's evaluation program is that findings are presented in a timely fashion and translated into terms that matter to managers: productivity and quality gains, dollar savings to the company, and improvements in job performance. Another factor is the company's commitment to use the results of evaluative research. Evaluation studies have often pointed to needed revisions in course content or teaching techniques, and, in most cases, the revisions are implemented. In a field where technological change occurs at a rapidly accelerating pace, training that can be easily adjusted to match fluctuating job needs is a must. New England Telephone's active and comprehensive training evaluation program—with its emphasis on quality control—has allowed this to happen.

Company Profile

Before the divestiture of AT&T in 1984, New England Telephone was one of twenty-one operating companies under the Bell System umbrella. Today, NET and New York Telephone are part of a totally autonomous corporate entity, known as NYNEX, which services Maine, Massachusetts, New Hampshire, Rhode Island, Vermont, New York, and parts of Western Connecticut. The two telephone companies still operate independently of one another, although certain departments, such as Operator Services and Information Services, have been regionalized.

The most tangible change at NET since divestiture has been a 37 percent reduction in staff size, from 41,000 employees in 1979 to 26,000 in 1984. In early 1987, however, several hundred technical jobs were added to the company. In addition, with the split from AT&T, the company no longer markets phone equipment nor provides toll services outside its local access and transport areas, the geographical regions that make up the operating companies' market areas. However, there have been other less visible, but equally important, changes.

"Everyone within the company is looking for new ways to reduce costs where it counts the most—training is one area which we feel can have a big impact," notes Martin Smith, district manager within NET's Training and Education Division.

Though efforts to evaluate training and education activities predated divestiture by over ten years, the breakup of the Bell System has made evaluation even more imperative: "The divestiture forced us to substantially reduce the overall size of our training organization, but, as a result, we're seeing much greater efforts in efficiency—a genuine attempt to do more with less," Smith says.

At its peak in 1979, NET's Training Department delivered 210,000 days of training per year; in 1986, that number dropped to 100,000. Despite this drop, training continues to play a central and vital role within the organization because of (1) the changing technology and its impact on job requirements, and (2) a corporate concern over how the corporation will be managed in the post-divestiture era.

In the past, NET relied almost exclusively on AT&T to provide courses in management development; today, corporate leaders are searching for ways to fill the gap. "We've got a lot of catching up to do," Smith concedes. "It's almost as if the company has belatedly awakened to the importance of developing interpersonal skills and managerial competence, especially in such corporate cultural areas as team building and proprietorship."

Though the overall volume of training at NET is down, training in generic management skills has increased by 70 percent since 1979, and Smith sees this trend continuing in the future. Management development courses currently make up over 10 percent of the training curriculum. In addition, there are development programs specifically for middle managers and executives. The overwhelming majority of courses are in job-specific, technical areas, including computer systems, marketing, and engineering.

One way NET has kept current with the latest technological developments is by recruiting course developers and instructors from other company departments. Employees with technical expertise in particular subject matter are assigned to training on a rotational basis, usually for a three-year period. Another way the company has stayed on top of new technology is by offering training courses when a new product is first conceived, before the actual marketing phase.

Though NET is headquartered in Boston, training is conducted at four major centers and several satellite locations throughout Massachusetts. Two centers are in Boston; one is in Braintree; and the fourth is in Marlboro, where the majority of management training takes place. The Marlboro Learning Center houses more than thirty classrooms and offers complete overnight, dining, and recreational facilities. In addition to these permanent centers, NET establishes temporary training facilities at work sites when the need arises.

The Evaluation Program: A Historical Perspective

One factor that has definitely favored the evaluation of training activities at NET is the centralization of resources and staff. Training operates out of a centralized division within the Human Resources Department. The training division contracts to provide services for "client" departments within the company. Consolidation was a gradual process extending over a four-year period, from 1979 to 1983. Before that, training and education activities had been fragmented into twenty-nine training groups, with nearly 500 full- and part-time employees. That meant that no corporatewide records were kept of training volume, staff size, cost, quality, efficiency, or future demands, says Smith.

In 1977, an interdepartmental task force, commissioned by a corporate council of vice-presidents, investigated the training operations and recommended the development of accounting procedures to assure better quality control. A second task force, chaired by Smith, adopted four major objectives to correct deficiencies inherent in the system: (1) establishment of quality-control procedures, (2) adoption of a cost-tracking system, (3) design of a forecasting process, and (4) definition of course development standards.

Thus, evaluation activities at NET evolved as a vital part of the process toward centralization. "Evaluation was used as a political tool to demonstrate the value of centralizing the training function," notes Smith. Today, efforts to assess the costs and value of training are generally supported throughout the company and are viewed as a necessary part of the job. The fact that NET employs full-time evaluation specialists is evidence of its commitment, Smith believes.

"Most organizations don't evaluate training activities on a regular basis," he points out. And, even at NET, evaluation can sometimes be a tough function to support. "You become the bearer of bad news. People will acknowledge the importance of evaluation, but you won't see any overwhelming enthusiasm," he says. Nevertheless, in the vast majority of cases, the training department gets good cooperation from line managers when it conducts evaluations. "A 60 percent return on our surveys is considered low," notes Smith.

Overview of Evaluation Activities

To appreciate the scope of evaluation activities at NET, a quick organizational sketch of the training division is helpful. Though it is centralized, the training function operates in a way that assures both flexibility and responsiveness to other company departmental needs. Six training districts are designed to meet the specific training and educational requirements of the operating departments within the company. A seventh district provides generic management training for all departments. Each district is responsible for the development, delivery, and evaluation of courses for its particular department. There is also an organizational consulting district and a training administration group. In addition, a core evaluation staff—consisting of two full-time employees—maintains evaluation methods and procedures and serves as a central information resource for the training districts.

The evaluation program revolves around six major activities: (1) internal audits or reviews designed to evaluate the operations of each training district; (2) client satisfaction or marketing measures, consisting of quick surveys to determine line managers' overall satisfaction with the quality of training, and focus groups to discuss managers' perceptions about particular courses; (3) course evaluation questionnaires, which cover both general knowledge taught in the classroom and relevance of course material to job task; (4) in-depth studies, which evaluate a course's economic impact on the company; (5) development of statistical indicators to measure costs, volume, and efficiency of training operations; and (6) evaluation of outside vendors.

Internal Audits. Of all the evaluation activities, the audit is the most comprehensive, generating the richest amount of data and enabling the evaluation to focus on a problem from a variety of angles. The 250-page *Training Evaluation Plan,* mentioned earlier, presents a complete set of job aids and exercises for evaluating the operations of training staffs. It is used in an audit to assess various aspects of training: courses, instructors, facilities, expenses, test procedures, and transition from the course back to the job. An audit may take up to three months to complete, but in the end it yields a comprehensive written report, highlighting both deficiencies and areas of strength. The report also includes concrete recommendations for corrective action when needed.

The evaluation staff conducts a special three-day training evaluation workshop, in which participants learn the skills and knowledge necessary to implement the evaluation plan and thus perform a comprehensive audit. The workshop is offered two or three times a year and is open to all levels of management with training responsibilities. According to Linda Littlefield, assistant staff manager for evaluation, participants have included managers from the other Bell operating companies, as well as from outside corporations.

Though the audits are directed by a member of the evaluation staff, personnel from the training district being audited are very much involved. "At one time, the evaluation of training districts was mandated from above. As a result, evaluation was something to be feared and was often viewed as a fault-finding mission," Littlefield explains. "Now an audit is performed only at the request of the training district and is a collaborative effort each step of the way."

Those conducting an audit can choose from a total of twenty-one data-collection exercises that measure forty variables or aspects of training. Usually three high-volume courses are selected for evaluation. An extensive audit might include classroom observations; observation of a graduate's performance on the job; interviews with graduates and their supervisors and with instructors; and analysis of classroom utilization, test procedures, course design, and training expenses. Among the variables measured are timeliness of training, seat cancellations, instructor performance, relevance of course content to job, post-training work assignments, feedback from field to trainers, cost of course development, quality of materials, and learning problems of trainees, to name just a few (see Table 1).

Since various data-collection exercises are used to investigate problems, evaluators are able to verify their findings or spot discrepancies that might lead to further study. For instance, at least three sources of data are available to determine whether or not trainees are applying classroom skills on the job: interviews with the graduates themselves, interviews with their supervisors, and observations of job performance by the evaluator.

When conducting the audit the evaluator first meets with the training district manager to jointly determine basic objectives and goals of the evaluation. The evaluator proposes appropriate data-collection techniques based upon the concerns of the training district being audited. Questionnaires, test forms, or any other data-collection instruments are prepared by the evaluator and submitted for review by the training manager. After collecting the data and then meeting with the training manager to discuss the interpretation of the data, the evaluator prepares a written report. Included are recommendations for any remedial action, with the following considerations taken into account:

> What is the probability that the action will correct the problem?
> Can the action be easily implemented?
> Will results justify the cost of implementing corrective actions?

The report is forwarded to the senior manager of the training district, who decides what changes to implement.

Table 1. Training Evaluation Exercises and Variables.

Variables	1 Trainee Questionnaire	2 Training Delivery Manager Interview	3 Analysis of Seat Cancellations	4 Analysis of Classroom Use	5 Analysis of Instructor Use	6 Instructor Interview	7 Analysis of Test Procedures	8 Analysis of Test Data	9 Observation of Instructors	10 Graduate Questionnaire	11 Methods Manager Interview	12 Review of Course Content	13 Analysis of Development Project Stat.	14 Compliance with Development Studies	15 Training Development Mgr. Interview	16 Graduate's Supervisor Questionnaire	17 Observations of Graduates	18 Field Manager Interview	19 Analysis of Delivery Expenses	20 Analysis of Instructional Design	21 Compliance with Adaptation GL.
Scheduling Process		X																X			
Timeliness of Training	X	X																			
Prerequisites (Compliance)	X	X																			
Pre-Training Briefing of Trainees	X	X																X			
Training Requests vs. Scheduled Training																					
Seat Cancellations		X	X																		
Curriculum Planning		X																			
Classroom Utilization				X																	
Instructor Utilization					X	X			X	X											
Instructor Performance (Evaluation)						X		X	X	X											

Procedures for Evaluating Instructors		X				X															
Testing and Grading						X	X	X													
Delivery Expenses																			X		
Learning Problems of Trainees						X		X													
Post-Training Work Assignments		X								X						X					
Post-Training Job Proficiency										X						X	X				
Training vs. Field		X														X		X			
Feedback from Field to Trainers		X																X			
Instructors vs. Developers		X													X						
Development Priorities		X													X						
Timeliness of Development		X											X		X						
Course Implementation Problems		X				X									X						
Instructor's Change of Course						X									X						
Productivity of Development Group													X		X						
Efficiency of Development													X								
Efficiency of Adaptation													X								
Cost of Development, Adaptation													X								
Compliance with Training Dev. Stds.														X							
Compliance with Adaptation GL																					X
Quality of Materials & Design		X				X	X			X				X						X	
Relevance of Course Content						X				X		X				X					
Evaluation of Development Projects															X						
Methods Staff vs. Instructors		X									X										
Methods Staff vs. Developers															X						
Conversion Training		X									X				X						
Special Expertise Required?	No	No	No	No	No	No	Yes	No	Yes	No	No	Yes	No	Yes	No	No	Yes	No	No	Yes	Yes
Preparation Time (in days)	1	½	¼	¼	¼	1	½	½	1½	5	½	½	½	½	½	5	1½	1½	½	1	½
Administration Time (in days)	3	½	0	0	0	1½	0	0	3	15	½	3	0	0	½	15	8	1½	0	6	0
Analysis Time (in days)	1	½	¼	¼	¼	1½	1½	1½	1½	3	½	1½	3	3	½	3	3	1½	1	3	1½
Sample Size (*per course)	10	1	NA	NA	NA	1*	NA	NA	1*	15*	NA	NA	NA	NA	1	15	5*	3	NA	NA	3

Source: New England Telephone Training Evaluation Plan (copyright 1984, New England Telephone Company).

Since 1979, nearly fifty audits have been performed, each having a definite impact. "I'm very confident of this approach because it enables us to really get at the root of a problem," says Smith. "As a result of audits, we've made specific changes in course content, teaching techniques, and in the way training is scheduled." Most of the changes, he observes, concern the adjustment of obsolete course content to match job needs, particularly when new technology is involved—a trend he expects will increase in the future.

Client Satisfaction Measures. Marketing measures, which directly tap the client or line department as a source used in the evaluation, are still in the experimental stage at NET. Client satisfaction surveys have so far been conducted in two departments: Operator Services and Switching Services. The surveys, administered by mail and/or telephone, are directed toward departmental managers and are intended to elicit only general information concerning the managers' reaction to training.

"The surveys provide a kind of quick temperature reading of the overall service provided by the training district," explains Littlefield. Among the issues examined are competency of the training staff, managerial perceptions of their own role in training activities, post-training performance of subordinates, responsiveness of the training district to departmental needs (that is, availability of course information, feedback from trainers), cost of training, satisfaction with training facilities, and quality of training provided by outside vendors.

After the customer satisfaction surveys of both operator and switching services, Littlefield met with training district managers to discuss the problems identified and to prepare a report. The reports are confidential and are not forwarded to the head of the Training and Education Division unless the training district manager wishes to do so. The initial detection of a problem usually triggers a more intensive effort to pinpoint causes and develop solutions.

"For example, one client felt there was a lack of information on available courses and little or no feedback from trainers on students' performance in class. While my job was to give a presentation detailing the problem, it's up to the training district to do something about it," Littlefield explains. In this case, staff members from the training district prepared a special form to be used for feedback purposes and a more extensive course catalogue.

Though some training managers at NET have criticized the surveys as being overly subjective, both Littlefield and Smith consider them successful. Nevertheless, in response to this criticism, the evaluation staff is modifying the surveys and plans to administer a revised form soon.

The other marketing research technique used in the evaluation of training is the focus group. In this case, members of the evaluation staff and the training district meet with the departmental managers to discuss their perceptions about particular training courses. Focus groups have uncovered some specific roadblocks on the job that might potentially thwart the application of skills learned in the classroom.

One group, for instance, evaluated the Proprietor's Workshop, which teaches lower-level managers how to become "risk takers" and develop more ownership for the job. The course was being tried out in the Distribution Services Department, and training managers wanted more feedback before offering it on a permanent basis. The focus group discovered that trainees were not applying the skills they had learned unless there was continued support on the job from their supervisors.

At the recommendation of the focus group, says Littlefield, both second-level managers and their supervisors now attend the workshop, and more meetings are held with upper management to act on the trainees' suggestions.

In a second application, evaluators met with six focus groups in January and again in June 1984 to discuss a curriculum of four courses. These sessions revealed the need for more visible support from higher management for using course-related techniques on the job and, secondly, for addressing coordination problems between departments.

Course Evaluation Questionnaires. While only a small number of the courses included in NET's huge curriculum are evaluated each year, the evaluation staff makes sure that these are the courses that need evaluation most. Representatives from each of the training districts select the courses they believe should be evaluated, based on a variety of factors. Two questionnaires—one for course graduates and one for their immediate supervisors—are mailed three months after the completion of the course.

Training managers are given a "menu" of categories from which they select the most appropriate topics to be included in the questionnaire. Standard items appearing on all the surveys include the general evaluation of the course as taught in the classroom and the relevancy of course material to job tasks. The training-district representative provides an up-to-date list of job tasks and the evaluator then selects the specific questions to be asked of graduates and supervisors, including how frequently certain tasks are performed on the job and how proficiently these tasks are performed—that is, whether trainees are able to perform these tasks unassisted or must be under the guidance of a supervisor.

Other optional categories that may appear on questionnaires are course design, timeliness of training, boss support, instructor performance, classroom environment, classroom activities, and course materials. Graduates and supervisors may also be asked to give their own personal comments about the training experience. The evaluation staff computerizes all course evaluation data and forwards a final report to the training districts.

An analysis of various course evaluations over the years has revealed an interesting trend concerning job performance ratings, Smith notes. When asked to rate the frequency and proficiency of job tasks related to skills taught in particular courses, the course graduates and their supervisors provide similar ratings for task frequency but markedly different scores for task proficiency. Graduates' ratings of their proficiency tend to be lower than their supervisors' assessments, and Smith suspects the graduates to be the more accurate judges.

"Supervisors don't seem to know how well a subordinate is actually performing certain skills learned in a training course, either because they do not have the opportunity to observe the subordinate's work or they simply are not qualified to make those kinds of judgments," Smith speculates. The more complex the job, he adds, the less the immediate supervisor is able to judge proficiency.

The importance of management support for training was also demonstrated in a survey evaluating a supervisory workshop on performance feedback techniques. The survey revealed an alarming number of supervisors who had made no attempt to apply the techniques they had learned in class. A second survey was sent out with an added question about support from the boss. The returns from the second sample showed that supervisors who had discussed the course and its implications with their bosses were almost twice as likely to see the feedback procedures as those who had not discussed the course.

Smith concludes: "Any kind of interest shown by the boss motivates people to do what they were taught to do." The Training Department has taken steps to encourage management support and involvement in training, such as the preparation of discussion guides for managers to use in reviewing courses with trainees. Nevertheless, Smith believes more work is needed to educate managers in making judgments about training and its relationship to job proficiency.

In-Depth Course Evaluations. The evaluation staff has occasionally conducted some very intensive in-depth economic impact studies of single courses, although these are considered time consuming and costly to produce. The few studies that have been completed, however, have produced useful results.

A course entitled Effective Listening, which was initially tried out in 1982 in one of NET's departments, is now offered in four departments and will soon be available at New York Telephone. The one-day course teaches listening skills to managers who, in turn, go back to the field and instruct their subordinates on the effective-listening process. A comprehensive evaluation of the course when it was first offered in the Operator Services Department showed it had a dramatic impact on the work efficiency of telephone operators. The course helped operators to reduce the number of questions they had to ask customers and generally enabled them to handle customer requests more effectively.

The success of the course is succinctly stated in the evaluation report: "The positive results to the company were both humanistic, in helping people develop better boss-subordinate relationships and teams, and financial, in producing an annual cost savings of $2,280,000 due to improved productivity occurring as a result of operators' more effective listening." The evaluation team was able to document dollar savings by measuring the course's impact on company indices of productivity and job effectiveness for directory-assistance operators, including average work time spent with customers, courtesy, accuracy, and attendance. Also documented were dramatic attitude changes, improved relationships (both at work and at home), and significant work improvement among some operators who had historically been unsatisfactory or marginal performers.

Development of Internal Measurements. Another evaluation activity includes the compilation of various statistical indicators to reflect the costs, volume, and quality of training. These statistical records, which are all computerized, help NET to control expenses, provide input for forecasting, detect problems that may trigger further investigation through internal audits, and develop a data base for establishing performance standards.

A detailed breakdown of data is available to trainers and line managers, depending on their particular needs. For example, efficiency indices may measure the amount of time instructors spend in the classroom; training expenses may be broken down to show the cost of administrative support for eight different curricula or the average cost of training one student in one hour.

The Training Department's comprehensive cost-accounting system, implemented in 1982, works on a basis of "cross-charging" client departments within the company. Each month the Accounting Department sends an expense record, including training expenses, to each manager in the company. As training expenses are distributed to the client departments, the balance in the Training Department's account is reduced by a like amount.

Billing rates are determined by the total costs of training divided by the number of students. Total training expenses include the costs of delivery (that is, training salaries and expenses, purchase of classroom materials, administrative support, data-processing charges), development costs (salaries and expenses for both course developers and subject-matter experts), and food and accommodation costs. Of NET's $15 million annual training budget, about 87 percent or $13 million is recovered through cross-charging.

"The aim is to deliver training as cheaply as possible without compromising on quality," claims Smith. The cost-accounting system helps in achieving that goal, since it allows line managers to more accurately budget for training expenses and forecast future demand. Nevertheless, Smith concedes, "forecasting is the part of training we do the least well."

Once or twice a year, a questionnaire is mailed out to line managers, asking them to forecast the volume of specific courses over the following year or six months. The Training Department adds some "fudge factors," says Smith, and comes up with a figure. "It's basically a way to cover yourself. Forecast figures are continuously adjusted throughout the year since, in most cases, managers underestimate the volume," he explains. The Training Department now employs several "account managers" to advise line managers and to develop long-range forecasts of training. The account managers also serve as channels for evaluative feedback.

Evaluation of Outside Vendors. The reduction of NET's training staff since divestiture has forced company trainers to rely more on outside vendors in developing courses. As with internally developed courses, NET keeps a vigilant eye on quality. Outside courses are never purchased sight unseen, and NET recently published guidelines for evaluating vendor courses and services. Evaluation includes, first, offering the course on a pilot basis, then observing the course and surveying course participants, and finally, negotiating any changes in course content with the vendor. Only after these steps are completed is a final decision reached on whether to purchase the product.

Future Directions

Predicting the future at any company can be risky business—at NET it became doubly difficult with the tremendous upheaval brought about by the AT&T breakup. Although the split from AT&T has caused a certain degree of confusion and nervousness within the ranks, it has motivated employees to seek new, creative ways to contribute to the company. "We're seeing a greater urgency about our business than ever before," Smith observes.

Training and education needs—particularly in the rapidly changing technological fields—will continue to grow. Smith sees, in coming years, a much greater turnover in course content as new technological developments come along. Especially crucial will be the relevance of training to job needs and the timeliness of training—qualities that will require ongoing evaluation.

"In one sense, this makes our job more difficult, since it means the findings of our evaluations are valid for shorter amounts of time," he says. Smith believes the trend will be toward the gathering of "little bits of data more quickly. We have to be willing to sacrifice precision for timeliness."

Evaluations that focus on the training group—those who develop and deliver training courses—will continue in importance at NET, but at the same time, Smith sees a tendency to involve the outside client more in deciding how evaluations should proceed and what training issues should be investigated. As one example, he cites the use of steering committees made up of line managers who are a major source of evaluative feedback. "Before, it was the responsibility of the Training Department solely," Smith points out. "We need something like this if managers are to feel a sense of ownership for training."

3

The Motorola Training and Education Center: Keeping the Company Competitive

F. K. Plous, Jr.

Motorola, Inc., is a worldwide manufacturer of electronic equipment, components, and systems. The company is headquartered in Schaumburg, Illinois, about twenty-five miles northwest of Chicago, and has approximately 100,000 employees. Manufacturing operations are conducted at Schaumburg, as well as at facilities in Chicago; Austin, Texas; Arcade, New York; Mesa and Phoenix, Arizona; Joplin, Missouri; Fort Lauderdale, Florida; and a number of locations overseas. With 1986 sales of almost $6 billion, net earnings of $194 million, and an average annual growth rate of 20 percent for the last ten years, Motorola is one of the world's largest and most continually successful manufacturers of electronic products.

Two major reasons often cited for Motorola's success are the continuity and stability of its management and its steadfast refusal to diversify into unfamiliar lines of business. The company

51

was founded in 1929 by Paul Galvin, Elmer Wavering, and
William P. Lear; Paul Galvin's son Robert now serves as its
chairman. The company was founded to build and market the
first automobile radios—hence its name—and although the company today produces a variety of products for automotive, data-
processing, communications, aerospace, and defense applications, all of those products represent more or less evolutionary
developments of Motorola's basic electronics business. A major defense contractor as well as supplier to the civilian market,
Motorola enjoys a reputation as an advanced research-and-
development organization on the cutting edge of high technology.

In a period when the products of many U.S. manufacturers are compared unfavorably with those produced by Japanese competitors, Motorola maintains a reputation for consistently
high product quality and competitive pricing. In fact, Motorola
has had a close relationship with the Japanese electronics industry since the end of World War II, when it helped restore
the industry by inviting Japanese manufacturers into Motorola
plants to study the company's operations. Not surprisingly,
Motorola is managed in ways that closely resemble the corporate
culture of the most successful Japanese firms: In addition to en-
joying a stable, committed management since its founding, the
company has a participative management program which gives
each employee a share in both decision making and distribution of profits. Moreover, since 1980, Motorola has operated
an in-house employee training and educational effort that has
improved the corporation's productivity and product quality
while raising the skill level and job satisfaction of its employees.

The centerpiece of that effort is the Motorola Training
and Education Center (MTEC), which was developed for the
specific purpose of providing Motorola employees with the skills
needed to keep the company competitive. My purpose in this
chapter is to examine the history, mission, operations, and effectiveness of MTEC.

Origins of the Motorola Training and Education Center

"We were founded to be the focal point of Motorola's
education and training efforts," says John Robinson, MTEC

manager of instructional resources. "The concept was that we wanted to drive the skills we needed into the company to support our long-range strategic goals and thinking. That required us to find out what we needed to teach. The original plan was to find out what's going on and develop the training we needed to support it. It was the business plan: Where are we going and what do we need to get us there?"

The idea of MTEC was originated by Robert Galvin, who serves as chairman of the 10-person executive advisory board that directs MTEC. Upon establishing the center, the board hired William Wiggenhorn, then the director of training at Xerox Corporation, to become director of MTEC. Wiggenhorn began his work at Motorola with a staff of only 8 people, housed in leased facilities about a mile from the Schaumburg headquarters. Today he manages a staff of 53 people who occupy three-quarters of a floor in Motorola's twelve-story headquarters tower, and the total number of trainers and administrators carrying out Motorola training and education is about 800.

To staff the organization, professional trainers and educators were brought in from outside. At the same time, Robinson said, "Six people from line operations were brought in for purposes of adding reality." These included Robinson himself, a twenty-year-veteran Motorolan with experience in product management, sales marketing, engineering, and manufacturing.

The mission of MTEC is to improve the corporation's productivity, performance, and profitability by developing the kinds of work-force skills that will support the corporation's strategic objectives. MTEC also has the responsibility for monitoring the impact of its programs on the company's bottom line.

"We're using a performance-based system," Robinson says. "That means the training you do has to have a measurable effect on the business, and you have to measure that effect.

"How do you ascertain if training has had an effect on the business? We do an audit. I would not mislead you into believing we have applied it to every program. We're still in a transition stage. But we have a control group and an experimental group, and we're starting to get our hands around the numbers. We're just now beginning to see a return on our investment. I can't get specific because the numbers are proprietary, but in terms of product quality (a major strategic objective at Motorola) we are seeing a return of several times on our investment."

MTEC's executive advisory board has determined that at least 1.5 percent of direct payroll should be allocated annually to employee training and education. Currently, that sum is over $40 million per year, which is closer to 2 percent.

Training Criteria

Decisions as to what types of training are to be offered are governed by the following considerations:

- All training must be job-related.
- All training must be applicable throughout the company rather than to specific types of tasks. ("We don't have a course on how to build Zener diodes," Robinson says, "because that's better done in Phoenix where they're made.")
- All training must support current corporate strategic goals as identified and communicated by the executive advisory board. (The two strategies currently receiving top board priority are product-quality improvement and inventory reduction.)
- All training is treated as a dual investment—in people and in the business. Employees are viewed as corporate assets that improve in value when appropriate investments are made in them.

In illustration of the last point, Robinson says, "With a lot of companies, you go into the lobby and it says something like, 'People are our most important asset.' You ask them what that means and they tell you, 'Oh, it means we like our people. We respect our people.' What we say at Motorola is, 'Look, an asset is a value carried on the balance sheet, but very few assets can be renewed with investment. Our people are a renewable asset, so we invest in our people, and as we do, their value grows, both to us and to themselves.' "

MTEC and Its Relationship
to the Participative Management Program

Like many of the most successful Japanese manufacturing companies, Motorola has a corporate culture that encourages a high degree of employee participation in corporate decision making. In fact, employee input is expected, and new employees are so informed upon hiring. In addition, all corporate facilities are structured organizationally to facilitate employee participation in decision making, and new employees are given a twelve-hour training course to familiarize them with the participatory mechanism. The mechanism itself is known as the Participative Management Program, or PMP, and it is involved with MTEC both philosophically and operationally: Philosophically, both the MTEC and the PMP embody Motorola's belief that a humane and mature relationship between employer and employee will result in substantial rewards for both parties. Operationally, the two are related because the basic unit of the PMP—the primary work team made up of six to twelve employees—is the arena in which the employee's performance goals are set and performance evaluated.

PMP features work teams, into which all employees are organized. Work teams, the basic organizational unit at Motorola, are the mechanism through which employees contribute to the decision-making process that assigns work and establishes production targets. Under PMP, the corporation's basic goals are laid down by management, which determines the production and profitability goals to be fulfilled by each PMP team. The individual teams, however, exercise considerable discretion over the manner in which they will reach their goals and, it is hoped, surpass them. They meet at least once a week to discuss their strategy and tactics, to decide by how much they can exceed their goal, and to plan the techniques they will use to accomplish their objectives. Motorola plants are not unionized, so no contractual language inhibits employees from optimizing job classifications or assignments.

"PMP is based on the idea that you know your job better than anyone else does," Robinson says. "So if you and your fellow employees can find a better way to beat the profit target of your operation, the employees and the company can split any profits beyond the target. Depending on how much the team exceeds its target, the team members can share up to 40 percent of the additional profits. The company gets the remaining 60 percent.''

It is in the context of PMP that employees are most likely to become interested in advanced training: By acquiring additional job skills they are more likely to improve the performance of their teams and increase their recognition and rewards. They are also more likely to gain an increased sense of participation in the operation of their workplace.

To promote this kind of skill building, Motorola uses a program called the Annual Performance Appraisal and Career Plan, which all employees are informed about when they apply for work. At that time, they are told that joining Motorola means more than just "getting a job." It means having an opportunity to develop a career. Once a year—more often if necessary—each employee meets with his or her supervisor to review the employee's performance and determine whether it has met the employee's own stated requirements for career development. It is at that annual meeting that the employee and his or her supervisor examine the training and education required for the employee to continue to be a productive team member.

Training as an Aid to Career Growth

Motorola's policy is that career planning is primarily the responsibility of the individual employee, while a review of employee performance and availability of training are the joint responsibility of the employee and his or her supervisor. The supervisor's job is to help the employee determine how personal career goals and the company's objectives can be brought into convergence and to familiarize the employee with company-sponsored training programs that can help both parties reach their goals.

Administration, Operations, and Coordination
of MTEC Programs with Corporate Strategy

The ten-person MTEC executive advisory board meets twice a year—in the spring and fall. "They meet in the corporate boardroom—which tells you something about how important this all is to us," Robinson says. At its meeting, the executive board looks at the strategic plan of the company and asks in what general directions training is required. It budgets accordingly in each broad function.

The general policies of the executive board are translated into specific policies by five functional advisory councils, each of which meets quarterly. The five advisory councils represent the five major functions of the company—manufacturing/materials, engineering/technology, management/executive development, marketing, and sales. The manufacturing/materials council is the largest, with sixteen members, followed by engineering/technology, with twelve. The marketing council has six members, while sales and management/executive development each has five.

"The functional councils meet quarterly and decide what particular training is required, and in what order of priority, in order to support the executive board's goals," Robinson says. "Their most important function is to identify training needs."

The burden of designing the actual courses, assigning trainers, and preparing course materials falls on the full-time professional staff of MTEC.

"Each course has two specific books that go with it—an instructor's guide and a student's manual," Robinson says. "We lay down the specifications for the books, but at any given time we have several hundred free-lance writers under contract to us to write them."

The MTEC staff also carries the ongoing responsibility for assessing on-the-job effectiveness of students who have graduated and for auditing and tracking the effectiveness of the different courses. Strengthening the documentation process is one of the major projects under way at MTEC at this time.

Course Subjects and Corporate Strategies

MTEC's instructional courses, films, and workshops are listed in a semiannual catalogue, of which the 1987 edition runs to 169 pages. The courses are summarized in a six-page alphabetized syllabus. The syllabus uses a six-column table to display the title of each program, the audience for which it is intended, the goal of the course, the business issue it addresses, the mode of delivery (lecturer, videotape, and so on), and the page on which the course is described.

The critical column is the fourth one—"business issue addressed." Entries in the fourth column tell which element in the Motorola corporate strategy each course supports.

The 1987 catalogue shows sixty-seven course titles covering instructional programs of varying duration and modes of delivery. Some are self-paced, self-administered courses (Introduction to Motorola Management). Some offer a choice of self-teaching or instructor-led teaching (Pareto Diagrams). Others run six to eight hours in a classroom (Line Balancing and Material Flow), half a day (PMP Goal Setting), or three days (Motorola Product Development). One very serious course is Juran on Quality Improvement. It meets for two hours each week over sixteen weeks and requires classroom instruction.

In addition to formal courses, MTEC owns a library of 105 film and videotape titles, which can be loaned out for showing on employees' request. Titles range from basic motivational films for sales reps to complex analyses of advanced industrial planning and management techniques (*Problem Solving Strategies: The Synectics Approach, The Effective Uses of Power and Authority, Theory X and Theory Y,* and others).

Currently, 8 percent of Motorola's expenditures are for courses conducted off-site at community colleges, universities, and technical institutes, and MTEC management would like to see more of such activity. ("We try to take advantage of off-site education whenever we can in order to be good citizens," Robinson says. "We also think it's good business sense.") Funding for these courses is provided by Motorola through tuition reimbursement. In the state of Missouri, a variation on this program is under way: Funding comes from the state, but classes meet at Motorola's facility in Joplin. Also at Joplin, employees can volunteer to take their training via computer tutorials like the PLATO system. They can also study in their homes at night, using a modem to connect their personal computer terminals with the Motorola plant.

MTEC also has authority to organize courses, seminars, workshops, and other instructional efforts whenever a need arises that is not being addressed by the current course catalogue.

"Typically, if we don't have a program internally, we go out and buy it," Robinson says. "If people locally see a course (offered by local college or university), and if it relates to their career objective, they can go and take it and we'll reimburse them if they get a mark of C or better."

How closely are MTEC courses, films, and workshops aligned with corporate strategic goals? Strategic goals, by definition, are broad and generic in nature. The long trajectory inherent in strategic planning often militates against the kind of specific practical materials required in a course to be pursued by an employee in his or her spare time during a period of, at most, a few months. Nevertheless, a review of the course listings in MTEC's 1987 catalogue reveals a high degree of congruence between course offerings and managerial goals.

Robinson says the two strategic goals currently being given priority at Motorola are product quality improvement and inventory productivity. In fact, of the sixty-seven courses listed in the current syllabus, twenty-five directly address the question of quality control and improvement.

As far as inventory productivity is concerned, none of the courses is explicitly described as addressing that issue, but materials management is mentioned frequently. In addition, twenty-six courses in the syllabus are designed to teach management planning, interpersonal skills, and related practices applicable to inventory management. These include the seven courses designed to teach PMP techniques.

Robinson explains how employees trained in PMP are translating their training into inventory reduction.

"Suppose a materials manager tells a production supervisor or manager, 'You're carrying too much inventory. You've got items in stock you're hardly using, but you've got a two-year supply in there. It's costing us money.' And the production department comes back and says, 'You're right, but we've got to do it that way because the supplier is unreliable.'''

At Motorola, Robinson says, that conversation would set off a problem-solving process involving employees in two or more PMP teams trained to analyze the problem and develop solutions.

"The materials manager says, 'I didn't know—let's get together and see if we can find a better way to do it.' So they convene a meeting of the PMP teams in both departments—materials and production—and they might find there's a supplier not far away, maybe just down the road, who's set up to deliver as required. They try the supplier, and his system works. They can stop relying on a vendor clear across the country. And all three parties—materials, production, and the new vendor—are winners."

The relationship here between corporate training and corporate strategic goals is demonstrated in two ways: First, the strategic goal of materials productivity has been served by MTEC courses, which prepare PMP teams to consider innovative and synergistic solutions.

But MTEC also serves an additional strategic goal: By helping PMP teams to be successful, it reinforces the pervasive corporate strategy of developing a participative culture.

Conclusion

The Motorola Training and Education Center is a major corporate training resource, and its activities have a direct relationship to the corporation's annual training budget of $43 million, or more than 1.5 percent of direct payroll costs. That sum is probably one of the biggest training-and-education allocations in U.S. industry. After five years of operation, MTEC and Motorola senior management seem to agree that the operation has effectively met its targets, although the development of monitoring procedures that will verify this claim remains one of MTEC's most urgent priorities.

Despite the success of MTEC, however, it is not clear whether the organization's programs could produce the same levels of success if transplanted to another organization. Indeed, there is some reason to suspect that, like certain delicate wines, MTEC courses might not "travel" well.

The reason is that MTEC is something of a "natural" at Motorola: It developed in an evolutionary fashion in a stable, healthy corporate culture already predisposed to the concept of an informed and involved work force and a supportive, accessible management. Motorola founder Paul Galvin originated the policy that "the chairman's door is open to any employee." His son maintains it. The Participative Management Program, unlike the employee-participation groups that some U.S. companies have started recently, is not a recent Motorola effort to play catch-up with Japanese competitors, but a contemporary example of enlightened employee-relations policies that Motorola has fostered for decades.

MTEC was an idea that fell on fertile soil and prospered in a favorable environment. Senior management, led by the chairman of the board, gave it their complete support—an absolute prerequisite for the success of any innovative corporate program, particularly an expensive one. Strong tracking and documentation add to MTEC's credibility, and ongoing guidance and commitment from the five functional boards seem to assure that programs administered by MTEC will be closely tailored to serve corporate goals.

This kind of careful, close relationship between advisory boards and MTEC professional staff is probably essential to the success of a corporate training program and should be carefully studied by any organization contemplating the establishment of its own employee training effort.

4

Corning Glass Works: Total Quality as a Strategic Response

John V. Hickey

Quality cannot be a final destination, only a continuing journey. This statement is one way to sum up both the strategic challenge faced by Corning Glass Works and its response through education and training. Corning has historically been its industry's leader in technological innovation, product quality, and management excellence, and it has made quality the keystone of its competitive strategy. In recent years, however, the company's quality leadership has faced a serious challenge. Not that quality has declined—management can say confidently that quality is better now than it was a decade ago, and Corning's reputation for quality remains untarnished. The challenge lies in the nature of the competition. Other companies in some of Corning's major markets—particularly companies in Japan and Europe—have improved their technology to a point where they can rival Corning's quality and also compete aggressively by price.

Corning's response is characteristic. Building on its historic area of strength, the company has undertaken a comprehensive change effort in pursuit of Total Quality. Based on the concept that quality is the sum of everything that happens in the company, the effort focuses on human transaction rather than technical tinkering.

Total Quality's chief vehicle is a companywide education and training campaign to build both awareness and skills. It is fully integrated into Corning's management processes. And although change is its goal, it is less an attempt to assert new values than to reinvigorate Corning's central value.

Some General Background

Corning Glass Works, in Corning, New York, with 1986 sales of more than $1.8 billion, ranks 193d in the *Fortune* 500. Net income for 1986 was $177.1 million, assets totaled $2.3 billion, and return on stockholders' equity was 14 percent.

The company employs a worldwide work force of more than 27,000, including more than 20,000 in the United States. About 55 percent of employees are engaged directly in manufacturing. Of the remaining 45 percent, a large proportion are engineering personnel, with others in research and development, administration, finance, and support activities.

Of employees hired for management positions, between 70 and 80 percent hold undergraduate degrees in technical fields. Most American production employees are members of American Flint Glass Workers Union of North America (AFL-CIO). About 16 percent of the manufacturing work force are engaged in apprenticeable trades.

Principal Products and Services. Corning is emphatically a technology-driven company. Its spending for research and development typically runs about 5 to 6 percent of sales, and the company has been the source of many important inventions. Its product lines fall into four basic categories:

1. *Specialty glass and ceramics*—the historical base of the company. Corning manufactures more than 50,000 different products in this sector, including ceramic substrates for use in automobile catalytic converters, television bulbs, sealed-beam headlamp parts, photochromic glass, and optical and ophthalmic glasses for lenses.
2. *Consumer products*—mainly glass and ceramic cookware under such well-known trade names as Pyrex ware, Corning Ware cookware, Corelle dinnerware, and Steuben, the best-known name in American art glass.
3. *Telecommunications*—optical fiber and electronic components such as capacitors and resistors.
4. *Laboratory sciences*—health and science products and services, including Pyrex labware, tissue culture products, MetPath clinical testing services, and Hazleton Laboratories, one of the largest industrial and analytical testing services in the country.

Corporate Structure. Corning's present chairman, J. R. Houghton, is the fifth generation of the founding family. Reporting to him are five group presidents responsible for specialty glass and ceramics, consumer products, telecommunications, and laboratory sciences, as well as finance and administration, research and development, and overseas operations.

The Strategic Challenge—and the Response. In October 1983, Houghton, who recently had been elected chairman, announced that the company would undertake a major, long-term effort to improve quality—not only of products and services, but also of management transactions. The goal of these efforts would be to make quality one of Corning's two main objectives—the other being profitability. The announcement threw the spotlight on several key quality-related issues:

• *Why emphasize quality now?* The company has long used quality as its chief competitive advantage, and its reputation for quality is high among customers and industry observers. However, Corning has found in recent years that other companies have dramatically improved quality and are able to compete on this ground as well as on price. Corning's customers demand quality—and since many of the company's plants might sell half their output to a single customer, it is vital to satisfy the customer.

- *Can Corning afford quality?* David B. Luther, senior vice-president and corporate director of quality, answers that the company has little choice. Since market share increasingly depends on quality, better quality equals a higher share. Moreover, as quality improves, unit costs decline for both Corning and its customers.

- *Is the pursuit of improved quality a true strategic direction—or just another "program of the year"?* Luther concedes that it would be easy to attack the quality situation with a program—and employees are likely to perceive it as a program. Success, however, will require years, and the effort must be treated and managed as a strategic direction.

- *How could Corning achieve its quality goal?* Chairman Houghton had provided a vision and a direction: to make Corning Glass Works a leader in delivering error-free products and services, on time, that meet customer requirements 100 percent of the time. He made a commitment to provide resources and he appointed a corporate director of quality. He directed each corporate group to appoint a quality executive. This team was charged with implementing a process to achieve the quality goal—and was told that the chairman and the management committee would review progress quarterly.

With direction and commitment clearly established, the challenge remained: to make the vision a reality in daily operations.

Corning's Approach to Education and Training. The burden of implementing this vision was borne by Corning's Department of Education and Training, which makes needed training available internally under one of the following conditions:

- The training is not available from other sources.
- It can be done by Corning itself at a substantial cost advantage.
- It can be done substantially better by Corning—and the advantage in quality is essential.

The department, whose director is Donald P. Hopkins, has an annual budget of about $2.0 million. This figure covers about thirty-five training and training support people at the facilities in and around Corning, New York, plus those at facilities elsewhere. At present, most of these field locations have only one or two in training staff. In recent years, however, Corning has made a policy of strengthening training capabilities at the local level. While some of the desired strengthening can be accomplished through wider use of video and other materials developed at Corning, the number of field training personnel is likely to rise.

The Department of Education and Training manages the Corning Quality Institute, a complex of classrooms, breakout rooms, offices, and related functions—but the institute operates under an additional budget of $2.0 million a year.

The New Employee Orientation Process: The First Step Toward Total Quality. Corning's orientation process for new employees was developed in response to a specific problem: high early-career turnover among professional personnel. The company hires 200 to 300 professionals a year for its domestic locations alone. It had been losing 30 to 50 percent of these employees within their first five years—at a cost estimated to run as high as $30,000 to $40,000 each. Both the turnover rate and some comments from recently hired employees convinced management that people were leaving because, in effect, they were not being adequately assimilated. So, in the fall of 1980, a steering committe was formed to research and develop an effective orientation system. Working with the Department of Education and Training, the committee set five specific objectives:

1. to reduce turnover in the first three years of employment by 17 percent
2. to reduce the time needed to learn the job by 17 percent
3. to improve the quality of the new person's contribution
4. to impart a uniform understanding of Corning's principles, objectives, strategies, and expectations

5. to build a positive attitude toward the company and the communities in which it operates

A pilot system was tested extensively in 1981. After some revisions and adjustments, Corning adapted, with permission, a basic design used successfully by Texas Instruments.

Corning's orientation is not a short, simple introduction. Phase I lasts for six months and is required of all employees. Phase II goes into considerable depth and may last as long as nine to twelve months longer. The process as a whole joins seamlessly to the employee's ongoing education and development.

Orientation is strongly based on self-guided learning, and the new employee takes the chief responsibility. However, Edmund J. McGarrell, Jr., program development manager, says that the employee gets a great deal of support from features built into the process, and that this fact—along with careful attention to timing—contributes largely to success.

The orientation process starts even before the new employee is on the scene. As soon as possible after hiring, he or she receives an orientation plan. The supervisor—who has been provided with a set of orientation guidelines and checklists—is in contact with the new hire, designing the job and conferring on a preliminary management-by-objectives (MBO) plan. The supervisor also advises on moving or housing problems, coordinates reception activities, and sets up an interview schedule.

The orientation is built around ten two-and-a-half-hour seminars. The timing of the seminars and the use of related employee workbooks, supervisors' guides, and orientation coordinators' manuals ensure, however, that the seminars are linked closely to the new employee's developing needs.

The first day on the job starts at breakfast with the supervisor. The new employee then goes through processing in the personnel department, attends a seminar called Corning and You, and has lunch with the seminar leader. The rest of the day is devoted to introductions to co-workers, a tour of the building, and first readings in the employee workbook.

During the first week the new employee has one-to-one interviews with the supervisor, co-workers, and specialists; learns the how-to, why, and where of certain job aspects; answers questions from the workbook; and works with the supervisor on details of the MBO plan.

Regular assignments start in the second week. Sometime during the third and fourth week, the employee attends two seminars along with his or her spouse—one on employee benefits and one on the community.

From the second through the fifth months, as job responsibilities multiply, the employee reviews progress with the supervisor every two weeks. During the second and third months, the employee attends the remaining seven two-and-a-half-hour seminars, on the following subjects: Corning's technology, Total Quality, financial and strategic management, performance management and salaried compensation plans, employee relations, valuing the individual, and information management. The employee answers workbook questions about each seminar and reviews answers with the supervisor.

The third month marks the end of Phase I. The workbook is completed. The employee receives a performance review—including review of the MBO list. He or she receives a certificate of completion for Phase I and makes plans for Phase II.

In Phase II, the orientation becomes increasingly specialized. It consists essentially of orientation for specific divisions and functions, plus participation in appropriate education programs, MBO reviews, and performance and salary reviews.

This orientation system has more than met Corning's objective of improving the retention rate of new employees during their first three years of employment by 17 percent.

In 1981, Corning designed a study to assess the effect that the new orientation system might have on early-career turnover. The retention rates of all salaried people hired in 1981 in Corning, New York, were tracked for a five-year period, and the rate of retention for two groups was compared:

> Group 1—Those people who attended all nine, or eight, or seven of the nine orientation seminars. (At that time, only nine seminars were offered.)

Group 2—Those who attended none, one, or two of the seminars.

The study shows that after three years the retention of Group 1 was 29 percent greater than Group 2. After five years the improvement was 34 percent.

Corning estimates that the orientation system kept twenty-four 1981 hires in the company who would have left without it. At a weighted average investment of $26,250 per new hire, savings totaled $630,000. Developing and installing the orientation system cost $170,890. So, the net saving attributable to the system for the "class of 1981" after five years' employment was $460,000.

Richard C. Marks, senior vice-president of personnel, sums up Corning's view of its orientation system this way: "Our drive to become a Total Quality company starts by doing things right the first time with every person who joins us. I believe our orientation process is managing by prevention at its best— one of the principles of quality."

Education and Training for Total Quality

Many manufacturing companies still consider quality a problem strictly for the manufacturing and quality-control people: "Why bother everyone else about it?" This attitude could never work as a basis for Corning's pursuit of Total Quality. Although Corning is a manufacturing company, David Luther points out that only about 20 percent of its salaried employees actually work in manufacturing plants. In other words, "everyone else" is most of the company—and a rich source of opportunities for quality improvement.

According to Luther, Corning management committed itself to a policy of achieving "Total Quality performance in meeting the requirements of external and internal customers. Total Quality performance means understanding who the customer is, what the requirements are, and meeting those requirements, without error, on time, every time."

Premises of the Total Quality Effort. Corning based its approach to Total Quality on four fundamental principles similar to those popularized by Philip B. Crosby's book *Quality Is Free.* Corning states the principles this way:

1.   The meaning of quality is simply meeting requirements specified by and agreed to with a customer.
2.   Any function, operation, or activity must be undertaken with the attitude that losses, reruns, or shrinkage are not to be expected. Error-free performance is the standard.
3.   Preventing problems once and for all, at the source, is the method of operation.
4.   The cost of making errors and not doing it right the first time can be calculated and tracked, and the calculation can serve as an indicator of problems and a measure of progress.

Corning recognized that Total Quality depended on making the best use of people resources. A first step toward this goal was to start persuading employees that quality was important, that better ways of operating were possible, and that their help would be needed and welcomed in finding those ways.

The emphasis on human resources by the Corning quality management system has three parts, interdependent and equally important:

1.   *Attitude.* There must be a major change in the way management thinks and acts: Plan and manage in a way that says errors are not expected or tolerated. Look for error sources, not scapegoats, in events or processes. Prevent errors— even if correcting them seems to be more fun.
2.   *Environment.* Attention must be paid to recognition, communication, education, and teamwork—factors that can make it attractive for employees, managers, and stockholders to be on the same team.
3.   *Process.* This part consists of specific actions that can be taken by individuals or groups to convert the vision and the principles into work tasks. For example:

- Identify the customer and requirements. Get agreement.
- Measure and display output needed to meet requirements.
- Use cost of quality as a measure of the impact of not meeting requirements.
- Set up a corrective action system to fix the problem.
- Set realistic goals to improve performance.

Once Corning had made a strong commitment to Total Quality and communicated it throughout the company, it had to create a structure to manage the effort and an education system.

Structures and Teams. The effort required appropriate units at every level of the organization. The following structure was adopted:

> The Management Committee, whose members were six top corporate managers, was formed to set quality policy, authorize resources, review results, and—most important—give the effort strong and visible support and leadership.
>
> The Corporate Quality Council, consisting of representatives from each of the five corporate groups plus leaders of the various functions, would convert broad policy to a more specific plan, manage companywide quality activities, and look outside the company for ideas, methods, and techniques that might help Corning.
>
> Division steering committees, including each division's general manager and staff, were expected to set the division's direction and establish expectations.
>
> Quality improvement teams from local units would manage the quality process at the unit level.
>
> Corrective teams and quality-control circles, drawn from among the workers, were staffed by the people closest to the actual fixing of quality problems.

Devising an Education System. Development of the Total Quality course began in October 1983 and was intensive. It was done by the professional education staff and members of the Corporate Quality Council, with help from a variety of consultants. A textbook was developed, using case material from within Corning. Six experienced, respected midlevel managers were chosen to be core faculty. They received eight weeks' training in how to teach and were supported by in-house training staff and outside consultants. All materials, print and videotape, were made available in Corning's six working languages, so that the quality training could be delivered anywhere in the world. A former office facility became the Corning Quality Institute.

The first Total Quality class was held on a weekend in January 1984. It was attended by the chairman, two vice-chairmen, and three group presidents. Classes were to be limited to twenty-five people, and each session required two instructors. Scheduling was a major challenge, but the system can now train 600 to 800 employees per month.

Quality Awareness Course Content. The quality awareness message was made available in packages for three different groups.

1. Quality improvement teams attend a three-day seminar. The first day's activities are opened by the group president. After that presentation, the team works with materials dealing with the questions "What is quality?" and "How do we get it?" Discussion then centers on the four fundamental principles of quality enumerated earlier.

On the second day, small discussion groups and workshops focus on ten actions that translate the four principles into a quality plan. The ten actions are commitment, communication, establishment of teams, education, measurement and display, corrective action, attention to the cost of quality, recognition, events, and goals.

On the third day, the team applies what it has learned to its own workplace situation by developing a quality improvement plan. A large segment of this day is devoted to the concept of change. The idea is raised that when change occurs, inevitably some people will feel threatened or hurt—and that help is available for them.

2. All other salaried employees receive the same training as the quality improvement teams, except that the third day is omitted.

3. Production and maintenance employees receive their quality training in four modules of four hours each. The modules focus on a general orientation combination of videotape and lecture materials. Designed for on-site delivery by trained local personnel—for example, department or shift foremen—the modules are backed up by a trainer's manual plus a one-day workshop for trainers. Although the package is designed to give local personnel every possible support in their training efforts, it also allows plenty of room for adaptation to local conditions.

Progress and Direction. Two years after the first quality awareness class, nearly all of Corning's employees, worldwide, had been exposed to the awareness training. But, according to Luther, Total Quality has generated training and education needs far beyond those that were originally anticipated.

For example, the team nature of the quality effort means that employees are typically involved in more meetings than before. More decisions are delegated to lower levels. Relationships tend to become less clear. As a result, employees need better and more varied skills in several specific areas.

And so, in the third year, quality skills training began. It consists of sixty hours of training divided into three courses: Communications and Group Dynamics, Problem-Solving Skills, and Statistical Analysis. The courses are designed to give people skills—actual tools—for Total Quality. The training—with the exception of statistics—is required for all employees; depending on one's background, a choice of statistics courses is offered.

This level of training effort put tremendous pressure on the delivery system, says Luther. To help meet the demand, Corning has undertaken a program of employees teaching employees on a widespread scale. Quality Institute instructors train new instructors, who are drawn from all levels of the organization. Some of the best are from the production and maintenance ranks and have a seemingly natural ability to convey their enthusiasm for Total Quality along with course content. With more than 100 new trainers, employee-taught Total Quality classes are now an everyday sight at Corning plants.

Quality Education in Context. Important as education is in achieving Total Quality, Corning sees it as part of a still larger process. Other parts include:

- *Recognition.* Leaders within the organization are advised to put greater emphasis on giving employees recognition for any useful contributions to the quality process. Unit managers are asked to hold recognition dinners and other affairs at which achievements are honored and talked about.
- *Listening to people.* Corning realized that its work force was becoming less homogeneous and that factors of age, race, sex, location, and other variables might give rise to differing viewpoints on the quality effort. The company instituted an attitude survey consisting of ninety-nine questions, some for the company as a whole and some only for specific units. Taking an average of one hour to complete, the survey was given to all Corning employees in North America in 1984 and 1985. The company has invested substantial effort to analyze survey results, form action plans based on the survey, and give both results and plans to the employees. To gauge progress and identify new issues, the survey will be repeated in 1988.
- *Sharing.* The company has made a major effort to exchange views internally as well as to learn what other companies have been doing. Four trips to Japan have allowed forty-five key managers to observe at first hand how Japanese companies attack the quality challenge. Corning has also set up many exchange visits to noncompetitor American companies. Internal activities include two-day meetings at which various groups share their quality experiences, and one-day clinics that focus on specific actions. Based on an increasing number

of inquiries, Corning has also set up a monthly half-day session to introduce outsiders to its Total Quality process.

The Strategic Position of Education and Training

A guiding principle at Corning is that every education and training effort should be "a process, not a program." The slogan means simply that training activities are viewed not just as short-term solutions to isolated problems, but as factors to be integrated into the larger management picture. The company is not satisfied that it has taken integration far enough. Taking it further is the first priority in the Department of Education and Training's long-term strategy.

This priority goes hand-in-hand with a corporate strategy of integrating the quality focus with key business goals. Corning's management committee has selected several long-term quality goals, to be met by 1991; the first of these goals is to increase employee training for meeting job requirements to a companywide average of 5 percent of work time.

Several Corning executives have expressed the view that the Total Quality campaign is demonstrating the true value of education and training as a corporate strategic tool. But while Total Quality has highlighted training's capabilities, it has also indicated that those capabilities may not have been used in the past as effectively as they could be. As Luther summarizes the situation, "In the past our training efforts have tended to be somewhat random and individually driven. Now the emphasis is on making them more strategic and organizationally driven."

David B. Groff, who is primarily responsible for developing an overall training strategy, says, "We are moving more rapidly than ever in the past toward making training content more job-relevant." He describes some specific goals for training:

- Course content should represent corporate policies and practices in general management and functional skills.
- Core courses should be targeted to specific job levels.
- Management course content should be determined by anal-

ysis of needs at specific levels, and functional course content by agreement on methods.

The primary input to course content development comes from the Corning workplace itself. Employees are asked what skills they need to perform well in their jobs. Supervisors are asked similar questions. Top management of a function or business is asked what characteristics are needed to manage it effectively. These inputs are analyzed against the background of what other companies are doing in training. All these factors are assessed to determine the skills needed at a given level in a given business. Courses are expected to meet the following criteria:

- Educational activities must convey corporate policies, practices, and values. They must emphasize ties to objectives of the business, as opposed to general developmental opportunities.
- Lower-level instruction is given by internal specialists who teach occasionally.
- A central automated system tracks career-enhancing education activities and is used in career decisions.

The Binding Force: Education and Training. Although Total Quality seeks to reinvigorate historic Corning values, it is emphatically a change effort. Not the least significant effect of the Total Quality campaign has been the change it has brought about in the company's education and training. By conceiving of quality as inseparable from greater awareness and improved skills, top management has made it mainly the concern of education and training, which have been accorded strategic status.

About three and a half years after the launching of Total Quality, Corning has seen the process emerge from the first phase, in which the main task was to build quality awareness. Attention has now shifted more toward the long-term challenges of developing the skills and mechanisms needed to institutionalize quality throughout the company and of integrating all of this into the broader management framework.

An observer at Corning gets the sense that tremendous sources of energy have been harnessed at every level of the company. Corning executives give credit for this achievement to individuals and groups throughout the organization. Top management is credited with creating the vision of quality, committing leadership and resources, and giving clear and consistent messages that quality is vital. The American Flint Glass Workers Union gets praise for informed support of Total Quality and an enthusiasm that matches management's. Numerous units and employees are credited with innovations and corrective actions that are already paying off in quality.

One also senses that without the strategic role of the Department of Education and Training, the vital connection among all these centers of energy would be far less effective.

5

American Transtech:
Learning as Part
of the Job

Nancy Rubin

American Transtech, a wholly owned subsidiary of AT&T, is one of the nation's most innovative new companies in its blend of state-of-the-art technology and participatory management style. Much of the company's success comes from its establishment of a facility in a new location, the incorporation of new technology in all phases of its operation, and a carefully designed cooperative work style. During Transtech's initial organization in 1983 at its Jacksonville, Florida, site, workers and managers received intensive on-the-job training from staff specialists in organization design as well as from computer-assisted training software.

Today, as Transtech continues to expand, training has been integrated into the everyday experience of its workers. At this writing, for instance, a select group of employees are designing a new team approach for the establishment of a particular customer account. In addition, each department has created a pilot work team of its own that monitors productivity and costs in an effort to improve existing work practices. Training is thus being treated as an ongoing part of the job rather than a separate effort in the company's daily quest for excellence. For these reasons, Transtech's training efforts seem elusive to the casual observer but are actually a vital part of the company's core efforts.

About the Company

American Transtech is a high-tech information management services company that was formed in 1983 to effect the transfer of 3.2 million AT&T accounts. With the divestiture's creation of 22 million shareholder accounts, Transtech had a unique opportunity to become the largest stock transfer company in America. In 1984, Transtech successfully accomplished that goal and began to diversify. At this writing, 65 percent of Transtech's business comes from AT&T and the seven regional holding companies. Recently, Transtech has focused on two lines of business: Financial Services and Direct-Marketing Services.

Transtech is located in a handsome new glass and steel building. The 2,400 employees of this state-of-the-art information and communications processing company are white-collar clericals and professionals; the only exceptions are the mailroom workers. The average age of Transtech employees is thirty-four.

One of the most unusual features of this company is its participatory management style, whereby workers perform in a nonhierarchical, cooperative work structure. This characteristic—the capacity to work as a team for the common goals of productivity and profitability—was carefully chosen by management during hiring and training, and it continues to be fostered among workers by ongoing managerial practices. The benefits of this collective approach are many—Transtech employees report not only that the quality of their work life has improved but also that they share in company profits over and above the financial commitment to AT&T.

Because the Transtech model was designed as a four-tier structure, there are few traditional distinctions between workers. In an atmosphere that stresses the team approach, the differences between professionals and clerical workers are difficult to sort out. Interdependence and role exchange are integral to the company's work ethic, and thus job descriptions and communications between executives and workers tend to flow more freely than they do in traditionally structured companies.

In its divestiture phase, American Transtech's hierarchy was composed of the president, Larry Lemasters, and four vice-presidents. These officers were responsible for the financial and administrative operation of the company. Beneath them were the people responsible for the various business functions of the divestiture—the directors of shareowner contact, stock transfer, dividend reinvestment and stock purchase plan, employee stock ownership plan, dividend payment processing, telephone response center, mailing and proxy services, computer management, and software development. This tier also included Transtech's staff heads—the directors of public relations and advertising, human resources, training, organization and development, marketing, strategic planning, and organizational communications. These individuals monitored each department's output and connected it to the company's overall purpose; because they worked closely with both the officers and the team managers, they were a critical link between the Transtech worker and executive.

Team managers work closely with company employees to facilitate productivity. Because of the company's emphasis on a cooperative approach to work, the manager functions as a facilitator rather than as an authority figure. If an individual worker has problems getting a task accomplished, a Transtech manager discusses the reasons for the problem with the worker and tries to help him or her find a solution instead of reprimanding the worker. Because so much of the work at Transtech is cooperative, the team manager often shares the worker's problem with the other team members to avoid repetition of the same mistake. In this environment, the team manager emerges as a skilled mediator of labor problems instead of a feared taskmaster.

Since personal initiative has been highly valued at Transtech from its inception, workers who wish to be promoted to team manager can respond to company notices for such positions. Worker proficiency is rewarded by increased responsibility and pay increases, rather than by a traditional job-promotion structure.

The In-Service Training Function

Prior to divestiture, Larry Lemasters, then assistant treasurer of AT&T's Stock and Bond Division, was already working to improve the quality of work life. Between 1979 and 1981, the Stock and Bond Division had also developed a new on-line real-time shareowner services system that allowed the division to handle large volumes of work at lowered costs. Although these efforts were already under way within the Stock and Bond Division, it was the divestiture that provided the catalyst for Transtech's unique work model. With the Justice Department's decision to divest AT&T, telephone stock accounts were expected to grow eightfold, thereby creating the potential for a giant new profit-making business. As the largest such transaction in history, the stock divestiture was a market that many of the nation's largest banks, such as the Morgan Guaranty Company and Manufacturers Hanover Trust, were eager to capture, but Lemasters was quick to present this opportunity to the officers of the AT&T board.

Lemasters was assisted in the development of a new company idea by four employees of AT&T's Stock and Bond Division: Andrew Abate, Nancy Dreicer, Frances Dramis, and Nelson Frye. To spearhead the training effort, Frye became head of AT&T's Organization, Development, and Training Division and reported to the vice-president of the Department of Corporate Resources. It was during the planning stage that Joseph Wiley was hired as vice-president to help plan the new company. Before long, Lemasters and his team presented a business plan to Charles L. Brown, then chairman of AT&T, for a new company that would act as transfer agent for the AT&T stocks and the newly created regional holding company stocks.

This business plan detailed how the proposed $100 million company would succeed and maintain its lead over potential competitors. At its center was a careful financial and managerial analysis of how high worker productivity for shareowner services could be achieved through the use of the on-line, real-time shareowner services system and a participative management style.

Within six months of the announcement of the divestiture, the plan had been approved by AT&T, and a site was chosen for the new company in Jacksonville, Florida. That city offered Transtech many advantages—because it was already a major East Coast banking and insurance center, it had a skilled labor force and a cooperative set of city leaders. In retrospect, Transtech managers claim that it was the selection of a new site, the construction of a new facility, and the hiring of new personnel that contributed to the company's immediate success.

The company's first year was, as Garo Mavian, director of Transtech's stock transfer operations, describes it, a "win-win" atmosphere, a time when people were willing to take risks and work together cooperatively for a common goal. The people who came to Transtech for employment at that time, according to Nelson Frye, were "risk takers, ones who liked excitement and were willing to take responsibility on their own." Initially, all 600 employees of AT&T's Stock and Bond Division in Piscataway, New Jersey, were offered new jobs in Florida; ultimately, 240 accepted. During this transitional period, the prospective Transtech employees didn't know the company's name, its charter, or even their own job descriptions. They were told, however, to prepare for a salary cut because of a lower cost of living in the new region.

As Frye observes, the hiring method that eventually took place at AT&T was really a self-selection process. "Essentially, they were self-managed people, not people who were into structure, or who needed guarantees about what they'd make and do," he said. With a core group of seventy or eighty people from AT&T, the company began to articulate its values of self-management and worker participation. When the company designers lacked knowledge in specific areas, they hired consultants to provide them with expert advice. By February of

1983, some of the AT&T workers had relocated and the training of new workers began.

Hiring. At the same time, a massive hiring process was begun in Jacksonville, resulting in the addition of 800 new employees by the end of 1985. Because of the large numbers of people to be processed, hiring occurred in stages. Candidates were selected by Transtech's human resources staff and then interviewed by team managers. These managers described the job thoroughly and offered examples of casework to the candidates. The team concept was also explained by the managers at that time, and some candidates automatically eliminated themselves because they felt they needed some structure and direction; others felt they were too competitive to work in such an atmosphere.

Training. During 1983 and 1984, approximately 1 percent of Transtech's total expenses was spent for training, organization development, and consultation.

From the beginning, managers were trained to hire their own personnel. This was done by stressing the importance of finding self-managing candidates and sensitizing managers to this quality in candidates during their interviews. Managers not only were instructed in these techniques by Transtech's organization and development staff, but were given opportunities to simulate those interviews before the hiring actually began.

At the same time, Transtech's organization and development personnel created three model work groups to experiment with the team concept. These groups engaged in participatory work groups in February, March, and April of 1983 to improve the Transtech team concept.

Once employees were hired, the training began in earnest. During a two-day orientation period, Transtech's five company officers met with new workers to explain the company's culture and values and to encourage them to fully participate in their work teams.

Workers were then placed in twenty- to forty-member work teams and began to learn their jobs through computer-based training programs specifically written for Transtech. These new programs enabled workers to learn their jobs in eleven weeks instead of the twenty-one it used to take in New Jersey. Because much of the company's work involves stock-account processing, workers were taught techniques to answer customer questions, correct account records on terminals, and produce rapid written communications with shareholders through the computer-training program. Although words like *self-managing, participatory,* and *egalitarian* had been stressed to workers throughout the hiring and orientation period, now the team concept quickly became a practical reality.

Coaches were present to acquaint workers with the computer-based training from the first day of work, but they were not always accessible when workers had questions. As a result, team members often found they had to ask one another for information. During this same time period, teams were also asked to develop their own work codes and policies on attendance, dress, and behavior. (Interestingly enough, the dress codes many teams developed were far more strict than those designed by traditional managers.)

"Through these devices people quickly got the idea that this was their show," said Frye. "We worked hard on the idea that we needed their participation and expected them to be part of the company's decision-making process from the beginning."

As the company hired more workers, Transtech continued to encourage its workers to be actively involved in its development and evolution. In the first months of operation, this cooperative approach was fostered through daily meetings of the company's work teams. Finally, in the last months before the divestiture, Transtech's teams held "dress rehearsals" for the massive work load that would begin on January 1, 1984. Even at this juncture, mistakes were observed and systems refined so that ultimately the divestiture process would go smoothly.

Since then, work teams have continued to meet regularly, although not necessarily daily, in answer to current group needs. These sessions are held within each department, often as workers sit in a circle around their work stations, or in one of the several conference rooms located within each division. The meeting atmosphere is nonjudgmental, and the meeting remains a place where workers and managers are encouraged to tackle problems and find solutions collectively. Workers are also encouraged to offer suggestions for improvements in productivity. As one employee observed, the beauty of the system is that anyone with a good idea "has a real chance to make a difference" in the way the company operates—an opportunity that enhances the worker's own self-esteem at the same time that it benefits the company.

It is this kind of open communication between team members and their managers that has generated worker enthusiasm and, ultimately, enhanced the company's productivity. By the end of 1984—the first full year of Transtech's operation—productivity for the processing of shareholder stock accounts had increased 60 to 80 percent over earlier performances in AT&T's Stock and Bond Division. During that same period, 5.6 million telephone calls were answered and 114 million checks, statements, certificates, and proxy cards mailed to shareholders.

As Frye notes, worker satisfaction soared, while absenteeism and job turnover were minimal. "The people loved it because they felt they were being trusted," he explains. Nevertheless, both Frye and Mavian point out that the establishment of such a system has required an enormous expenditure of time and energy by managers and workers. Designers of the Transtech model point out that they were able to do this because there was little need to develop a traditional monitoring system within the company to tally absenteeism or tardiness.

Instead, the company strategy has been to help managers run counseling sessions with workers and "catch people doing things right." As one employee points out, the company has taken a lot of time to help develop the individual worker. She says, "The feeling here is not as it is in most organizations, that as the company grows you grow, but rather that as you grow, your company grows." Her perception tallies with the company's long-term training goals to develop highly efficient work teams that are essentially self-managed. Thus, when problems do appear in the company's work teams today, Transtech managers—or team members—routinely present them to the group for a solution.

Through the marriage of a participatory management style and the use of computer technology, Transtech achieved a unique record of productivity in its first year of operation.

Long-Range Strategy for Training

Company Expansion. With the successful completion of the AT&T divestiture in 1984, Transtech entered a new phase as an information management services company. As the seven new regional holding companies began to individualize and require more customized services, Transtech management began to see the need for a different kind of team approach—one that would coordinate the various subsets of services that were being uniformly offered to shareholder accounts. Simultaneously, as Transtech began to reach out to acquire new accounts and diversify its services, competitive profitability became a critical priority.

Under the leadership of William A. Hightower, who became Transtech's president in May 1984, the company began to evolve into an aggressive information management services organization. This competitive orientation has, in turn, created the impetus for a new organizational design. In Transtech's postdivestiture phase, the Organization Development and Training Program focused more on management skills development and teamwork than on technical training. At the same time, the concept of a "business team" was developed to unify company goals.

This team—composed of the president, vice-presidents, executive directors, and heads of the various business units—is responsible for setting the goals and direction of Transtech in the competitive marketplace. Ultimately, the business team's long-range goal is the growth and diversification of Transtech's information management services.

Current Training Efforts. In this second developmental phase, the company reorganized its services around the customer's needs, rather than around a particular organizational function, as it did in the first years of Transtech's existence.

In keeping with the company's commitment to participatory work teams, Transtech hired a consultant to work with the Human Resources Department and called upon its workers to facilitate the creation of new team designs. By early April 1985, 150 employees offered to participate in the company's first sociotechnical design team, which was to serve BellSouth within the Financial Services Division. After an extensive application and interview process, eighteen workers were chosen for that team. The team members then met daily and studied the particular requirements of BellSouth. Since that time, the sociotechnical team design has been incorporated throughout the entire organization.

There are several obvious advantages to the sociotechnical team approach; the first, according to Barbara Moulding, assistant vice-president of financial services and former head of the BellSouth team, is that the workers will be acquainted with the larger picture and hence less likely to make mistakes; the second, that they have become quite familiar with customer needs and preferences; the third, that since the workers have designed the work procedures themselves, they will have considerable control over its functions; and the last, that because of their planning, these employees have eliminated replication of effort.

In this first customer-oriented unit, team members from various functions, such as telephone response and stock transfer, worked together in one group and drew upon the services of a pool of managers. Transtech managers and employees have consistently pointed out that such a design effort would not have been possible without the earlier history of a participatory work style. By the summer of 1985, the BellSouth account became operational.

Along with this effort has been the establishment of pilot work teams within each department. Within the Financial Services Division, for instance, a pilot team for a telephone response center experimented with the shifting of workers from phone response to paperwork during periods of low demand: that group also tracked the time and costs for call processing. Similar experiments to lower costs and raise productivity were conducted in pilot teams throughout the company.

Because the participatory work style has been such a success, management and workers are enthusiastic about the sociotechnical design-team concept, seeing it as a way both to deliver better customer services and to enhance the considerable resources of its staff. Although there is little information on Transtech's long-term training strategy, the company's vibrancy and commitment to a participatory work style suggest that training for a new technology is a rudimentary part of its workers' daily experience. As Transtech's business needs continue to evolve, the concept of a participatory work style and a team-training approach will undoubtedly remain one of the company's greatest strengths.

6

Improving Operations and Employee Opportunity Through Technical Training: Gilroy Foods, Inc.

Russell W. Scalpone

Several key management strategies have emerged over the past decade for improving business operations and thereby enhancing competitive position. These strategies include: improving productivity through automation; upgrading product quality while simultaneously reducing costs through the use of in-process quality monitoring and statistical process control techniques; and involving the hourly employee in the job of maintaining and improving quality. Companies pursuing one or more of these innovative strategies, however, are finding them difficult to put into practice. The reason for this difficulty is that all of the strategies have an unseen common denominator, a hidden criterion for success that is usually overlooked in both planning and implementing them. They all require a work force trained with sufficient technical knowledge and skill to make the strategy work.

Gilroy Foods, Inc., a major subsidiary of a *Fortune* 200 company, is a leading producer of high-quality food products such as dehydrated onion, garlic, and capsicums. The main processing plant is located in Gilroy, California, and has a medium-sized work force. The actual number of employees varies widely within a given year due to the seasonal changes inherent in growing, harvesting, and processing food. A key requirement of the business is the careful monitoring, control, and grading of product quality at each stage—from initial growing through harvesting, processing, packaging, and final delivery to the customer.

Improvement Strategies and the Need for Technical Training

At Gilroy Foods, advances in both production and quality-control technology had reached the point where they necessitated a more structured and focused approach to technical training for hourly personnel in several key departments. Within operations, process control and product flow were becoming increasingly computerized through the extensive use of electronic control devices and programmable controllers. The installation of a computerized maintenance-management system made possible better tracking and control of recurring maintenance problems as well as better planning of maintenance work. A major capital project was also undertaken to construct a steam cogeneration facility. This project would provide better efficiency and more precise control systems that would have to be fully understood by operating and maintenance people alike.

A number of trends in the area of quality control (QC) were changing the role of the QC technician and related skill requirements. Customers were requesting more varied and advanced QC tests for special product studies. At the same time, customers were certifying Gilroy products for shipment without incoming inspection, based on more extensive reporting of test data. These trends required more advance testing knowledge as well as more extensive analysis and reporting of test data.

New technology was making some tests easier to perform on the production line. This trend, coupled with expanding use of statistical process control techniques, was in turn fostering greater involvement of production line people in routine QC activities. The effect of all these trends was a more complex and less routine QC technician job—one that required more grounding in hard laboratory sciences, statistics, computer science, and electronics as well as greater skill in training to prepare production people to carry out new, quality-related responsibilities.

Thus, at Gilroy Foods, the stage was set for a fresh look at how technical training could help the company and its employees better cope with, and benefit from, changes that were occurring in the business. The task confronting Gilroy Foods management was to design workable, cost-effective programs that could meet company objectives while responding to the personal career development goals of employees. To assist with program design, the company hired a consultant.

Program Benefits, Objectives, and Critical Requirements

A large-scale technical training program with a curriculum linked to the employee career ladder can have significant benefits for both the company and its employees. Benefits for the company include the following:

- obtaining high utilization from technically sophisticated equipment
- improving quality of products and services produced directly by skilled workers
- increasing the productivity or value of output per worker
- reducing the cost of recruiting skilled workers from outside the company

Conversely, benefits of the training program for the worker include:

- enhancing self-confidence and self-esteem
- increasing the meaning, importance, and responsibility level of work that can be assigned to the employee

- increasing the individual's potential for advancement and higher compensation
- improving the individual's employability within the company as well as in the labor market as a whole

These dual benefits for company and employee make a technical training curriculum linked to the job progression structure one of the most powerful tools available for aligning employee goals and motivation with the business goals of the company.

While management within both the QC and Maintenance departments at Gilroy Foods remained convinced that these benefits were achievable, they were in agreement with their consultant that more tangible, clearly defined criteria would be required for justifying and planning a comprehensive technical training program. Thus, a set of working objectives was adopted to be used in evaluating specific program features. These objectives required that the training should:

- help to maintain Gilroy Foods as the leading quality producer of food products in its field
- achieve significant reductions in unnecessary costs
- ensure a high level of technical support services
- minimize disruptions in production through better handling of problems
- create means and opportunities for both existing and new employees to develop skills, enhance their contribution to the company, and achieve the highest possible job level to which they might aspire

With objectives stated in this manner, it was possible to define needs and focus technical training curricula based upon measurable criteria keyed to specific cost and service areas. This approach to stating objectives and measures was aimed at demonstrating costs and benefits for the program and will be described further when we examine the details of the program in each of the two departments.

While a positive cost/benefit ratio is one make-or-break requirement for a technical training program, it is not the only one. At least two other factors are critical and need to be considered in planning and implementing the program. These factors are program administration and employee acceptance.

Whenever a technical training curriculum is linked to career progression, questions arise regarding the administration of promotions. When is an employee ready to advance? Should anyone who completes training be advanced, or should an on-the-job skill demonstration be required? Should a paper-and-pencil test be required for promotion, or should we rely upon supervisory judgment to determine that the employee is ready?

At Gilroy Foods, a decision was made to permit every employee in the skill progression to advance automatically, based upon objective criteria of knowledge and skill attainment, without dependence upon paper-and-pencil testing, subjective supervisory ratings, or mere seniority. Objectivity in the administration of the program was required not only to alleviate undue pressure on first-line supervisors to make subjective judgments, but also to establish the credibility of the program in the employee's mind. It was felt that employees must have the expectation that their effort and achievement in learning will produce tangible recognition.

A final requirement for the Gilroy Foods program was that it be accepted by hourly and supervisory employees. A fair and objective approach to administration will go a long way toward defusing potential criticism of a technical training and progression program, and will foster quality control in the process of training and advancing people. But fairness and objectivity are not enough to ensure acceptance. Employees who participate in the training and administration of the program must feel a sense of ownership for the process.

It has long been recognized that participation by affected parties in the planning of an organizational change is the best way to create in them a sense of owning the change; planning a new training program is no exception to this rule. Hourly employees and first-line supervisors have the biggest stake in seeing that the program succeeds and will, in fact, be the ones who determine whether or not the program *does* succeed. Therefore, it made sense that they should participate in the design of the maintenance and QC technical training programs at Gilroy Foods. Consequently, mechanisms were established to allow participation by employees and supervisors in the definition of training needs, program content, and administrative procedures.

Three critical requirements were addressed in both the maintenance and QC technical training programs: providing for cost-beneficial program content, employee participation in program development, and fairness/objectivity in program administration.

Case Study 1: The Gilroy Foods
Maintenance Training and Development Program

The maintenance department at Gilroy Foods consists of a large staff of mechanics who are responsible for the preventive care, overhaul, and repair of plant utilities and equipment, as well as fabrication and construction work to maintain the buildings and grounds.

The maintenance program was initially conceived because of a mutual desire on the part of both maintenance management and the employee union to provide a more structured and reliable means for developing new apprentice mechanics into journeymen. As program planning began, however, it became clear that a comprehensive program would also have to address the training needs of existing journeyman mechanics, their work leaders, and even the maintenance supervisors, if the program were to have significant impact on operations and the working objectives described earlier.

Cost Benefit, Staffing Analysis, and Program Content. Cost and staffing analyses were seen as ways of relating training to the needs of the entire organization, and were therefore critical for justifying the program as well as directing the training content toward meaningful areas. The working objectives mentioned earlier covered such things as cost reduction, level of technical support service, and minimizing disruptions to production. The analyses investigated these needs in two ways.

First was a review of the maintenance budget, staffing level, departmental performance, and work load in terms of dollars and hours by category, including extent of use of outside contractors and categories of services they provided. This analysis was helpful in positioning the Gilroy Foods maintenance function in relation to maintenance departments in other companies and industries.

The second cost analysis focused on maintenance repair records in different areas of the plant, comparing the frequency of occurrence for different categories of repair jobs, along with their total cost in parts and labor. While actual results of this analysis are proprietary, the format of the analysis is depicted in Figure 1. It should be noted that each cost exhibit ranked the repair categories from greatest cost (at the left) to least cost (at the right), to facilitate easy identification of those "vital few" categories responsible for the greatest proportion of total cost in that area of the plant.

Needless to say, those vital few items with high repair costs were singled out for special attention in the design of training for both hourly and supervisory people in maintenance.

In addition to the cost and operational budget of training, another important consideration is the opportunity training creates for employee advancement. To implement a large-scale training effort that will stimulate upward mobility, certain questions must be answered. How many people will be needed in the future at each job level? How many can realistically be developed and promoted from within? What kinds of skills cannot be developed in-house and should be recruited from the outside?

To answer these questions in quantitative terms, a detailed staffing forecast was constructed. This consisted of looking at the number of people at each job level: new apprentice, mechanic-in-training, journeyman, work leader, and supervisor. Then, for each of the next five years and for ten years out, three numbers were developed for each job level:

1. *Staffing demand:* the number of people that will be needed based upon expected plant capacity, capital plans, projected work load, and so forth

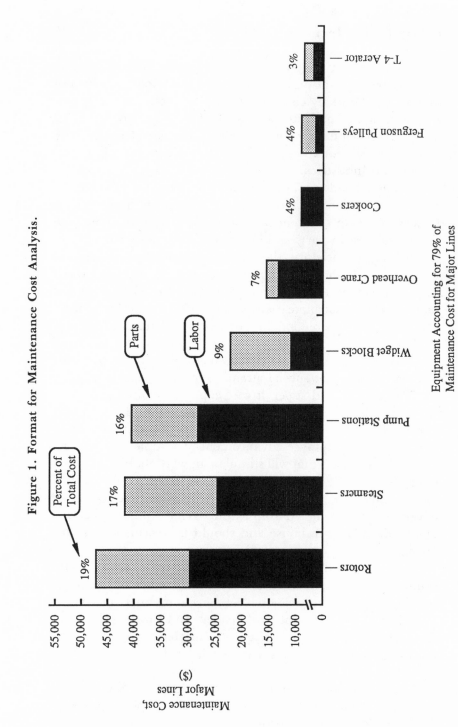

Figure 1. Format for Maintenance Cost Analysis.

Equipment Accounting for 79% of
Maintenance Cost for Major Lines

Note: Equipment categories and dollar values are fictitious. Percentages have been rounded.

2. *Staffing supply:* the number of people available if nothing were done to fill staffing needs (based upon the existing number of people at a given job level minus those lost due to turnover, attrition, retirement, and the like)
3. *Supply minus demand:* the net number of people who must move into a job level each year to meet projected needs

This analysis revealed the number of apprentices needed each year and the rate at which people had to progress in the program to meet the demand for journeyman mechanics within a given year. One finding of particular interest was the discovery that more journeyman mechanics would be needed in the near future than were previously anticipated. As a result, this analysis was invaluable in planning the program budget and reinforced the original rationale for the program.

While the cost and staffing analyses were highly useful in planning the overall direction of the program, they did not provide sufficient detail regarding the knowledge and skill needed to perform satisfactorily as a mechanic in the Gilroy Foods plant. Thus, the next step was a detailed analysis of the mechanic job. This entailed interviewing maintenance mechanics, work leaders, and supervisors to identify the following:

- most critical types of maintenance tasks and repair work performed on a routine and emergency basis
- knowledge, skills, and abilities needed to do the work
- personal and physical characteristics required to succeed as a mechanic
- problems encountered in the past with the delivery of maintenance service

Due to the importance of coordinating maintenance repair work with production needs, several production managers were also interviewed to determine how maintenance training might be used to improve support provided to their departments.

At a later stage of the study—just prior to implementing an apprentice selection program—mechanic knowledge, skills, abilities, and personal/physical characteristics (KSAPs) and mechanic's tasks were formally defined, listed, and submitted to mechanics and supervisors in questionnaire form so that the KSAPs and tasks could be rated, listed in order of priority, and evaluated. Based upon this rating process and the elimination of incorrect or unnecessary items, it was possible to describe the mechanic's job with approximately twenty-five tasks and an equal number of KSAP statements.

Based on the results of the job analysis, a *Practical Skills Manual* was prepared, detailing the course curriculum and practical skills that constitute the full range of achievements expected of a mechanic during the training period to become a journeyman. The mechanic course curriculum consisted of approximately fifty skill-training modules, ranging from two to sixteen hours in length, grouped into five categories (mechanical, electrical, pipe fitting, buildings and grounds, and steam handling) and graded by job level. Practical skills consisted of several hundred specific troubleshooting, repair, and preventive maintenance tasks grouped into categories based on the knowledge area (for example, hydraulics, fabrication, electrical, and plumbing) or on the specific types of equipment found in a plant area (for example, belts and conveyors, fans, mills, and dryers). Each practical skill was graded by level of difficulty and stated in concrete terms to facilitate an objective assessment of the individual mechanic.

Project Management Mechanisms and Employee Participation. The project to develop the training program was planned to permit all affected organizational levels and departments to participate both in providing input and in reviewing program content and design features as they emerged. Overall direction for the developmental project was provided by a steering committee, consisting of the vice-president of operations, two operations managers, the director of human relations, the manager of employee relations, the plant engineer (maintenance manager), and the maintenance superintendent. This group provided overall policy direction, received status reports, reviewed project deliverables, and ensured coordination between the needs of production and maintenance.

Actual program development work was carried out by a project team consisting of the plant engineer, the maintenance superintendent, the maintenance training and systems supervisor, an outside consultant, and a production manager with extensive prior work in plant labor relations.

To facilitate employee participation, two advisory teams were established. One consisted of maintenance supervisors (all salaried) and the other of a journeyman mechanic and several work leaders (all hourly). Hourly advisory team members were selected to ensure representation of key plant areas and technical skills. One member of this group also served as union steward, although the charter for the advisory teams excluded from discussion matters pertaining to the labor-management agreement.

The process of developing the program was characterized by a high level of communication and participation at all levels. Initially, the plans for developing the program were presented by the plant engineer to the entire maintenance department in a general meeting. At critical stages of the project, key deliverables—such as project methodology, job analysis results, the *Practical Skills Manual*, planned administrative procedures, and the apprentice selection program—were also presented to the advisory teams for questions, comments, reactions, and suggestions. Some items, such as the *Practical Skills Manual*, were distributed to advisory team members for critique and revision. In the advisory team meetings, group members were polled by circulating index cards to obtain written comments for subsequent posting and discussion, by recording comments on a flip chart, or by gathering comments orally in both guided and open-ended discussions.

Mechanics, work leaders, and supervisors also provided input on an individual basis in the job-analysis interviews. These interviews were originally aimed at fact finding regarding job content, but due to the general level of excitement and interest connected with the training program, the interviews often elicited discussion of many ideas related to both training and the improvement of maintenance.

The most widely used communication channel, however, was the old-fashioned informal conversation. One-on-one exchanges occurred between project team members and all levels of maintenance people in the hallways, the photocopy room, the maintenance office, and the cafeteria—and more than once they raised an issue or consideration that had been overlooked during formal fact gathering.

Administrative Approach. The approach to program administration was designed to provide automatic career progression based upon demonstrated achievement, with minimal room for subjective interpretation. In the program, advancement from apprentice to mechanic-in-training and from mechanic-in-training to journeyman was based upon four factors:

1. satisfactory completion of prescribed course modules, as indicated by a supervisor or training instructor
2. minimum time in grade, to ensure adequate exposure to a full range of on-the-job experiences
3. demonstration of practical skills by performing the task in question under the observation of a supervisor, training instructor, or other qualified individual
4. a satisfactory performance appraisal that covers areas such as attendance, safety, and other observable aspects of performance

While subjectivity can enter into a performance appraisal, the appraisal process is designed to minimize bias by involving not only the immediate supervisor, but also the production supervisor (the user of maintenance service), the work leader, and the employee in the appraisal. Moreover, individuals will be held back only in the event that documented instances of substandard performance are recorded.

Practical skills are signed off when the individual is observed to perform the task in question. Bias in this case is reduced through the use of a written procedure for observing the task and, in the case of more complex tasks, by providing the observer with a written procedure for the task itself.

A few additional component parts of the administrative package should also be mentioned. These are the developmental plan and the developmental file. The developmental plan is a list of the courses and practical skills an individual agrees to complete in a given time period. The accumulation of these plans is one basis for future planning of departmental training activities. The developmental file, on the other hand, is the record of an individual's training achievements. The accumulation of the developmental file provides management with an inventory of skills and achievements for the department as a whole and is also useful in planning and budgeting.

All program administration is overseen by a maintenance skill committee consisting of the plant engineer, the maintenance superintendent, the maintenance systems and training supervisor, and the plant human relations manager. This group plans training strategy, approves training expenditures, monitors progress of individuals in the program, and communicates with supervisors, instructors, and others regarding plans or any problems. The maintenance systems and training supervisor provides support for both the program and the skill committee by administering a training center, maintaining training files and records, researching and contacting training program vendors, and following up with maintenance supervisors, mechanics, and other involved parties in order to ensure that the work of training gets done.

The Apprentice Selection Process. The single greatest concern voiced by employees both informally and in advisory team sessions was the need for a better way of selecting maintenance apprentices. In the past, apprentice selection had been based upon employee seniority and an aptitude test battery administered by a local college. Because of widespread concern about this method, a new and more comprehensive process was devised.

Each step of the new procedure was based on a determination of the specific knowledge, skills, abilities, and personal or physical characteristics (from the job analysis) that could be assessed at that step. A key step in the process was the interviewing of candidates by a member of the skill committee. This interview was considered vital, not only from the standpoint of the selection process but also for communicating about the program with candidates, all of whom were company employees. Thus, it was decided that every qualified candidate would be interviewed, regardless of how many applied.

Another key step in the planned apprentice selection process was a week-long pre-entrance objective program (POP)—an assessment of a candidate's trainability through actual participation in a simplified form of apprentice training. In the POP, a small group of candidates would learn basic skills, such as tool usage, simple welding, and basic electricity, as taught by an outside instructor. Throughout the week, the instructor would evaluate learning and progress through written and oral questioning as well as through simple projects demonstrating newly learned skills. A passing score in the POP would be an average of 70 percent across the five one-day modules.

Current Status and Evaluation. At this writing, the Maintenance Training and Development Program has accomplished the following:

- A multiroom training center, including both shop and classroom facilities, has been constructed. Furnishings and audiovisual equipment have been installed.
- The initial group of apprentice candidates has been selected and is currently participating in the POP.
- The *Practical Skills Manual* has undergone several stages of review and revision and is considered to be in final form (although it will be updated on a continuing basis).
- Skill committee and advisory team members are currently reviewing commercially available skill training modules, placing them in order of priority and jointly making purchase decisions.
- Supervisory training in the observation and evaluation of practical skills is scheduled to begin in a few months, as will formal apprentice training.

While long-term results of the program are not yet available, preliminary indications are very positive. The program has visibly improved the communication of managers with supervisors and hourly workers. Comments and concerns regarding the way maintenance work is done, the skill requirements for handling the work, and the nature of the promotional system have flowed freely in both directions, with visible response and a commitment by management to ongoing personnel development. Moreover, the skill committee and advisory teams continue to meet on a regular basis and have become permanent vehicles for developing and implementing a wide variety of improvement-oriented activities.

Evaluation of the program is a continuing process and will be based upon careful monitoring by the skill committee of indicators such as the following:

- overall departmental costs
- frequency of the high-cost repairs in each plant area, by category
- frequency of production stoppages due to maintenance-related problems
- completion of courses and practical skills by program participants as indicated in their developmental plans
- advancement of apprentices to higher-level positions within the maintenance department

Informal feedback from hourly and supervisory people will, of course, continue to be the most important kind of evaluation input on a day-to-day basis, and responding to this input will be the primary means of ensuring that the program will continue to be effective in achieving its goals.

Case Study 2: The Gilroy Foods
Quality Control Training and Development Program

The Quality Control (QC) Training and Development Program at Gilroy Foods was, at this writing, newer and thus less developed than the maintenance program. Nonetheless, a brief comparison of the QC and maintenance programs, together with their similar and dissimilar features, will illustrate how the principles of program design described earlier can be applied to a different type of department.

The QC Department at Gilroy Foods consists of three

laboratories and related support personnel. The total work force in QC is approximately half that of maintenance. Three distinctions between the QC situation and that of maintenance are noteworthy. One is the work situation and environment. In maintenance, the mechanics are usually spread out over the entire plant, responding to work requests and moving to a new job when they complete the one they are working on. The mechanic fabricates, services, or repairs a variety of equipment, often alone, in many different locations: atop ladders, under conveyors, inside drying ovens, and so forth. Conversely, technicians in the QC labs normally work in one location—the lab— alongside other technicians, completing very precise tasks and following exacting written procedures. Where the mechanic needs to understand the functioning of many different types of equipment and to have skill in using different tools and materials, the technician must know the specifications and procedures and be able to recognize when a test result is unusual.

A second distinction between QC and maintenance is the nature of forces that generate a need for training. In maintenance there was a need to raise the individual's skill contribution in the face of changing equipment and plant technology. In the QC labs, the technician's role and the tasks that constitute it were actually changing. Both customers and other departments within the company were demanding that the labs perform more complex testing, more nonroutine testing, and more *information processing* in general.

This increased complexity, together with the advent of new instruments and new technology in QC, demanded a greater quantity of technical knowledge on the part of the individual worker, but the technician's role was also changing qualitatively, due to the inescapable economics of prevention versus cure. The sooner a potential quality problem is corrected, the less costly and troublesome it becomes. Thus, a problem discovered in final product testing is extremely costly to correct. A problem discovered early in the production process is easier to correct, and a potential problem that is detected and prevented from becoming a problem is the easiest problem of all to deal with. Thus, the logic of prevention dictates moving QC testing from the lab to the production line to shorten reaction time and improve control of the production process.

The implications of this trend for the role of the QC technician are profound. The new technician role requires a number of new capabilities, most of which must be used outside the traditional, controlled laboratory setting, including:

- extensive knowledge and use of both electronic instrumentation and process-control statistics
- ability to go beyond merely performing repetitive test procedures to carrying out special research projects, such as process capability studies
- ability to teach testing, data recording, and control techniques to production line personnel

Because of these emerging role changes, a major aim of the cost-benefit analysis for the QC training program was to investigate the potential gain of training technicians for their new role.

A third difference between the QC and maintenance situations was the lack of a true job progression structure. In maintenance, an employee moved through three job levels to become a journeyman mechanic, whereas in QC, almost all technicians were in a single grade level. Thus, another task of the QC project team was to explore the appropriateness and feasibility of creating new job levels to permit a skill progression within the department.

Cost Benefit, Staffing Analysis, and Program Content. As in the case of maintenance, working objectives for the QC program were stated in terms of cost, support service, minimizing disruptions to production, and creating advancement opportunity for employees. Another similarity to the maintenance program was the desire to quantify the impact of quality training on the rest of the organization. This was achieved by analyzing the cost incurred by Gilroy Foods in producing a quality product.

Experts in the quality field, such as Crosby, Feigenbaum, and Juran, have long advocated the establishment of quality cost accounting systems within companies as a means of identifying

improvement opportunities and measuring the gains from a companywide total quality program. The approach of quality cost
accounting is a useful one, because the costs incurred in meeting
required quality levels are usually lost in the labyrinthine structure of most company accounting systems. By accumulating
quality costs, it is possible to identify specific areas where quality
improvement strategies are likely to ''pay off'' for a company.

The QC project team examined quality costs in two categories. First was *appraisal cost,* the cost of inspecting, measuring,
or testing the product. Appraisal cost is normally most closely
associated with the operating budget of a quality-control department and the activities performed by QC inspectors. At Gilroy
Foods, appraisal cost is examined by first collecting data on the
frequency of various tests performed in the micro and analytical
labs and then multiplying the frequency of each test times their
cost in labor and materials. The result is similar to the chart
in Figure 2. As with maintenance cost analysis (see Figure 1),
activities were ranked with the highest cost items at the left.
Thus, it became clear which tests were likely to pay the biggest
dividends due to improvements in technician skill, methods, or
procedures.

A second category of quality cost examined was what quality
theorists call *failure cost,* that is, the cost incurred when product
does not meet specifications. Failure cost occurs when product
must be returned, reworked, recycled, or scrapped because there
is a problem with it. This source of cost is usually the largest
single source of quality cost in most companies, but it is often
poorly measured or simply considered to be part of normal production cost. Once failure costs have been identified as such,
however, they become amenable to reduction by means of early
problem detection, as well as preventive and corrective action.

At Gilroy Foods, the opportunity to reduce failure costs—
that is, to produce a quality product—was sufficiently large to
support the conclusion that QC technicians' new roles outside
the lab were a step in the right direction. The failure cost analysis
also enabled the project team to identify the kinds of technician
tasks, projects, and skills likely to impact the bottom line. The
format for the failure cost analysis is depicted in Figure 3.

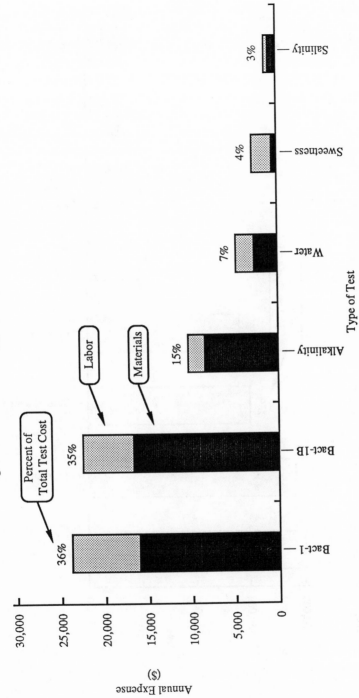

Figure 2. Format for Appraisal Cost Analysis.

Note: Test names and dollar values are fictitious. Percentages have been rounded.

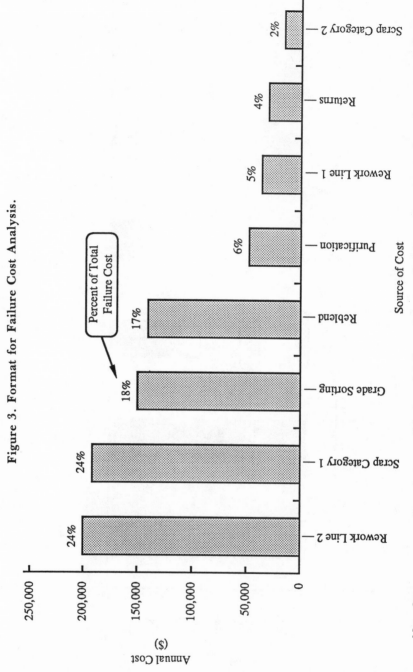

Figure 3. Format for Failure Cost Analysis.

Percent of Total Failure Cost

2% Scrap Category 2
4% Returns
5% Rework Line 1
6% Purification
17% Reblend
18% Grade Sorting
24% Scrap Category 1
24% Rework Line 2

Source of Cost

Annual Cost ($)

250,000
200,000
150,000
100,000
50,000
0

Note: Category names have been modified, and dollar values are fictitious. Percentages have been rounded.

The QC staffing analysis was similar to that performed in maintenance, except that it also considered the changes in the technician role described earlier. An interesting finding of the QC staffing analysis was that while the overall number of people in QC would remain constant over the next ten years, most technicians would have to advance to a higher skill level if the QC Department was to meet the demands of both customers and in-house users of its services. This finding reinforced the conclusion that training should be used to upgrade the overall capability of the technician work force over time.

The job analysis approach utilized in QC was similar to that employed in maintenance. Technicians and their supervisors were interviewed. Then technician tasks, knowledge, skills, abilities, and personal physical characteristics were listed and rated, placed in the order of priority, and evaluated. A *Practical Skills Manual* was prepared, similar in format to that for maintenance, listing the courses and specific tasks required of technicians. The twenty-three recommended courses for QC differed from those for maintenance, however—not only in content but also in that many of them, such as chemistry, microbiology, statistics, and quality information systems, would have to be conducted by local community colleges or outside professional organizations. This fact suggested the need for a strong liaison between the QC Department and outside educational organizations.

Project Management Mechanisms and Employee Participation. In QC, the project team for the training program consisted of the quality-control manager, three QC supervisors, a QC training administrator, and an outside consultant. Because QC is smaller than maintenance and because of the face-to-face proximity of all technicians to one another, a formal advisory team arrangement was not deemed desirable, so the project team was instead assisted by individual technician project advisors. These advisors were senior technicians with extensive job knowledge, and they were considered by all to be the best informed regarding historical development, procedural requirements, and training needs.

While a formal steering committee was not designated for this project, a top management advisory group was formed to receive status reports and make recommendations. This advisory group was composed of the vice-presidents of operations, the vice-president of technical services, the director of production, the manager of human relations, the manager of cost accounting, and the chairman of the company's Quality and Productivity Committee.

The project began with an orientation and discussion session for lab technicians, during which the project proposal was presented and discussed. Next, the project advisors and all supervisory people in QC were interviewed to solicit comments and suggestions concerning the project. Following these interviews, job analyses were conducted for both the micro lab and analytical lab technician jobs, with several feedback cycles to supervisors and senior technicians to review and comment on job content as defined by the consultant. Lastly, the *Practical Skills Manual* was prepared, reviewed, and finalized by supervision.

Before the final report was presented to upper management, it was first presented in a general meeting to the entire QC Department for review and reactions. Due to the size of this meeting, group discussion was not feasible, so a reactions questionnaire was distributed to all attendees. The results of this questionnaire were tallied and conveyed back to employees by their supervisors for discussion in smaller groups. While the overall reaction of the QC people to the presentation was extremely positive, a number of concerns and constructive suggestions were gleaned from this feedback process, and these were incorporated into the implementation planning for the program.

Administrative Approach. The approach to program administration for QC was similar to that in maintenance, with advancement based upon the same four criteria: course completion, minimum time in grade, practical skills mastery, and a satisfactory performance appraisal.

The process of evaluating practical skills was greatly aided in QC by the existence of detailed written procedures for each quality-control test. Nevertheless, some new procedures will have to be developed, particularly for project-related skills or skills that cut across several testing procedures.

As in maintenance, the training program will be overseen by a skill committee, in this case supported by the QC training administrator, who will be responsible for liaison with educational and professional organizations, maintaining technician development plans and development files, researching and developing courses, following up with QC supervisors, and monitoring the training process.

Current Status and Evaluation. At this stage of the QC training and development strategy, a combination training facility and QC library has been constructed in the QC Department, and the QC skill committee is revising its detailed implementation plan for the program, selecting initial courses, and preparing budgets for the implementation phase.

Evaluation of the QC program, as in the case of maintenance, will be based upon both bottom-line cost improvements (appraisal and failure costs in the case of QC) as well as the extent to which program participants complete courses and master their practical skills. The QC program is unique, however, in that its ultimate success will depend upon the ability of QC management and technicians to foster operational improvement by transferring QC testing, data collection, and problem-solving skills to other departments, such as production.

Conclusions

This case study has shown how technical training can be used as part of a company plan and strategy to improve quality, reduce cost, and provide opportunity for hourly workers to advance in their personal development and in their careers. The lesson of the case studies presented here is that a large-scale training effort can seek such lofty benefits only if it is well planned with an eye to cost benefit, objectivity in administration, and the need for employees to participate in the development of the program and thereby have a hand in shaping their own destiny. And while training alone will never be the sole means by which a business succeeds, it remains as a powerful tool for joining the interests of management and the hourly worker in the common pursuit of excellence.

PART TWO

CONTINUOUS LEARNING FOR ALL EMPLOYEES

In past years, organizations have usually had to plan for some degree of change as a part of doing business. Today, however, so many aspects of business are changing, and so rapidly, that many companies are having trouble coping. The rapidly accelerating pace of technological change, in particular, has profound implications that have caused many companies to reassess their training strategies. Employees and managers must develop the capacity to learn new skills and upgrade their old ones more quickly than in the past. And more critical than ever before will be learning skills not simply related to the operation of new technologies, but to the most innovative and profitable applications of those technologies.

Traditional training methods—in which trainees are viewed as passive recipients of ideas and information—no longer suffice in today's corporate environment. In response to continual change in products, technologies, markets, and competition, leading-edge companies are gravitating toward a new mode of operation—continuous learning—in which everyone in the organization is actively involved in an ongoing process of learning new skills.

Continuous learning methods are distinguished from more conventional types of training by the following characteristics:

113

- Learning, rather than being solely confined to special training courses or seminars, becomes an everyday part of the job and is built into routine tasks.
- Employees are expected to learn not only skills related to their own jobs but also the skills of others in their work unit and are also required to understand how their work unit relates to the operation and goals of the business.
- Employees are expected to teach, as well as learn from, their co-workers. In short, the entire work environment is geared toward and supports the learning of new skills.

While the research for "Training for New Technology" did not uncover any one company that exhibited all these features or that had consciously implemented a policy labeled as *continuous learning,* it did find several companies that had established programs or processes reflecting some of these characteristics to varying degrees. Most notable are employee involvement programs, in which voluntary interactive teaching and learning are encouraged. Case studies focused, for the most part, on mechanisms that foster continuous learning and on participative approaches to training.

Companies employ a variety of structures and mechanisms that help foster continuous learning and permit participation of everyone in the organization:

- *learning by objectives,* usually related to management by objectives (MBO), in which employees and managers jointly identify educational needs and how to meet them in conjunction with a periodic performance review process
- *train-the-trainer* programs, in which in-house content experts (rank-and-file employees, managers, or technical personnel) are trained in skills to teach and sometimes design courses
- *semiautonomous work teams,* composed of members who routinely train and are trained by one another
- *pay-for-knowledge* incentive schemes, in which employees receive pay increases as they acquire new skills

An example of the learning-by-objectives approach is the Continuing Engineering Education Program (CEEP) at General Electric's Aerospace Electronic Systems Department. This program keeps company engineers abreast of emerging technologies through an advisory council of engineers, technical managers, and marketing representatives. The council reports on developing trends in technology and ensures that the program's course curriculum meets the needs of the business. By linking the course work to business objectives and by making the successful completion of courses an important factor in yearly performance appraisals and career advancement, General Electric has motivated increasing numbers of engineers—of all ages—to participate in its continuing education program.

An even greater degree of employee and managerial involvement in the training process is evident in train-the-trainer programs, in which in-house content experts are taught how to train others in the organization. Companies that have used such an approach find not only that it is more cost-effective than sole reliance on internal or external professional trainers but that it also helps to sustain continuous learning by cultivating and expanding the organization's own resources for more and more of the teaching. At several General Foods plants, teams of line managers and hourly production employees regularly participate in train-the-trainer programs, in which they are taught how to assess training needs, analyze jobs and tasks, develop course materials, teach courses, and evaluate training results. At one of the General Foods plants where the participative approach to training is extensively used, quality and efficiency indices have markedly improved. While these results may be partially due to new technology start-ups, the quality of training is reported to have had a major impact.

The most extensive degree of employee involvement in the learning process exists in semiautonomous work teams. At the S. B. Thomas English muffin plant in Schaumburg, Illinois, training is one of several supervisory duties routinely shared by team members. Organized into "action groups" according to specific functions, team members rotate through various managerial duties, including cost control; attendance; hiring, firing, and promotion; work assignment; counseling; safety; and communication. As a regular part of the job, members exchange ideas and information concerning their current duties. The plant's pay-for-knowledge-and-skill system serves to reinforce the continuous learning process. Team members are paid bonuses as they acquire new skills.

In a few instances, unions have become actively involved in the training process. Union involvement in training programs enhances work participation, improves the quality of training and learning, and paves the way for further cooperation. Most effective are partnerships in which the union and the management are equally responsible for the control, planning, design, development, and evaluation of training programs. In a small number of cases, major corporations and unions—such as AT&T and Communications Workers of America (CWA), and General Motors, Ford, and United Auto Workers—have diverted large sums of money annually from the wage/benefit package into jointly administered training funds. Labor-management control over funding strengthens the joint commitment to long-term training and employment security goals, regardless of economic fluctuations. Also, the existence of jointly controlled funds provides labor and management with additional opportunities for reaching agreements about the nature and timing of technological change and the management of retraining and placement programs to cope with these changes.

The breakup of the Bell System in 1984 and the quickening pace of technological change within telecommunications have forced the new "baby Bells" to become more competitive by developing additional products and services, reducing the number of jobs, and sharpening the skills of existing employees. The 1983 AT&T/CWA pact had stipulated that $36 million be set aside for training and retraining workers and that the programs be administered by joint union-management training advisory boards. Described here are the efforts of one such joint board at Pacific Bell, one of the new operating companies serving all of California. By joining forces to retrain and relocate surplus employees to new jobs, labor and management have successfully introduced new technologies, while either avoiding layoffs or keeping them to a minimum. The participation of community colleges and the California Employment Training Panel, an innovative state program to prevent job loss, has further enhanced the quality of training.

7

A Participative Approach to a Technological Challenge: General Electric Company's Aerospace Electronic Systems Department

John V. Hickey

The specialized knowledge of engineers is the key to the technological leadership and the marketing strategy of General Electric Company's Aerospace Electronic Systems Department (AESD). This indispensable asset, however, is highly vulnerable: AESD estimates that a newly recruited engineer's professional knowledge will be largely obsolete in about five years.

AESD has found a unique solution to this problem. It has created a Continuing Engineering Education Program (CEEP) with an advisory council of engineers, managers, and marketing representatives to steer curriculum decisions and make sure CEEP courses meet the needs of the business. The courses are directly linked to performance appraisal and development.

AESD sells airborne military electronics to a single but complex customer, the United States Department of Defense. The nature of its business means that AESD has a relatively small number of competitors. But since the stakes are high, the competition is intense. Technological leadership is the crucial competitive edge.

The threat of obsolescence in itself creates a tremendous need for refreshing, updating, and improving engineers' mastery of their fields. The training and education task is made even tougher, because engineers joining the company from even the best technological institutions bring little exposure to the kinds of technical challenges they will face at AESD—and little experience with the state-of-the-art computer support that General Electric (GE) can provide.

Appropriately enough for an aerospace electronics company, AESD meets some of its educational needs through courses beamed in via satellite from the National Technological University (NTU). NTU is a consortium of universities formed to deliver instruction to graduate engineers at their workplaces and to award master's degrees.

This is the space-age side of AESD's training technology. Most of the department's engineering education needs, however, are met by a much more earthbound method—human instructors in conventional classrooms. The method of delivery is dictated by the nature of the material and the technologies available. It is effective because AESD has taken particular pains to make it participative and fully responsive to engineers' needs.

Aerospace Electronic Systems Department in Context

General Electric Company had total sales of nearly $36 billion in 1986 and was ranked third in *Fortune* magazine's list of the largest American corporations. In number of employees—about 300,000—GE was ranked fifth. Its sales of appliances, both small and major, have made the company's name literally a household word. The company is more diversified than its name might indicate and is involved in such disparate fields as jet engines, plastics, and financial services. So large and complex a corporation calls for effective organization. The company is organized into groups, which are made up of divisions, consisting of departments. Within the departments are sections, subsections, and units. The size and scope of these entities may vary.

The Aerospace Electronic Systems Department in Utica, New York, has annual sales of about $400 million. It belongs to the Avionic and Electronic Systems Division, whose sales exceed $1 billion a year. Within a department, sections represent various functions, such as engineering, manufacturing, marketing, and finance. Subsections, usually organized by product line, might include 100 people in five different units—the smallest organizational entity.

Although the organization is strongly and clearly hierarchical, GE grants its various parts a high degree of autonomy. In fact, the company is often cited as a demonstration that so large and complex a system can work effectively only if its major parts have substantial autonomy.

GE maintains a corporate education and training function, which provides courses in general management areas such as finance, employee relations, and manufacturing management, and in engineering disciplines with broad application. In all areas, the corporation provides broad guidelines for training and education, but gives the local trainers discretion in administering and developing courses to meet their specific needs. Engineering education consists of two major programs, one corporate, one local. The arrangement in nonengineering areas is often similar.

Of the 3,500 employees in AESD, about 1,000 are in the engineering section. Of a total training budget exceeding $1 million a year, engineering accounts for about $500,000—an indication of the importance attached to engineering training.

The Continuing Engineering Education Program

The centerpiece of engineers' training is the Continuing Engineering Education Program (CEEP). This program was devised to deal with the rapid obsolescence of the knowledge of engineers. The challenge, as summed up by Richard W. Abbott, administrator of CEEP, is "to keep our engineers abreast of emerging technologies, and to introduce them to what is brand new and not available anywhere else."

CEEP courses—about thirty-five in any given semester—are open to all employees in the department, not just engineers, as long as the applicant receives his or her supervisor's approval. Since the courses are conducted outside regular work hours—most often, immediately at the end of the work day—employees must have the motivation to use their own time both for classes and for whatever outside preparation is required.

In recent years, CEEP has attracted some 1,800 applicants a year, and of that number about 75 percent have completed their courses. Generally, about half the enrollees are from engineering.

Engineering Education Advisory Council. One distinctive feature of CEEP is a special advisory council to ensure that engineering training meets the needs of the department. Abbott is chairperson of the Engineering Education Advisory Council, which plays a key role in the development of curriculum.

The council has twenty members, including Abbott. About half the members are senior engineers and the rest are managers, including two subsection managers. All technical areas are represented, as well as business planning and marketing. In response to Abbott's request, section managers choose their representatives to the council, based on the extent of their technical knowledge of certain areas and their interest in education.

The thinking behind the inclusion of both the marketing and engineering functions on the council is explained by Oskar Schriever, manager of engineering resources and training: "Marketing has to ferret out the customer's ideas, and then work with engineering to develop the applications. Many times technologies that are critical to our future business opportunities will determine the direction of our training programs. That's why we have marketing people on the education advisory council."

CEEP and the advisory council were developed over

several years in response to perceived shortcomings in AESD training. Raymond W. Zukowski, manager of integrated logistics support and services, explains: "Before the mid 1970s, training was in a reactive mode. Management would ask us to run a course, and by the time we were ready, it was almost too late. There was no real time connection between training and the department's needs which would enable us to make good decisions about the future. The lack of connection was reflected in the low participation rate of our courses."

The situation became worse in 1977–1980, as the pace of change picked up, along with the training demands. A technological trend of particular importance was the shift from analog to digital and large-scale integrated (LSI) technologies. In the business-planning cycle of 1976, AESD projected that the ratio of analog to digital technologies in its products—about 2:1 at the time—would be exactly reversed by 1980, and that the trend would continue. Meeting the challenge would require massive application of digital and LSI techniques. But as of 1976, only a half-dozen engineers in the department were knowledgeable in LSI applications.

Response to the Knowledge Gap. AESD responded to this knowledge gap by developing two specifically targeted programs:

1. *Technical Renewal Program.* This was a two-year, on-site concentrated program to provide existing technical staff with in-depth training for selected technologies. Many of the courses were conducted on company time, attendance was frequently mandatory, and the consequences of not attending were clearly specified: limitation of advancement potential, demotion, pay cuts, or even possible layoffs. According to Ray Zukowski, the program filled critical gaps cost-effectively—for one-third as much as it would have cost to lay off technologically obsolete engineers and hire new personnel.

2. *Very Large-Scale Integration Training Program.* The program of training in very large-scale integration (VLSI) was a natural sequel to the Technical Renewal Program (TRP). It met AESD's specific technological need and was ultimately extended to other GE locations as well. More than 1,000 employees attended.

A Proactive Approach. Effective though these two ad-hoc programs were, the department managers saw the need for a more proactive approach to training that might eliminate the need for crash training programs in the future. Experience with TRP and VSLI had persuaded management that a successful program would have to overcome certain obstacles:

• *Inadequate management support.* Before TRP, according to Zukowski, management had given employee education and training relatively lukewarm support. TRP made it apparent that top-management support was essential and that lack of it could reduce the effectiveness of the training efforts.

• *Lack of involvement in the business/technology planning cycle.* AESD's training effort was unprepared for the technology shift that was identified in the mid 1970s. If the training function had been more closely involved, crash programs might have been avoided.

• *Lack of technical depth in administration.* Mere administrators are not adequate for high-tech training programs, according to Zukowski. Only a director with solid technical background is prepared to understand the technology requirements and develop the appropriate courses. Richard Abbott, the full-time administrator of CEEP, has the appropriate technical background.

• *Unclear goals, directions, and needs.* Like any essential part of a business, a training operation must have clearly stated objectives, measurable goals, and definite funding requirements to bid for management support.

• *Poor basis of motivation.* AESD had required some employees to take part in TRP and VLSI. But, while coercion may be justified on a crash basis, only motivation from within can be maintained over the long term. Zukowski terms motivation "a very sensitive area" and warns that unless it is properly handled, "a negative reaction to training will result."

All these considerations were kept in mind as AESD developed CEEP, which was adopted in fall 1981 and was launched in spring 1982. Its five major features include the following:

1. *A full-time, technically qualified administrator.* Abbott has primary responsibility for planning present and future engineer-

ing education needs. He is also responsible for choosing and training instructors, and assists in developing and scheduling courses.

2. *The Engineering Education Advisory Council.* As noted earlier, this council is chaired by Abbott and includes nineteen additional members, chosen to represent all major technical areas plus marketing. Members are expected to report trends and changes in technologies relevant to AESD, identify emerging areas of potential business, and help to develop needed courses through an informal give-and-take process. Members suggest needed courses, while others join in evaluating the suggestions. When a course has been approved in principle, Abbott draws on the council for guidance in developing course materials and choosing instructors.

3. *Qualified instructors.* For the most part, course instructors are available within AESD. Often, says Abbott, the person who identifies the need for a course—whether a council member or not—ends up teaching the course. If a qualified instructor is not available within GE, outside resources, such as a college or university or a professional training organization, may be tapped. As many as fifty engineers serve as instructors in a semester.

Noting that "the best people tend to be the busiest," Abbott says that the instructor of first choice may not always be available for a given course. However, he has never been unable to find an instructor for a proposed course. In searching for instructors, Abbott always seeks the guidance of the most knowledgeable people in the subject area. In many cases, an instructor is chosen by self-nomination; in other cases, the recommendation of the advisory council provides the initiative. In general, Abbott finds, "the people who teach are the people who want to teach."

The instructors receive train-the-trainer support in a three- to four-hour course given by Abbott. Focusing on presentation skills, this course works mainly by bringing seasoned and new instructors together for structured but informal interaction to develop those skills.

Instructional activity is not part of an engineer's job

description. It is done on the engineer's own time and brings additional pay for developing and teaching courses. (Abbott comments, however, "If a potential instructor's first three questions include one about pay, he slides a long way down the list.") Instructors are paid from engineering's budget.

4. *Analysis and evaluation.* New methods and techniques of training are constantly being evaluated and reviewed in a quest to keep training cost-effective. Schriever, manager of engineering resources and training, notes, however, that AESD makes little use of independent, computer-based training. The reason: Most CEEP courses run in a given form only once or twice, and then are either dropped or revised. By the time computer-based courses could be devised, their material would probably be obsolete. Even if such methods were applicable, they would require, he estimates, a full-time staff of about twenty-five people to do programming. Similarly, Abbott adds, use of videotaped materials is limited.

5. *Multiple feedback.* The relevance and effectiveness of CEEP are maintained by mechanisms for feedback to instructors, participants, participants' superiors, and AESD management.

The first feedback mechanism is a course-evaluation sheet. Each student, upon completion of the course, fills out a two-page questionnaire that is returned anonymously to Abbott. Individual questionnaires are consolidated into a report for the instructor. Thirteen questions ask the student to rate, on a five-point scale, such aspects as accuracy of the course description, sequencing, relevance, adequacy, attitudes and approach of the instructor, and the interest of the subject matter. Five more questions cover overall ratings of the course and instructor, recommendations for changes and improvements, and suggestions for additional courses. The final section is an open-ended call for comments.

A second questionnaire is sent to employees who have dropped a course. It asks the reasons for dropping the course: personal, inaccurate or misleading course description, level too high or too low, and other reasons to be specified. Comments and suggestions are invited. The questionnaire, with signature optional, is returned to Abbott.

Feedback to the participant on course performance occurs through scoring of homework assignments, quizzes, and exams, as appropriate. Furthermore, the courses are made an integral part of performance appraisal and employee development. At the end of each year, managers receive printouts showing employee enrollment in various courses. Performance appraisals note which courses have been taken and may serve as a basis for recommending further courses. Schriever notes that although "employees are not forced to take courses, the recommendations are made, and the courses are a factor in appraisals." Zukowski adds that it is clear to employees "that if they don't take certain recommended courses, they risk falling behind in the credentials they need for advancement."

Increased Course Offerings and Enrollment. By creating an array of educational offerings tied closely to the needs of the business and to the incentive value of improved performance and advancement, AESD has tapped the motivation Zukowski sees as essential to successful training. This achievement shows up in figures for both course offerings and enrollment.

By the 1980–1981 term—the period of first substantial movement toward the objectives of CEEP—the number of courses available reached forty-two, about three times as many as in any previous year. The number continued to rise and exceeded sixty courses in each of the following five years.

Enrollment has also grown. In the late 1970s, before TRP, course enrollments averaged between 200 and 300 a year, and the trend was downward. TRP set off a turnaround, and on the basis of the latest semester figures, AESD projects an enrollment of around 2,000 for 1988.

One indicator of the CEEP's motivational power is the age distribution of enrollment. Participation is not by any means concentrated only on younger engineers who are in the early stages of career building. Enrollment encompasses all age groups. The 51–55 age cohort is as heavily enrolled as the 36–40 age cohort. The combined 51–60 age group accounts for fully 25 percent of the total. And even among employees age 61 and above, interest in self-development is strong enough to make up 3 percent of total enrollment.

Some Other Aspects of Engineering Education

Although the Continuing Engineering Education Program is the keystone of the Aerospace Electronic Systems Department's effort, it is not the whole picture. Both corporate and local training resources provide additional ways for engineers (and other employees) to pursue self-development for their own benefit and the company's.

For example, newly graduated engineers with bachelor's degrees have the opportunity, under GE auspices, to pursue a master's degree in a three-year advanced-education program. During the first year, the program has a highly standardized curriculum that is mainly corporate driven. In the later years, the curriculum is more adapted to local needs. To some extent, courses in the program are offered in cooperation with local institutions. For example, some of the courses taught at AESD are listed in the catalogue of Syracuse University. The number of engineers enrolled in this program reaches as high as fifty in some years. In addition, a smaller number have pursued doctoral degrees.

A recently available educational resource used by GE is the National Technological University (NTU), a nonprofit, private educational corporation set up by a consortium of sixteen universities. Its purpose is to grant master of science degrees to graduate engineers for studies based largely on courses offered via satellite broadcast. Participants must meet NTU's academic prerequisites, and they must be employed by a sponsoring company that is part of the NTU network. Courses are under way in five academic areas: computer engineering, computer science, electrical engineering, engineering management, and manufacturing-systems engineering. Students not pursuing the master's degree may take NTU courses as auditors or for credit. In many cases, the NTU courses are structured so that students may interact with instructors via a two-way telecommunications link.

The Impact of AESD's Engineering Education Efforts

Although AESD's end product is hardware, ideas are what it sells. A long process occurs between the first concept for a system and its eventual delivery. The process embraces several competitive stages, from the idea to the prototype to pilot models and, finally, to approval for full-scale production. At each stage, the U.S. Department of Defense and the department's prime contractor must be convinced of the benefits of procuring the system from AESD. Zukowski comments that each of these stages has implications for training: "Part of our engineers' job is to keep ahead of the customer and say, 'Here are some areas in which we may be asked to bid, and here are the things we should be doing to prepare.' If we haven't done at least two years of homework on a potential customer need, we'll never win that contract. Training has to prepare engineers for that kind of role."

Continuing education is a useful tool in another kind of competition—attracting and keeping the best available engineering graduates. The importance of this competition has been increased in recent years by the age demographics of AESD. The department was established in 1953, and many of its engineers are close to retirement. In addition, a business downswing in the 1970s kept hiring down and created a situation in which the department now has plenty of engineers in their twenties and in their forties, but fewer in their thirties. So, at the time of TRP, training had to reach all the way to the senior group of engineers. Now, faced with the imminent retirement of many of those engineers, the department is hiring about fifty new graduate engineers a year, searching for the best graduates from the best schools. The prospect of continuing-education opportunities and technological challenge is a powerful lure for the top graduates.

Historically, AESD has experienced low turnover among its engineers. In recent years, turnover has tended to rise because of a short supply of engineers and tough recruiting competition. AESD has found that in many cases, however, engineers hired away by other companies are eventually brought back to GE by the technology-education combination.

AESD has avoided the strategy of hiring primarily experienced engineers to fill technology gaps in its own staff. Schriever notes that "training works faster than recruitment." Zukowski adds that, leaving aside the question of technical knowledge, a newly hired engineer "may take years just to learn how the department functions"—not a problem with engineers already on board. Besides, it is motivating for employees to see that the company is committed to developing them rather than replacing or supplementing them.

In summary, AESD believes that its educational programs—especially the CEEP, with its emphasis on broad participation and self-motivation—have been crucial to its ability to meet the technological challenge. And while the impact of training on productivity is hard to gauge, Schriever notes that in a period when the department's business had increased by 45 percent, its staff increased only 20 percent.

8

Training and Development
at General Foods:
A Participative Process

Jill Casner-Lotto

Training and development at General Foods (GF) is no longer an isolated function carried out solely by professional trainers stationed at corporate headquarters. Instead, as a way to encourage learning throughout the organization and link training more directly to individual and business goals, training at GF today is a process in which line managers, hourly employees, and technical personnel play a critical part. In fact, in attempting to separate the training successes from the failures, one GF official observes that when managers and employees have actually helped to plan, design, and implement programs, "the training sells itself. Plants that operate under a 'Thou shalt train' directive invariably find little or no success for their training dollars."

Through a variety of novel approaches—such as a corporatewide training network to share resources and ideas among GF manufacturing plants based in the United States and Canada; the Hourly Training Program, in which operators, line mana-

131

gers, and technical experts work as a team in the design and delivery of training; and annual "technology roundtables" for manufacturing managers—General Foods seems to be well on its way toward achieving a learning and teaching environment in which training becomes a work-oriented activity.

A Commitment to Employee Development

One could hardly walk down the packaged and frozen food or beverage aisles at any supermarket and miss the GF name. Jell-O brand desserts, Birds Eye frozen vegetables, Kool-Aid soft drink mixes, Post cereals, Maxwell House coffee, Oscar Mayer hot dogs and luncheon meats, and Entenmann's baked goods are among the major products manufactured by the food and beverage giant. General Foods, which is headquartered in Rye Brook, New York, had net earnings totaling $317.1 million in 1984, almost 10 percent above the $288.5 million earned the previous year. The corporation had broadened its product portfolio by introducing new products within existing GF divisions and by acquiring several new businesses, including the Ronzoni Corporation and Oroweat Foods Company.

About 55,000 employees work in more than 100 locations worldwide. General Foods itself was recently acquired by Philip Morris, Inc., but GF officials anticipate the takeover will have little or no effect on employees' work lives and on management styles and philosophies. This is significant, in that much of the success of its human resource programs, including training and education, derives from a strong top management commitment to employee growth and development.

General Foods president Philip L. Smith emphasizes the development of personal leadership skills and over the past two years has led a managerial seminar on business leadership. His active involvement in the program has sent a powerful message throughout the organization. "Our president clearly favors the notion of 'managers as trainers' and believes this should be a major managerial responsibility," remarks Kathleen Hanson, organizational development associate. "And his actions speak louder than words."

Another indication of the corporate commitment to training is that it has remained a high-priority item, even in times of economic austerity. This commitment is part of a philosophy in which the development of employees is an ongoing process.

Training Roles and Responsibilities

Since there is no single, centralized training department or training director at GF, it is considered a joint responsibility of the personnel manager and line managers at each plant. Line managers, working closely with subordinates, are primarily responsible for identifying training needs in their units or departments and communicating these needs to the personnel department. The personnel manager oversees the design, development, and implementation of training. However, line managers and selected technical experts are actively involved in these stages, helping to design specific training modules within their areas of expertise, reviewing and approving training materials before they are used, providing data for the evaluation of training, and acting as instructors in some cases. A further degree of involvement is evident in GF's Hourly Training Program, in which operators, managers, and technical specialists join forces in the planning, design, and implementation of training for machine operators and other production employees.

Division personnel managers are responsible for supporting and encouraging plant training activities, while at the corporate level, organizational development specialists act as consultants to the plants, providing training resources and advice and communicating corporate initiatives. The Organizational Development (OD) Department, based in the corporate headquarters, also runs GF's management development program, offering fifty courses in a variety of generic management skills.

Since each plant absorbs its own costs for training, it is impossible to arrive at one overall figure reflecting the total amount spent on training at General Foods. Corporate training costs, including direct costs (materials, program and course development, off-site training, outside consultant fees) and indirect costs (travel expenses, time away from job, and so on), are estimated to be around $800,000. The OD Department is composed of four staff members whose job duties include, but are not restricted to, training, and two additional staff members who are involved in training on a full-time basis.

The Training Network

The training function is deliberately decentralized since General Foods feels it is the only way to make training a truly participative and work-focused process. "In the past, corporate trainers tended to focus more on the needs of corporate-level management, rather than on individual plant needs. We wanted to avoid that," says Anthony Olkewicz, senior OD consultant. The OD Department also wanted to shed its role as "corporate trainer telling people in the field what to do," he adds. With the creation of the Operations Training Network, established in 1980, both issues are addressed.

The training network represents the corporatewide vehicle for coordinating and sharing knowledge, experience, skills, and other training materials and resources throughout the GF organization. Seventeen manufacturing plants out of a total of twenty-two are actively involved in the network. Personnel managers or staff representatives are the official members of the network, though the training activities and programs initiated through the network often include manufacturing and line managers, hourly and professional employees, and, on occasion, the plant managers. The members meet formally twice a year, but the sharing of resources and ideas is a constant process, according to David Kakkuri, operations training manager, who coordinates the network out of the Midwest Training Center, located in GF's Battle Creek, Michigan, manufacturing facility.

"At any time, a network member can call upon another member, requesting information on a particular training program or assistance in actually designing and facilitating a program," Kakkuri explains. The network often sponsors training sessions that include representatives from four or five plants at a time, further reinforcing the exchange of ideas and resources.

The training is usually carried out at a centrally located work site, thereby making plant equipment and other resources readily available to trainees. About 1,200 individuals received training in 1984 in a variety of technical and management skills. Without losing sight of the specific needs and goals of the individual plants, the network has helped lend a sense of corporate vision and continuity to the training function, notes Kakkuri.

Managers as Trainers—and Trainees

At GF, the participation of managers is considered a vital component in the training process—a component that can affect both the quality of training and the behavior of trainees. Kakkuri works closely with a steering committee of five plant managers to keep abreast of training issues in the field. "I use them as a sounding board, discussing my ideas and responding to their suggestions," he notes. The committee has also proven to be a valuable aid in drawing upon managerial expertise, since members often recommend line managers they believe would make effective trainers. Line managers have acted as facilitators in several training exercises, and they have come from a variety of departments, including engineering, accounting, sales, production, and research.

"Their participation as instructors lends a lot of credibility to the subjects being taught—more so than just a personnel representative—since they have lived through these experiences and so relate better to trainees, and because they are viewed as good leaders," Kakkuri states.

Another organization-wide activity that strengthens managerial involvement is the roundtable discussion held once a year for top-level manufacturing managers. Participants discuss the latest technological developments, exchange ideas, and make presentations on new projects under way in their plants. Each year a volunteer task force of five or six manufacturing managers sets the agenda.

Training issues often come up at these sessions. An important focus for the group has been GF's statistical process-control program, in which all employees—from operators to the vice-president of operations—are learning statistics as part of a corporate campaign to boost quality. One topic discussed was managing change, as it relates to both technology and the work force. In addition, representatives of the Illinois Institute of Technology presented a national update on productivity. The sessions have proven to be extremely popular both for their educational value and as a forum for discussing manufacturing issues, according to Kakkuri. "Each year I get hounded by the managers if I haven't gotten the meeting notices out well in advance," he notes.

In addition to these activities, the Organizational Development Department is taking steps to make managerial participation even more prevalent throughout the General Foods organization. One way is through encouraging effective use of the Management Process, defined as a GF philosophy of management, which involves the identification and communication of organizational and employee development needs and goals through employee-managerial dialogues, regular performance reviews, and timely feedback. While the Management Process can be a valuable tool in shaping career development plans and matching these to key business objectives, managers have not always used it in this manner.

"Managers and employees have looked upon the Management Process as 'something extra,' rather than as a part of their job responsibilities, which it really is," says OD associate Hanson. She and others in the OD Department are attempting to change this attitude by training line and personnel managers to integrate Management Process discussions with the organization's business planning procedures at regular quarterly intervals. "When people realize that this is not just another personnel system, but something that can improve business results—and we've already seen it happen at some of our Canadian plants—I believe the Management Process will be better accepted and more widely used," Hanson notes.

On another front, the OD Department is offering and aggressively marketing managerial seminars that emphasize techniques in coaching subordinates and teaching on-the-job skills. Courses have been piloted and received favorably among midlevel managers and will soon be offered to the corporation's top 400 senior-level executives.

There are also initiatives under way at the plant level, independent of the OD effort, to increase the manager's role in training. At GF's Modesto, California, facility, line managers have been recruited to train hourly and salaried employees in leadership and management skills. Employee involvement in production decisions has been encouraged at the plant for some time, but this latest effort takes employee involvement one step further, according to Zachary Stiles, personnel manager. "By providing management skills to employees, we hope to develop a key group of production-line leaders and create an environment where people are capable of supervising themselves," says Stiles. Line managers were selected only if they were highly respected among the hourly group, related well to the work force, and were considered to be good trainers. So far, four line managers have attended off-site train-the-trainer sessions and have begun to train twenty-five hourly and eighty salaried employees in one department of the plant. If this pilot effort is successful, says Stiles, the program will be expanded throughout the Modesto facility, as well as to another GF facility in California.

Hourly Training Program

Training strategies that involve not only line managers, but hourly and technical employees as well, are no longer in the experimental stage at GF—they are proven successes. The Hourly Training Program, in effect for about five years, exemplifies joint managerial-employee participation in the entire training process, including data gathering to determine training needs, analyzing tasks, writing training manuals, acting as instructors, and evaluating training results. Twelve plants out of the total twenty-two are training their hourly employees in this way, though the plants are in various stages of implementation.

One GF location that is very involved is the Dover, Delaware, plant, the corporation's most diverse manufacturing site. Jell-O brand gelatins and puddings, Log Cabin syrup, Minute Rice, and Bakers Chocolate are just a few of the major goods produced at GF/Dover, which employs 900 hourly people and 325 salaried personnel. According to Stuart Marcus, personnel manager, the program was implemented two years ago to train hourly employees to operate new or upgraded production equipment and to improve their skills on existing equipment, with special attention given to quality, productivity, and safety issues. Management and labor, represented at the Dover plant by the United Food and Commercial Workers, had prior experience in working together on a joint problem-solving committee (still in existence at the plant today). Thus, cooperation on a training program, rather than being viewed as a breakthrough effort, was considered instead a natural extension of the plant's operating environment.

When new training manuals are needed at Dover, the department manager selects a team of employees and managers representing various areas of functions in the plant, depending on the specific job for which the manual is being written. All types and levels of employees—operators, supervisors, quality-control personnel, engineers, and mechanics—take part. The team, usually consisting of about five members, spends three full days learning skills in task analysis and then two days in train-the-trainer sessions led by a personnel staff member and a representative of the training network, who teach presentation and organizational skills. One team member, usually selected by the department manager, then spends another two to three weeks writing the manual, drawing upon fellow team members, other plant employees, and outside experts as resources. University of Delaware instructors, for example, have acted as consultants on training projects.

The author of the manual often trains other employees; trainers have included both supervisory and hourly personnel. The entire training procedure takes about three weeks, and during this period team members are relieved of their line duties in order to carry out their training responsibilities. "It just couldn't work any other way," says Marcus. "If we asked people to take on both responsibilities, one of the areas would suffer." Marcus adds that training is often done during slow periods to avoid any serious work conflicts.

So far, 100 employees have been trained in this manner and about twenty training manuals produced for a variety of hourly positions, including packaging machine operation, production processing, and equipment cleaning. The Dover management and employees are convinced that this is the best way to train. "The results are very encouraging," says Marcus. "For the first time, operators are learning why they are doing something—not just the routine steps. We've received nothing but positive feedback on training both at the monthly departmental team meetings, in which 'state-of-the-business' issues are discussed, and at joint labor-management problem-solving meetings."

As coordinator of the Hourly Training Program throughout the GF organization, Kakkuri directs the classes that are designed to teach plant employees and managers to become effective trainers. Participants, usually drawn from several plants, are organized into teams, each consisting of two to five people. Kakkuri outlines in detail the eight-step training model used by the teams in these train-the-trainer exercises: (1) task analysis, (2) development of objectives, (3) identification of specific training segments (safety, troubleshooting, and so on), (4) design of each of these segments, (5) testing of design through presentation to another team in the class, (6) revision of design, (7) application of revised design through presentation to employees at the "home" plant, and (8) final evaluation.

Step 7 is especially important since it represents, in effect, the trial run before the actual training takes place at the home plant, according to Kakkuri. "The team tests the training design by piloting it on a small group of experienced operators at the plant who can offer suggestions and ideas for improvement. At the same time, these sessions act as a refresher course for these operators—it's really a two-way street," he notes.

Training manuals and procedures have been developed for a variety of technical positions, including the operation of sophisticated high-tech equipment. In these instances, engineers and R&D personnel provide considerable input, in both the design and implementation of the training.

Line efficiencies and quality indices have increased considerably at the plants where the supervisors and employees are directly involved in the training of other employees. "While some of the results are due to new technology start-ups, according to the comments I've received from operators, plant managers, and personnel managers, a large part is due to the training," Kakkuri remarks.

Why does this sort of "peer training" seem to work better than more traditional approaches? It may be attributed to the benefits it brings not only to the trainee, but to the trainer as well. Kakkuri offers this insight: "In a sense, the person cast in the role as trainer is relearning the job every time he or she trains another employee. Under a more traditional mode, a certain amount of knowledge is inevitably lost and new employees may eventually end up absorbing only, say, 50 percent of what their predecessors knew about a specific job. You get a higher-quality training program by taking content experts and teaching them to become trainers rather than the other way around—plus you're adding to the personal growth and development of those trainers who are learning how to teach others and, in so doing, learning more about their own jobs. It's a real motivator."

Conclusions

Despite these benefits, there are some precautions to note when attempts are made to make training a more participative, work-focused process. Kakkuri emphasizes the collaboration that is necessary between the personnel and line-management functions. "Line managers have to feel comfortable as instructors. That's why we have these extensive train-the-trainer programs— to make sure they are adequately prepared. In addition, personnel and line managers often act as co-trainers, sharing the teaching and training-design responsibilities," he explains.

Most important, however, is the need for managers themselves to find or make the time that is required for training— not always an easy task. "We're in a difficult transition period," Olkewicz notes. "We now have fewer staff members at GF identified as professional trainers, so it means more people are wearing many different hats. No one is going to tell managers they have to train their employees—it's up to them to make sure this happens." To encourage managers' participation, Kakkuri plans his own calendar a year in advance so he can alert managers of future programs and give them plenty of advance notice to arrange their schedules.

"It definitely makes life more complex," Olkewicz concludes. "But I think when managers see the connection between the training process and their own long-term success, they're going to make the investment."

9

Training
in a Team Environment:
S. B. Thomas, Inc.

Nancy Rubin

From its modest beginnings in a lower Manhattan bakery in 1880, S. B. Thomas, Inc., has become the largest producer of English muffins in the United States, capturing half of the national market by 1985. Most of Thomas's growth has occurred within the last eight years and is the result of a deliberate and ongoing managerial effort to transform the company's operations from an old-line family business into a leading national corporation. At the heart of the Thomas philosophy is a commitment to change and a responsibility to manufacture high-quality products in a timely fashion with well-trained personnel. Since baked goods are a highly perishable, fast-turnover product, competition is brisk and profit margins are traditionally low.

It is strict attention to these three elements—consistently high-quality baked goods, time limitations, and an innovative use of human resources—that characterizes Thomas's recent managerial efforts and that has given the company its edge in the marketplace. Participatory management is the key to Thomas's training efforts, which are ongoing at every level of operation at its newest plant in Schaumburg, Illinois.

Since the opening of the Schaumburg plant in January 1984, Thomas's workers have engaged in a self-managing model of the various aspects of muffin making—baking, packaging, and shipping. The fifty Schaumburg workers rotate through various managerial duties in specific work teams and continually search for new ways to improve internal systems. Employee selection, termination, and promotion decisions are made by the workers: the company's nine managers serve as facilitators and advisors rather than as "directors" of worker activity.

Employee turnover was high during Schaumburg's first year, and the new management system was initially met with skepticism from other managers within the organization. Although Schaumburg had to operate at full production capacity soon after hiring workers, it has since become economically competitive with the other four Thomas factories, which are managed traditionally. Today, as the participatory-management style continues to be refined at Schaumburg, the bakery's sociotechnical-design concept is gradually being introduced to managers at other S. B. Thomas sites as a model for long-term corporate development.

A Growing Company

Located in Totowa, New Jersey, S. B. Thomas was acquired in 1970 and became a wholly owned subsidiary of CPC International, Inc., a multinational company primarily engaged in grocery products and corn-wet milling, a process used in grain production. For the next five years, the company continued to be run as a family business with a traditional management hierarchy; the products also continued to be sold as consumer bakery goods with profits of 3 to 5 percent a year. Thomas's first transition began in 1975 when CPC appointed David Newstadt as company president to improve the company's profits and position in the marketplace. Newstadt set about doing this in two ways: first, by extending Thomas's sales boundary beyond the New York metropolitan area into the Washington-

Boston corridor; and second, by reducing the number of products from thirty to four. Today, Thomas produces four varieties of English muffins and four varieties each of toaster cakes, pita, and protein bread.

As the company expanded its sales effort during the late 1970s, two new factories were built—one in Placentia, California, and the other in Frederick, Maryland. (A fourth factory was acquired by Thomas in 1980 when CPC International obtained the Sahara Baking Company in Weymouth, Massachusetts.) In the late 1970s, Newstadt also hired a group of middle managers and sales and advertising representatives to help convert Thomas's baked goods from a regional bakery product into a national specialty item.

In the wake of these changes, the old-line population of Thomas's workers at Totowa expressed concern as they watched the company evolve from a family business based on the apprenticeship system into a market-driven corporation with an aggressive new breed of middle managers. One symptom of the company's difficulties was its high turnover rate, particularly among the company's "new-breed" managers, who had been hired from the outside during those transitional years.

In 1978 Michael Hogarty, former vice-president of operations under Newstadt, became Thomas's new president. Under his aegis, Arthur Weren, vice-president of human resources, began to develop new strategies to bolster the company's human resources while improving its competitiveness in the marketplace. To this end, a labor-management council—or plant advisory team—was created by the newly appointed plant manager, Carl Bay.

The team was composed of a small group of S. B. Thomas workers and managers who met regularly with top-level executives to air their problems and offer suggestions. Although this open-ended approach sometimes degenerated into a painful gripe session between labor and management, Thomas executives claim that it was a necessary step in the company's transition— one that demonstrated the company's commitment to its workers and, in so doing, established a precedent for the company's subsequent support of participatory management. It was at this juncture, observes Jack Collins, Thomas's current director of operations, that labor's attitudes toward changing corporate priorities evolved from adversarial to cooperative.

Brainstorming sessions designed to improve leadership and worker morale followed from these original discussions and, in the next several years, senior managers attended workshops for personal effectiveness training. Key managers—such as Collins; William Sholl, Thomas's present human resources director; and Stanley Zaranski, who would become Schaumburg's plant manager—attended a special workshop designed to help managers assess and improve their interpersonal skills through a team-building method.

Since CPC International was also experimenting with new management concepts in some of its other subsidiaries with management consultant Louis E. Davis, Thomas's executives were able to observe several models, such as CPC's Skippy Peanut Butter plant in Little Rock, Arkansas, where employees worked in self-managed teams. There, senior management became acquainted with the sociotechnical-design concept, or the deliberate blending of worker tasks with management duties and technical design. Convinced that this concept could be successfully adapted at S. B. Thomas, company officials then asked Hogarty for a "philosophy of operations" statement upon which to build such a plan. The ensuing corporate philosophy states Thomas's five unifying principles:

1. Business is satisfying consumer needs.
2. Human resources are the key to success.
3. Open communication is essential to good management.
4. Thomas is responsible to the communities in which it operates.
5. Workers are responsible to company owners.

A corporate steering committee and a bakery-design team were created to plan Schaumburg's technical layout, the organizational structure, teams, career-progression patterns, payment systems, and selection and training. The corporate philosophy served as a guide in the work of this design team.

Plant Design and Organization

By the spring of 1983, the S. B. Thomas steering committee was working cooperatively with the five-member team
that would manage the Schaumburg plant. This team included
Zaranski, Schaumburg's plant manager; David Oakes, a human
resources director; Gene Flynn, facilities administrator; Gary
Willis, controller; and Brandon Deane, quality assurance manager. With Davis's help, the team developed a philosophy based
on a sociotechnical system and self-managed concept that would
serve as a guide for the various design decisions at Schaumburg.

Since the creation of a sociotechnical design tailored to
the needs of a particular company usually takes months—or even
years—to plan, Thomas's managers knew at the beginning that
the speed of Schaumburg's construction and the targeted operation date would mean deviations from an ideal planning process. Nevertheless, the managers were committed to the idea
of participatory management and decided to go ahead with it,
with the understanding that the plan would be refined when the
bakery was on line.

At completion in 1983, the facility was an 85,000-square-
foot plant designed to produce muffins four days a week that
would be marketed in the midwestern states. Because baked
goods must be delivered to the store fresh and have only a nine-
day shelf life, Schaumburg planned to offer workers a staggered
ten-and-a-half-hour-a-day, four-day workweek—Saturday, Sunday, Tuesday, and Wednesday. Monday, Thursday, and Friday
were designated as cleanup and preventive-maintenance days.

Hiring began in late August 1983, based on a recently
designed recruitment and selection scheme, with newspaper
advertisements that described the S. B. Thomas Company and
introduced the concept of participatory management. Interested
individuals attended open-house meetings, where the organization was described in greater detail. A total of 450 attendees
who returned the mailing cards handed out that day were invited back for an interview. In keeping with Schaumburg's
management design concept, applicants were interviewed by
a team consisting of a corporate recruiter and a Schaumburg

coordinator, who asked applicants about their previous work experience and the way they handled peer and managerial requests. Those applicants who successfully completed the first team interview were also questioned by Zaranski, Willis, and Oakes. Finally, in late September 1983, fifty-two people were hired.

Today, Schaumburg's work force is predominantly made up of blue-collar male employees, most of whom live within an hour of the facility. They belong to Local 2 of the Bakery, Confectionary, and Tobacco Workers Union, which also represents employees at Thomas's four other sites. Schaumburg's workers, or associates as they are called, are organized into teams, or *action groups,* according to their function. These groups are defined as associations of individuals who are "responsible for the quality, quantity, and cost of a defined output." Thus, workers assigned to muffin production belong to the process action group, while those working in the packaging area are members of the pack action group. Associates involved in Schaumburg's environment belong to the systems action group. The plant's administrative assistants are members of the administrative action group, while the managers belong to the management action group. These action groups encourage a sense of ownership for their members through self-regulation and cross-skill applications. They are responsible for decision making at the activity level, total information sharing, development of self-regulating mechanisms, and individual growth.

The Training Process

Self-management pervades every aspect of the action group and is integrated with training at Schaumburg. In fact, because Schaumburg is still rapidly evolving, it is probably safe to say that the plant is in a constant state of training and self-refinement. Schaumburg's action groups meet once a week to air grievances, set new goals, and find solutions to problems. And at least once a quarter, representatives from the different work teams meet together. There are also periodic joint meetings between shifts, presidential breakfasts, and bakerywide meetings at various times of the year. After its initial set-up, training costs at Schaumburg have been running at 7.5 percent of its direct manufacturing expenses and 1.5 percent of its administrative budget.

Social Training. Two types of training occur daily at Schaumburg—the first involves social learning, and the second, task function. Social learning, the "people" side of Schaumburg's sociotechnical design, is accomplished in several ways. Workers perform the managerial functions, such as supervision, dispute settlement, and attendance, along with their production-related tasks. In the traditional workplace, these functions are assigned to a supervisor or line manager. At Schaumburg, managerial functions have been broken down into certain roles carried out by individual associates. They include: communicator, work assigner, recorder, discussion leader, counselor, and facilitators for such functions as sanitation, safety, training, cost control, fire prevention, first aid, security, and attendance. In addition, some associates serve as representatives to various company committees concerned with the technical and social aspects of the plant's operations. Of these tasks, training, cost control, attendance, work assignment, counseling, safety, and communication are considered most important, and an incentive to assume them is provided in a ten-cents-an-hour wage increase.

By serving in these different capacities for a period of weeks or months, associates not only increase their knowledge of the work teams and act as nonthreatening comonitors for each other, but also obtain a distinct sense of pride for their part in the team's productivity. As team member Joan Groneman says: "I enjoy being involved in the facilitator functions because it's so interesting and gives a new dimension to factory work. Here, we're responsible for our actions, and we learn to use peer pressure positively." Thus, it is through this combination of open communication and assumption of facilitator roles that associates become trained in self-management.

With the maturing of Schaumburg's system, it should be noted that social training now actually begins at the associate's moment of employment. Today, when an individual applies for a job at Schaumburg, he or she is interviewed by a team from the work group that has the opening. Usually the applicant is asked to role play a simulated cooperative work situation and is then assessed by the interviewing team.

Once applicants are hired and appear on the bakery's production line, they are taught about the participatory work process through observation and on-the-job experience with their work team. In addition, the weekly reports they receive during a sixty-work-day probationary period provide associates with feedback on the behavioral aspects of their performance, as well as on the fulfillment of their tasks. In this way, the new associate is quickly integrated into the participative management system.

Training for Technical Tasks. In contrast to the routine task training that takes place in traditional factories, Schaumburg's task training is complex. When a new associate joins the Schaumburg bakery, he or she spends the first weeks or months under the supervision of the work team's training facilitator to learn the job. Although training facilitators are selected by each work team and are familiar with all the jobs performed in their action groups, they do not necessarily conduct all the training for the new associate. They either personally train an associate on the job or they assign that person to work with an individual who is skilled in the job. Eventually, the training facilitator evaluates the new associate's skills; once the facilitator finds that the associate's performance is satisfactory, the associate may perform the function independently.

In addition to the initial training assistance given to the new associate, all Schaumburg workers are continually encouraged to develop their potential and extend their skills beyond those they learned shortly after being hired. At Schaumburg, associates are paid for the acquisition of new skills and knowledge through an incentive system. Compensation is based on the concepts of pay-for-knowledge and demonstrated skill. The system applies to unit skills (those within a work action group), craft skills (electrical, plumbing, mechanical, hydraulic/pneumatic, welding, refrigeration/electronics/controls), or community skills (CPR and other first-aid techniques). If Schaumburg associates want to improve their skills and knowledge beyond those required for their particular function, they can study them and be compensated for their new knowledge—whether they are actually using the skills on the job or not.

Associates acquire new skills at Schaumburg in a carefully designated series of steps. They may simply take a test on a given skill and, if they can pass it, are remunerated for that new demonstrable knowledge level. Usually, however, they first learn how to run a particular machine, fix a piece of equipment, or administer CPR, for example, by working with their training facilitator or other workers who already perform that function. They may also acquire the theoretical knowledge for a given task through a series of self-paced training manuals. Associates are then given a test on their practical and written knowledge of the skill and, when they pass, are paid for their new skill.

This training and compensation system is now in place on the associate level at Schaumburg, but is not yet in effect in the administrative and managerial action groups. At this writing, those two groups are currently developing an alternative compensation system for acquired and demonstrated skills.

Usually several associates within a work team are simultaneously training and being trained to learn new skills. An associate who has been assigned to monitor the final inspection before packaging, for instance, might be training another associate in this same function. As that associate trainee becomes skilled, the training associate may then spend several hours learning a new task, such as how to monitor the packaging machines. Through this kind of ongoing training process, associates are constantly upgrading their skills and learning different aspects of the functions in their action groups.

As one member of the pack action group says, "It really keeps you learning all the time. And you don't get bored the way you might if you just kept putting the same screw in the same hole for the next twenty years, the way you do in other factories." Adds John Szymoniak, an associate from the bakery floor who was recently promoted to the management action group, "This way, too, you don't have to just rely on one or two people to perform a function, and then have difficulty if that person happens to be sick. Because many of us know the various functions, we can take over in an emergency or give someone who's having a problem a hand.'' Eventually, he explains, the ideal is that everyone within a work team will have had experience with everyone else's job.

Three Training Stages

There have been three training stages at Schaumburg since its beginning. The first began in late 1983 with a formal companywide training period during which associates learned the rudiments of the muffin-making process through demonstrations, videotapes, films, and on-the-job training; at that time, they were also introduced to the concept of sociotechnical design. As the various work teams and action groups have matured, associates have continued to refine particular functions and procedures related to technical tasks and behavioral dynamics.

The second training stage began with an effort to reduce turnover and improve productivity. In October 1984, monthly meetings were held with the seven key facilitators from each action group. During these brainstorming sessions, facilitators worked with managers who held similar roles in the management action group to solve problems particular to each function. For instance, Willis, the management group's cost facilitator, met with cost facilitators from Schaumburg's six other action groups to help find ways to reduce overhead. Oakes, the counseling facilitator, discussed behavioral problems and their solutions with the bakery's other six counseling facilitators. After five months, Schaumburg's facilitators reported that they had a clearer idea of their functions within each work team and a sense of how to get their goals accomplished. Since then, facilitators have continued to make efforts to improve their job-training methods.

By October 1985, associates had produced a series of training films explaining and illustrating their various tasks. They also created an activity list, which described each task in detail and accompanied each training film. And Dawn Hamersly, a training facilitator for the process action group, wrote a manual on Schaumburg's cooling system to help new workers pace themselves during the production cycle.

In the third training phase at Schaumburg a formal training method for new workers was developed. At this writing, nine people from Schaumburg's action groups have formed an orientation committee to develop a standardized approach to training. According to this plan, the new worker spends the first day of work briefly observing what each team member does: at that time the new hire also receives a package of pertinent information about the Schaumburg bakery, including the company's work policy, union contract, managerial functions, associate responsibilities, security and safety practices, and a monograph on sociotechnical design. The second morning, a training film is shown on the particular function the worker is expected to perform, and the worker receives a written description of that function. Although training films now exist for the various task functions within each work team, new films on the social or behavioral aspects of Schaumburg's system are being planned.

Making the Social System Work

The sociotechnical-design concept demands that workers be provided with a social system in which they can develop and grow on a job that is coordinated with an effective technical system. According to Schaumburg's statement of philosophy, "The foundation and spirit of the social system is based upon the assumption that individuals are capable of making decisions given they have sufficient information and proper training. This premise, we feel, will develop a sense of ownership . . . leading to excellence."

Schaumburg associates are expected to demonstrate a flexible attitude in the workplace that recognizes few status differences between workers, accommodates criticism, maintains a positive feedback system, and stresses the efforts of individuals for the greater good of the group.

To promote a sense of ownership, associates were initially encouraged to define and understand the nature of their tasks even before the plant officially opened in January 1984. Those involved in the muffin-baking process, for instance, were clearly instructed in the various steps in the procedure and the acceptable outcomes. As work teams grew more experienced, individual associates demonstrated improvement in their ability to spot trouble, institute changes, and create better products with less waste. But such self-regulatory skills took time to develop at Schaumburg and necessitated a cooperative attitude on the part of workers and management—one not always easy to find in those who had previous experience in a traditional work environment.

It is for this reason that Schaumburg associates say that it takes a special kind of worker to participate in a self-managed group. Since Schaumburg first opened, hiring methods have been refined to include an elaborate role-playing interview, as noted earlier, to identify the highly cooperative worker.

Often, particularly in the bakery's early months, associates expected managers to solve disputes within work teams as they might have done in traditional work environments. Since a basic tenet of the sociotechnical design is self-regulation, managers had to continually stress that such disputes should be solved between the associates within their action groups. Essentially, this means that if an associate feels another is not performing his or her job adequately and is thus jeopardizing the team's output, the two associates should first deal directly with one another.

Through an open dialogue, the problem can be shared and a solution discovered. If this approach is not successful, Schaumburg associates follow a prescribed series of steps to effect a solution. First, there is a counseling session with the group communicator and counselor. If that proves unsuccessful, the work team studies the situation and makes a recommendation. If satisfaction still is not obtained, "problem" workers are asked to make a *success commitment* over a designated period of time—or face disciplinary action, written notice of suspension, and, finally, termination.

The Union Role

The union has played a similarly unique role at Schaumburg. Because Schaumburg's self-managing system places the managerial functions on the associates and holds them responsible for task performance, the union serves a consultative role, in addition to monitoring contract compliance. As mentioned above, Schaumburg associates serve in various supervisory functions, which immediately enhance their understanding of individual workers and group dynamics. In accordance with union procedures, two Schaumburg workers currently serve as shop stewards. Although these workers must frequently "switch hats" when they serve union functions, their ongoing service to the group in facilitator roles often coordinates smoothly with their union duties.

As of this writing, Zaranski and Oakes note that the relationship with the union has proceeded quite smoothly since the plant's beginning. In fact, as Joan Groneman, one of Schaumburg's shop stewards, points out, the only time the union is likely to intervene is when the action group's own grievance procedure is not carried out properly; this, however, is a rare event, particularly since the strength of the sociotechnical design derives from the individual worker's own sense of control over his or her daily work conditions.

Reaping the Rewards

In summary, it is clear that while the initial steps to establish Schaumburg's participatory management system were cumbersome compared to those in conventional management systems, Schaumburg workers have begun to reap personal and occupational rewards from that system. As Ursula Karcz, a member of Schaumburg's process action group, says: "The beauty of it is that you get feedback about your performance. Usually, if something has to be decided by the group, it's a fair decision. You don't take the criticism as personally as you might if it was a supervisor who you felt always picked on you. What you come to learn quickly is that what's your job is everyone else's too—that all of you count at work."

Workers have been almost universally enthusiastic about this system, especially those who have previously worked under traditional management hierarchies. "This is much better. There's much more room in this kind of cooperative system to grow and be recognized," says Dawn Hamersly, an associate in the process action group. "In the other system, you're clearly stuck in a particular job and therefore don't take on additional responsibility. Here you're encouraged to. And you're constantly getting feedback which gives you lots of opportunities to do better, so that it's almost impossible to get fired."

Others do note, however, that some people—particularly those who have spent a lot of years in traditional factory work, and who prefer structure and dislike taking initiative—have difficulty adjusting to the Schaumburg system.

Thus, while initially awkward, the sociotechnical approach does have many advantages, not the least of which is that it enables the worker to be self-motivated. Observes Louis Davis: "If people are responsible for achieving a goal, they should have a great deal to say about how they're going to achieve it."

Impact on Managers

For the first year of Schaumburg's operation, the plant managers were heavily involved in the training and in technical aspects of productivity. All the equipment had been transferred from the Totowa, New Jersey, plant and placed in the new Schaumburg facility, where it required innumerable technical adjustments. Concurrently, the new social system was being applied to a group of workers without any experience in work teams and, thus, needed constant refinement and attention from managers like Stanley Zaranski and David Oakes. Turnover ran at 40 percent the first year, and it took twelve to eighteen months for the plant to reach the operating norm for other S. B. Thomas plants.

During this period, managers were understandably cautious about ceding control to the workers, and the sharing of power came only gradually. At this point, Schaumburg had also lost two managers, which put considerable strain on the remaining seven. After consultation with corporate headquarters and recommendations from Louis Davis's group, several managers were hired from within the Schaumburg facility and promoted. In the second year of operation, turnover dropped to 20 percent and is expected to decline to 10 percent or less as the action groups refine their internal management mechanisms. In most cases, managers are assigned to loosely oversee the action groups; currently, however, one group has developed into such a smoothly running team that it no longer requires any managerial support. Eventually, it is anticipated that truly "managerless" groups will become the norm at Schaumburg, rather than the exception.

While the sociotechnical-design concept at Schaumburg connotes a "flattened" corporate structure, or few boundaries between workers and managers, the design ideally allows the company's few managers to concentrate upon critical tasks. As Davis explains, the appeal of the sociotechnical design is that it allows workers to manage themselves in small groups, while company managers can focus on their proper functions—connecting with the outside world and handling resources essential to the business—that is, people, money, materials, or equipment.

Now that Schaumburg's work teams are running more smoothly, its managers have been able to turn their attention to those functions. Stanley Zaranski has been able to concentrate more fully on affairs that affect Schaumburg's sales area and its relationship to the larger corporation, instead of the day-to-day running of the bakery. Similarly, controller Gary Willis has watched members of the administrative action group assume many of the reporting and payroll functions for which he was once solely responsible. Consequently, he can now spend more time concentrating on the improvement of Schaumburg's transportation and distribution system.

In this way, Schaumburg managers claim that the system ultimately works better than traditional management hierarchies. "My job here is to communicate goals, not to make decisions for the teams about how to reach those goals," explains Zaranski. "As these groups have improved, I've been able to relax because I can trust them to carry out those goals efficiently." Adds Willis, "The proper role of the manager here is that of a consultant. It's true that it takes lots of time to set up the system, but what you finally get is an operation that works better in the long run because you have people in place who really care."

Long-Term Implications

As previously mentioned, the time-consuming development of a sociotechnical plan and the high turnover in Schaumburg's first year of operation initially led to skepticism among managers in other S. B. Thomas sites. Yet, Schaumburg's recent performance record, low number of labor disputes, and lower production costs have begun to cause a turnaround in their thinking. In addition, corporate leaders at S. B. Thomas, such as Jack Collins and William Sholl, are committed to the concept of participatory management and have begun to introduce it on a corporatewide level. Currently, for instance, S. B. Thomas trains its managers by function in the participatory management concept. Controllers from the five Thomas facilities meet to exchange and develop more efficient strategies. Formerly, meetings were held for plant managers, production managers, production supervisors, and plant engineers. By developing these action groups in cross-plant functions, Thomas executives hope to strengthen the company through its various employee levels, and develop a uniformity of purpose and objective to ensure its continued growth.

10

Pacific Bell and Communications Workers of America: Retraining for the Computer Age

Jill Casner-Lotto

At Pacific Bell, employees whose jobs may be phased out due to technological change or economic downswings are being retrained and successfully "recycled" into the company. In a field as volatile as telecommunications, projecting future job opportunities and responding quickly through retraining efforts take an extraordinary amount of skill, planning, and, most important, cooperation. The retraining program in place at Pacific Bell Telephone (Pac Bell) represents a cooperative venture between the company and the Communications Workers of America (CWA), which has contracted with several California community colleges to develop courses and provide instruction. Another party is also involved in this venture—the state of California's Employment Training Panel (ETP), an innovative program to prevent job layoffs. The panel finances retraining projects in the private sector by diverting $55 million a year that otherwise would go into the state's unemployment insurance system.

The collaboration that exists among these various parties— plus the motivation and drive of individual employees—are the key elements contributing to the success of the Pac Bell/CWA program. In operation since 1984, the program is making impressive headway: As of July 1987, about 750 employees in the Los Angeles area had been retrained, many of them going from nontechnical jobs to more highly skilled, better paying technical and marketing positions. Many more employees will have the chance to improve their skills now that the program has been expanded throughout the state.

The Pact Between Pacific Bell
and the Communications Workers of America

Although both Pac Bell and CWA had been involved in training for some time, this latest move to retrain is due largely to two major forces: the court-ordered divestiture of AT&T in 1984 and widespread technological change, particularly in the clerical and technical fields. Like many of the other new operating companies that spun off from the breakup of AT&T, Pacific Bell—now part of the Pacific Telesis Group—is undergoing fundamental changes in order to become, according to company officials, a more competitive and entrepreneurial business. Pacific Telesis is a corporate entity composed of various subsidiaries, the major ones being the two operating companies: Pacific Bell, which services all of California, and Nevada Bell, which serves most of that state.

Other subsidiaries under the Pacific Telesis umbrella are involved in marketing various goods and services, including computers and computerized switching systems sold to domestic and international markets, property management services, cellular mobile telephones, and publishing services. The corporation is headquartered in San Francisco.

Prior to divestiture in 1984, there were 110,000 employees at Pacific Bell. Today, the company employs 67,000—40,000 of them nonexempt employees in a variety of clerical, operator, sales, and technical positions represented by the CWA, and 27,000 in management slots. To meet its revenue objectives, the company's strategic plan calls for a further shrinkage of the work force to 60,000 employees by 1990. Because of retraining and placement efforts, there have been only 500 layoffs since 1984. As of 1986, when the new Pac Bell/CWA agreement established a policy of employment security for the term of the three-year contract, there have been no layoffs.

The 1986 contract expanded the existing joint labor-management mechanisms for retraining and relocating surplus employees both inside and outside of the company. Employee assistance may include not only job-specific retraining, relocation to new positions, job fairs, and career guidance help, but also generic retraining that gives former Pac Bell employees a significant head start in the highly competitive telecommunications job market. As a last resort, company and union officials have also worked out a process for outplacement counseling.

Joseph Richey, human resource development manager at Pac Bell, emphasizes that these retraining and placement efforts stem from a strong corporate commitment to the individual, as well as from their inclusion in the collective bargaining agreement between Pac Bell and the CWA. Union officials believe their involvement in developing retraining programs will give them more control over the content. "The union believes that as the company relies more and more on outside colleges to develop training courses, the training will become generic in nature and broad enough to have application outside the company," according to the late Edmond Bishop, former administrative assistant to the vice-president of CWA District 011. "We feel we can encourage this by entering into joint agreements with management and by spreading the word to our members through the local union structure."

Management agrees that union involvement in structuring the retraining program enhances its credibility among employees. "Employees tend to listen when the union carries the message to its membership. And in a company that was a 'cradle-to-grave' organization, many people just can't believe that they must be retrained if they want to be successful," Richey notes.

Two Types of Training

The nature of technological change in telecommunications is difficult to characterize, since the changes have occurred so rapidly and because the field itself is so highly complex. While computer technology has eliminated jobs in certain categories, such as traditional clerical, typist, and operator positions, in other categories it has led to an increased demand. Service representatives, for example, who possess a thorough understanding of the new telephone technology and, at the same time, are able to relate well to customers, are needed now more than ever. Technicians' jobs, while fewer in number, have undergone dramatic changes, and, as a result, require increasingly sophisticated skills. "Cable splicing has now become fiber-optic splicing," notes Richey, "and technical problems are no longer solved through manual rewiring of equipment, but instead by careful analysis of computer software data."

To best prepare for the onslaught of new technology and achieve the maximum fit between employee skills and changing job needs, labor and management have organized training activities into two major categories: generic pretraining aimed at preventing possible layoffs, and job-specific training. Beginning in May 1986, some pretraining for customer service representatives was funded by California's Employment Training Panel (ETP). Currently, most of the pretraining is funded through the company's tuition-aid plan, though some pretraining courses are funded through the Employer-Based Training Program (EBT) run by the Los Angeles Community College District. Job-specific training is paid for by the company, as well as by the Employment Training Panel, which currently funds retraining programs for four occupations. Pretraining is voluntary and conducted after or before work hours, while job-specific training takes place on company time once the employee has been transferred to the new position.

Pretraining activities serve two very important functions. First, by including general skills in electronics, computer technology, mathematics, logic, and other technical areas, the pretraining courses equip employees with knowledge that applies broadly to telecommunications rather than being tied to one particular job or employer. Pretraining also benefits the employer. Designed to prepare employees for the job-specific training they receive once they are transferred, pretraining gives employees a chance to "try the job out" on their own time. As such, pretraining is the best assurance the company has that employees are adequately qualified for the job and will stay once they are placed.

"This has been a problem for us in the past," notes Richey. "Once employees transfer to new jobs they have the right to return to their original positions within a six-month period. In certain jobs, the retreat rate was as high as 40 percent, because employees were not qualified or didn't like their new job. We've now gotten that rate down to 5 percent."

As a result, training costs have been reduced as well—not an insignificant factor for a company that spends between $20 and $25 million a year on job-specific training. At Pac Bell, the job-specific training function is carried out under the 400-member Training Department, while the pretraining activities are organized under the company's Placement Center, which operates on a much slimmer $6.5 million budget with a staff of 80. The reason for the difference, notes Richey, is that the bulk of training expenses comes from the highly sophisticated equipment used in the job-specific training courses. Nevertheless, pretraining—even though it represents a much smaller portion of overall training expenses—is viewed by labor and management alike as a crucial link to both individual and company success.

Between 8,500 and 10,000 employees receive some form of training per year in a variety of management, clerical, or technical skills. Several training methods are used, including instructor-led classes, correspondence courses, and self-paced courses, often utilizing computer-interactive video systems. Training may be conducted at the work site, on the campus of a nearby community college, or at one of Pac Bell's five training centers fully equipped with classroom, library, video, and other training facilities. Two of these are located in southern California, while three are in the northern part of the state.

The Training Advisory Board

Union involvement in retraining at Pac Bell is facilitated through the Training Advisory Board (TAB), a jointly administered body created as a result of the 1983 contract between AT&T and CWA. The national agreement called for the establishment of TABs to generally oversee training activities at each of the new operating companies—but specific issues, such as board composition and responsibilities, were left up to each of the individual companies. The training board at Pacific Bell is currently composed of three management and three labor representatives. The board's major responsibilities include curriculum review and approval, projection of future job trends, training, site selection, and discussion of key issues affecting the training process. The 1986 contract also specified that the board explore alternative funding sources for retraining programs.

The major issue currently before the board concerns the needs of surplus employees whose jobs are threatened by new technology, market changes, or other economic forces. The board has responded by developing generic pretraining courses that prepare surplus employees for new opportunities within the company and—if that's not possible—outside the company. In recent years, community colleges have increasingly become a partner in the actual design of these courses. Thus, course development is very much a collaborative process, involving board members, college officials, and company department heads.

The process begins with an informal meeting between two or three members of the board (which may include both management and labor representatives) and the dean or director of vocational education from a community college. The dean is presented with a general course outline or overview stating the training needs and content guidelines. College officials then prepare an "approximate" curriculum, says TAB member Richey, which is reviewed by board members as well as by appropriate company department heads. Using that feedback, representatives from the community college develop a more detailed curriculum. This curriculum is then presented before the full board, which meets quarterly, for any further modification and final approval.

For the most part, labor and management have had no serious differences over the way training is conducted, and only minor adjustments concerning course content or site location have been necessary. The greatest value of the Training Advisory Board is that it has provided both parties a forum for airing whatever issues or disagreements—however big or small—may come up before they become major sources of conflict. "The big change is that we talk before we do things," Richey observes. "In the past, the company might have done something and then discussed it with the union—and it might have been okay—but the union was not involved in the decision."

Two very successful pretraining projects at Pacific Bell are programs for electronic technicians and service representatives. The pretraining curricula for both the electronic technician and the service representative courses were developed in cooperation with two California community college districts. The electronics pretraining was funded by the Employer-Based Training Program. And a major source of funding for the service representative pretraining came from the ETP.

A key requirement for ETP funding is that the training lead to known jobs in stable or expanding occupations that provide a decent living. Minimum-wage or dead-end occupations are unacceptable. The panel's stated purpose is to "help workers learn the skills needed by employers and thereby help to stimulate and revitalize the California economy." In operation since 1982, the ETP has proven enormously successful, awarding more than $220 million to more than 5,000 employers involved in more than 500 training projects around the state (Gutchess, 1984, pp. 93–99).

Still another party that proved instrumental in getting the retraining project off the ground was the Los Angeles Business Labor Council, a group of top-level management and labor leaders from various industries. In the beginning stages, the council served as a broker, bringing together the various parties involved in the effort. The council's input also helped,

Richey notes, in addressing the needs of surplus employees and developing the right kind of retraining, since many council members had experience in handling similar problems in other businesses and were aware of existing job opportunities in different industries.

From Telephone Operator to Technician

One of the most striking features of the electronics technical training program is that it is directed toward employees in nontechnical jobs, many of them occupied by women. So far, 750 employees have been retrained, including former telephone operators, secretaries, and clerks. The electronics pretraining program opens up opportunities in ten different jobs ranging from communications technician to splicer. For many employees, successful completion of the course and relocation to one of these technical positions can represent a significant move up the career ladder, in terms of both skills and pay. Union official Edmond Bishop noted that jobs in the clerical field average about $9 per hour, while the craft rate is about $17 per hour.

For employee Janet Alonzo, the prospect of being in the technical end of the company is exciting. Quoted in a *Los Angeles Times* article describing the program, Alonzo noted that she enrolled in the electronics training course since her present position—in which she monitors the progress of installation work—might eventually become "surplus." "There will be more mechanized ways to check information, so fewer people will be needed," says Alonzo. By fitting in the training either before or after the workday, she estimates that the 160-hour rigorous course will take her about eight months to complete (Weinstein, 1985).

"This type of training is good for only the most motivated employees," according to Joe Richey. He notes that in addition to the basic training course, certain job titles require qualification on the electronic switching systems minicourse test—a grueling six-hour exercise in which there has been a 35 to 40 percent failure rate.

Participants who enroll in this electronics training course

receive computer-interactive training in basic electronics, digital techniques, transmission fundamentals, logic, and numbering systems. Employees are fully reimbursed upon completion of the course. The course is self-paced and takes between three and twelve months to complete, depending upon the number of hours per day or week the employee is able to devote to it. It provides employees with individualized, competency-based instruction that is presented in a series of modules. The work stations, located at seven different Pac Bell sites and costing approximately $8,000 each to install, consist of a videotape player, a color monitor, a microcomputer with disk drive, and electronic test equipment.

According to the course description, trainees move through the exercises under the watchful eye of the computer:

"The student responds to the questions on the video screen; the computer replies and directs the student in appropriate handling of the test equipment. The computer-interactive instruction includes theory, hands-on lab jobs, and quiz materials on videotape with computer-generated text and lesson control. . . . Traditional textbook homework is regularly assigned and a computer-guided homework review is provided for all assignments."

If students have questions that the computer can't answer, human help is merely a phone call away. Community college instructors—many of them Pac Bell retirees or former employees—are equipped with beepers so they can readily respond to students' inquiries.

Reliance upon this type of work-based computer system has greatly increased employee access to the course, says Paul Stansbury, associate director of occupational and technical education for the Los Angeles Community College District. "We've changed the delivery method to make it as convenient as possible for employees who might otherwise find it difficult to commute to the campus."

Richey agrees that the community college's flexibility—in scheduling classes, tailoring its courses or creating new ones, or just adjusting its program to whatever fits the situation— has greatly contributed to the success of the retraining project. "It really is a unique change in the educational system," says Richey. "Prior to 1979, we moaned a lot about their product—

about students being unprepared for the business world. Now, at least the wall between us is breaking down. We're still stumbling around in the rubble—but things are happening.''

Training for Service Representatives

Unlike its impact in the clerical field, where the number of jobs has been reduced, computerization has sharply increased the demand for well-trained service, or customer, representatives. ''For starters, just think of some of the phone bills today—they're pages and pages long and often extremely confusing,'' noted Bishop. ''Service reps today need to be especially well-prepared to field customer questions. It's become a very demanding, tension-driven job.''

The combination of technological and ''people'' skills taught in the generic pretraining class for service reps reflects the kind of versatility needed on the job. Along with computer keyboarding skills, the course teaches techniques of selling, customer-interaction skills, how to handle stress in the workplace, and clerical-overview skills. The classes are highly compressed, with a great deal of information taught within a short period of time.

The 120-hour course has attracted a wide variety of employees, ranging from telephone operators to engineering aides. According to Richey, the course has proven enormously successful and cost effective. Before pretraining was instituted, as few as 55 percent of enrolled employees successfully completed a forty-five-day job-specific training program. Currently, with pretraining in place, 85 percent succeed in the job-specific training. ''Before pretraining was implemented, we were losing as many as 45 percent of those who had already gone through on-the-job training. Now, we've reduced the failure rate by 30 percent and our costs have come down significantly,'' explains Richey.

Placement of Surplus Employees

As of mid 1987, 860 retrained employees had been placed in new positions at Pacific Bell. While the company is required to place trainees in order to secure state retraining funds for the community colleges, labor and management have devised their own systematic approach to job placement of so-called surplus employees. The first discussion of surplus employees occurs at meetings of local common interest forums, which are joint labor-management groups established in each major geographical area of California. The forums, headed by the company's regional vice-president and the local union president, meet regularly to discuss the impact of technological changes and office closings on the work force. If labor-force reductions and relocations are necessary, they occur in an orderly fashion according to the jointly developed and managed Inter and Intra Vice-President Movement Plan, which provides for the transfer of surplus employees within the geographical area headed by a company vice-president and throughout the state. All retraining issues are directly referred to the TAB for further action.

If still more attention is needed to bring about a smooth relocation process, the companywide Upgrade and Transfer Plan is used. This plan also ensures that job placements take place in a fair, controlled, and timely manner. Transfers are not based on seniority alone—qualifications play an equally important role. Employees who want to be retrained for new positions must first enter their names in a transfer file that rates them by category: Category 3 refers to those who possess only minimum skills for the job in question and who, in certain cases, have passed a basic qualifying test in order to become eligible for pretraining. Category 2 applies to employees who have successfully completed the pretraining course or courses, and who are considered substantially qualified for the job. Category 1 refers to the job incumbents. Thus, to be trained an employee must have a Category 3 rating; to be placed, a Category 2 rating.

Files of potential transferees waiting for requisition are kept well stocked for any given job. "As a result, the company seldom has to hire off the street—only in the case of entry-level positions. That's been a big plus," notes Richey.

The Upgrade and Transfer Plan gives first preference to laid-off employees who have retained recall rights and to surplus employees whose jobs may be displaced by new technology, but who are still employed by the company. A primary function of the TAB is to project the job categories where a surplus is expected and notify employees whose jobs are in jeopardy at least sixty days in advance of any layoffs. Department heads submit the names of surplus employees to a surplus-control center, established in the company's Placement Center. Any job requisitions that are generated go to the control center before the normal placement process is set in motion.

The surplus-control system is not perfect, but so far, judging from the figures, it is working well. During the first three quarters of 1985, 2,000 employees were in jobs declared surplus. Out of these, 80 percent were recycled into stable jobs at the company. It is unclear, however, whether that rate of placement can be improved—or even maintained—in the future, Richey notes. The offering of early-retirement packages to employees aged fifty-two and older has opened up jobs at the company, but opportunities will become increasingly limited as these slots become filled and the number of near-retirement-age employees levels off. The company and union are developing alternatives, such as working with local Private Industry Councils to find job opportunities at other companies in the area and to provide generic pretraining before employees leave Pacific Bell.

Forecasting

One of the weakest links in the system is forecasting areas of job growth and decline, labor and management agree. "In this respect, I don't think the system is up to the speed it should be," noted union official Edmond Bishop. "We've got to fashion some improvements that utilize our electronic communications skills to get the word out." Recently, CWA officials met with AT&T and Department of Labor representatives to discuss ways of applying the new electronics technology—in the form of job banks, hot lines, and other computerized systems—to disperse relevant job-trend information.

"We're honing our forecasting skills," says Richey, adding that a goal is to come up with five-year forecasts in major job categories. The company currently has a computerized system that notes either positive or negative one-year growth trends in any given job category.

"The reality is that you can't always read the future," Richey admits. "The important thing is that the union is involved in planning for the changes ahead. Whatever numbers we come up with, the union knows up front what those numbers will be and is in a position to carry that information to its members. There'll be no surprises."

Providing Career Direction

Pac Bell's Employee Career Center, which, prior to the 1986 contract, was sponsored by the company and is now jointly operated by labor and management, has encouraged recruitment from within through employee growth and development. (For a more detailed description of the Employment Career Center Program, see Chapter Eight of *Training—The Competitive Edge,* by Jerome M. Rosow and Robert Zager [San Francisco: Jossey-Bass, 1988].) The program employs "career specialists," whose role is to give employees a broad overview of the job picture—where the jobs will be, the content of these jobs, and the qualifications needed—"in short, where the opportunities are and how to get them," notes Richey. Employees are made aware of the full spectrum of retraining and other options, but ultimately, according to the corporate view, their future depends on their own initiatives. "From the corporate perspective, a program like this separates the achievers from the sustainers—it's for the highly motivated individual who wants more and needs help to get it," he states.

The Employee Career Center, initially offered only in the Los Angeles area, has now been expanded statewide. A regularly issued newsletter, entitled *Career Center News,* publicizes information on retraining programs, job trends, career workshops, and registration dates for courses offered through the community college. The same information is also available in a computerized system called "Career Wise"; highly user-friendly computers are located at work sites throughout the state.

The union has also marketed the concept of career growth through its own network. Letters to the locals and stories in the union newspaper regularly include information on job projections and retraining programs, and how members can take advantage of these programs. Union stewards, added Bishop, are taking an active role in informing the membership.

"We may be moving slowly, but we are making progress," concluded Bishop. "This is something that neither side can achieve in a few days. It takes a lot of front-end time and planning—on both sides—to be successful."

PART THREE

MANUFACTURER-USER
TRAINING PARTNERSHIPS

The manner in which the manufacturers of new technology approach users can make an enormous difference in the application of that technology. When the relationship is a cooperative one—in which manufacturer and user share information and ideas about the design, implementation, and training for a new system—the opportunities for both parties to learn about the product increase, and more creative applications of new technology result. Unfortunately, in today's corporate environment, that scenario is the exception rather than the rule. More frequently, users are on their own when it comes to implementing the technology and integrating it into the functions of the work unit. Usually, training in the operation and application of new systems is not even part of the package deal; more commonly, training is considered an ''extra'' and is only provided at considerable cost to the customer.

Such a policy can be disastrous, resulting in training that is superficial and irrelevant to the customer's needs; delayed start-ups in which millions may be spent in debugging complex computer systems; long periods of equipment downtime; employee resistance; and management frustration. Service-sector companies, in particular, are experiencing setbacks in the introduction of new technology, and the disappointingly low productivity yields are convincing many of them to spend less on office automation systems.

173

The absence of a close working relationship between manufacturer and user has seriously hampered the spread of new technology. This part focuses on this crucial, yet frequently overlooked, aspect of technology transfer. The cases presented here demonstrate the advantages—to both users and manufacturers (or vendors)—of joint responsibility for training, as well as for the design, building, and implementation of advanced technological systems. The users benefit from faster implementation, increased flexibility in the application and adaptation of new systems, and more uptime. Customer satisfaction is the obvious benefit to the manufacturer. However, there is another, often unexpected outcome of a genuine learning partnership beween the two parties—namely, the creation of a kind of synergy, in which the user learns new, innovative applications that exceed the manufacturer's standards and the manufacturer uses this information to modify and improve its products for future sales.

The first case described in this part represents a breakthrough approach to vendor-user cooperation. At Control Data Corporation, input from customers is helping to solve some complex training problems. Though best known for its computer hardware, Control Data also develops and markets computer-based training courses and provides consulting services in support of the automated production equipment used in heavy manufacturing. To improve its responsiveness to customer needs, Control Data sponsors a training advisory board, composed of its major customers, and conducts site visits at customers' workplaces. Through the board and the site visits, Control Data receives continuing feedback of customer concerns and has consequently both developed more flexible, cost-effective ways to deliver its courses and modified course content to more closely match customers' needs.

Two other cases—the General Motors plant in Linden, New Jersey, and Goodyear Tire and Rubber—illustrate the kinds of initiatives users can take to develop successful training programs. In each case, the company obtained a training commitment as a condition of the equipment contract and then jointly developed and carried out training strategies with the manufacturer. Training programs included written specifications that required demonstrated performance of tasks by trainees as the test of compliance. Both companies also sent their employees to equipment vendor schools for train-the-trainer courses. Employees then designed the training course, and taught co-workers to operate, maintain, and repair the new system. Such an approach proved less expensive than providing vendor training for all employees and was also more responsive to the needs of the workplace.

While formal training sessions at the time of equipment installation are essential if employees are to fully understand the potential range of applications, knowledge about the new technology can be gained through other, less formal channels. Often, the quality of learning that occurs at various stages of the vendor-user relationship—such as the design, building/testing, installation, and start-up phases—exceeds that which could be absorbed solely through structured classroom sessions or conventional on-the-job training. For example, at Ford Motor Company's truck transmission plant at Sharonville, Ohio, a team of salaried and hourly employees visited the vendor's plant during the building phase of new technology to identify any operating problems before the equipment was installed at the Sharonville plant. Ford production and manufacturing engineers met biweekly with the vendor, Lamb Technicon, and contributed to the design of the equipment. Involvement in the technology as it was being developed and tested gave the users an understanding of the underlying logic of new systems and helped them immeasurably in diagnosing and remedying equipment problems.

The successful application of computer-integrated manufacturing (CIM) systems poses an even greater learning challenge for the user due to several factors, including the complex nature of the technologies involved and the fact that, in any one factory, many different vendors usually supply the network of machines, computers, and software systems that constitute the integrated systems. Both Caterpillar Inc. and Miller Brewing Company were implementing multivendor integrated systems and both turned to third-party specialists, who were chosen for their technological and training expertise. Allen-Bradley, which specializes in programmable controllers and communications networks, was selected to carry out Caterpillar's training program even though it supplied only a relatively small number of components in the Caterpillar system. In addition to its long-established reputation for producing high-quality equipment, Allen-Bradley also emphasizes training as part of its customer-support services. The supplier's special expertise in CIM technology plus its willingness to organize a comprehensive approach to CIM implementation convinced Caterpillar executives that Allen-Bradley was the best choice.

Miller Brewing Company, which introduced new technology into all phases of the beer production process, has worked closely with Amatrol, Inc., a vendor of bench-training equipment and courses, in training for and implementing integrated systems. Though it was not even one of Miller's suppliers, Amatrol was chosen to assist in training because of its experience in building integrated systems, its skill in training, and its willingness to develop with Miller a complete training program tailored to Miller specifications. A unique feature of the program is its use of Miller supervisors to train hourly workers. Amatrol trainers also stay in close touch with Miller supervisors after the training and provide help when system-related problems arise on the shop floor.

11

Learning from Customers: Control Data Corporation's Training Advisory Board

Jill Casner-Lotto

A new approach at Control Data Corporation's Training and Education Group (TEG) is proving extremely effective at eliciting customers' views on the training needed in the manufacturing environment. TEG develops and markets computer-based courses, including a series of courses known as the Industrial Automation Training Program (IATP). The training group also provides consulting services to support a variety of automated production equipment and systems. To make sure its offerings meet customer needs, TEG sponsors a Training Advisory Board, which is made up of representatives of Control Data's customers. Another crucial aspect of Control Data's attempt to improve its responsiveness to customer needs is a schedule of plant visits, in which professional training consultants from TEG spend an entire day on the shop floor, interviewing and observing the actual users of its training products and services. According to Keith Johnson, IATP program manager, the board meetings and the on-site visits are helping Control Data obtain a more detailed analysis of customer needs and problems—a prerequisite, he says, to becoming more competitive in the training field.

In this case study, Control Data is the training vendor rather than the equipment vendor, but the model adopted—an advisory board of customers supplemented by on-site interviews with the end users—is one that is applicable to any vendor-customer relationship. In fact, at least one Control Data customer is so pleased with the arrangement that he is trying to persuade equipment vendors with whom his company works to establish similar mechanisms to get at customer needs.

At a recent board meeting, Johnson unveiled plans for Control Data's development of a new, more cost-effective training delivery system—a direct response, he says, to customer input received via the advisory board. Another less tangible—but equally important—benefit of having the Training Advisory Board and the extensive network of end users is that both have prompted some thoughtful discussion of training issues that might not otherwise have received such close attention. For example, the board has discussed the need for more and better equipment-specific training in computer-based formats, as well as the need for more cooperative efforts among equipment vendors, customers, and third parties, such as Control Data, to develop and market computer-based training courses. Although there is not always agreement on what is needed to solve the problems—indeed, very often there may be more disagreement—both Control Data and its customers see the advisory board as a useful vehicle for reaching solutions and compromises.

The Industrial Automation Training Program

IATP specialists develop both standard and customized training courses delivered by Control Data's computer-based PLATO system. IATP is marketed to companies involved in heavy manufacturing, including those in the automobile, food and beverage, aviation, petroleum, and chemical industries. Most of the IATP course material is aimed at providing generic skills to maintenance personnel, since it is in this group that the need for generic training has been most acute. Johnson explains: "Many maintenance employees are not adequately prepared for the more specialized equipment training provided by the equipment vendors or by the employers. Our goal is to provide maintenance personnel with the prerequisite knowledge and skills needed to get the maximum out of the technology in which companies have invested. We do this by bringing their technical skills up to the level required to understand and benefit from the equipment-specific training."

A wide-ranging curriculum is offered: basic technology courses in electronics, microprocessors, computers and data processing, hydraulics, and pneumatics; more advanced courses in programmable controllers and robotics; and "prebasic" remediation courses in math fundamentals, blueprint reading, learning techniques, and maintenance skills. Courses may be delivered on IBM-PC-compatible devices, which Control Data will sell to customers. Another option is Control Data's time-sharing system, in which phone lines connect customers' terminals to the company's mainframe computer in its Minneapolis headquarters. In addition to offering off-the-shelf courses, Control Data has developed an authoring package that enables customers to design and develop courses tailored specifically to their needs. A training course typically sold to customers consists of various instructional formats: computer-based software, written text, videotapes, and lab activities to simulate actual on-the-floor applications and increase hands-on experience. For example, the lab hydraulics course includes a five-foot-long, 500-pound hydraulic lab, with various types of valves, cylinders, filters, and tubing, so trainees can perform exercises with real hydraulic systems.

Beyond offering courses, however, Control Data considers itself a full-service vendor, meaning, says Johnson, that "we will help customers solve complex training problems" concerning the delivery and management of the training, skill-level assessments, and performance and productivity difficulties. Typically, consulting services include a needs assessment, in which TEG staff conduct plant-floor surveys to determine present skill levels and also perform in-depth task analyses to decide on the level of training needed. In solving productivity and performance problems, TEG consultants must address such issues, says Johnson, as the level of knowledge and skills required in order to properly maintain some highly complex automated equipment. "The maintenance employees need to understand how digital circuits operate in order to maintain a programmable controller. They also have to understand how that programmable controller is used in a particular system in the plant—for instance, a controller that operates a conveyor system requires knowledge of the conveyor's role in the plant, how its sensors get input, how the output decisions are made, and what happens at various points in the process," explains Johnson.

As part of a high-technology company specializing in computer-manufacturing, disk-drive, and computer-services businesses, the Training and Education Group is well positioned to offer the kinds of technical training service it does. Many of the course developers and training consultants have backgrounds in technical fields and have worked with computers, observes Johnson, citing his own experience at Control Data installing and maintaining computer systems before assuming his present position as IATP program manager. "This helps us to pick up and understand the processes that go on in the plant. A computer is a control system and that's what an automated plant is—a big control system," says Johnson.

Customers agree, adding that whatever Control Data staff may lack in its understanding of industrial technology, the company's industrial customers—through such channels as the training advisory board and plant-floor networks—can fill in. "We're feeding them a lot of technical information," notes a maintenance engineer with John Deere, one of the five companies represented on the board. That basic concept—listening to and learning from customers—is central to the board's operation.

How the Training Advisory Board Works

The Training Advisory Board was formed in March 1986, following months of discussion between Control Data and several of its customers who expressed the need for some kind of forum in which to talk about training problems and share ideas. Johnson credits the sales personnel with playing a key role as intermediary between TEG consultants and customers. "Our sales reps deal with these people on a day-to-day basis and are right out there on the plant floor, so they are able to put us in touch with customers who are most vocal about their needs," says Johnson. The ongoing communication and close working relationship between sales and the training staff are important factors in making the board work, he adds. "We act as consultants to them, providing information on course content and prerequisite entry skills, and they—through their help in getting contacts for the board—are a major source of market-input data."

Five companies, each represented by at least one individual, currently participate on the board: General Motors, John Deere, Chrysler, Procter & Gamble, and AT&T. Most of the board members are training directors, although the Chrysler representative is a production manager and one of the two GM reps is an hourly employee and union member responsible for the coordination of computer-based training at the plant.

The Training Advisory Board meets semiannually at Control Data's headquarters in Minneapolis. The issues vary widely, depending upon the priorities and concerns of customers, TEG staff, and the sales representatives. At the beginning of the board meeting, there may be a formal, fifteen-minute presentation on a particular topic of concern—troubleshooting techniques, for example—but this is always followed by a free-form discussion between board members and Control Data personnel.

Opening some more structured and direct lines of communication has been a major advantage of the Training Advisory Board for both Control Data and its customers. "Until the formation of the board, our channels for receiving any kind of customer input were mostly informal. This resulted in the lack of any real understanding between us," Johnson notes. "We felt there was a need for a more formal interchange of views in order to lead to a better understanding of our customers, and I think our customers felt they would gain from sharing similar problems and needs across industries."

According to Lyn Paris, John Deere's manager of technical education and training, participation on the Training Advisory Board has not only improved communications between John Deere and Control Data, it has also enhanced communications between the corporate and plant-floor levels within John Deere itself. To be more effective on the board, Paris says he is in touch with the end users at the plant sites to discuss and better understand any training problems they may be experiencing. ''This gives them a direct pipeline to Control Data.''

Another plus has been ''rubbing shoulders'' with trainers from other industries. Even though the industries are different, the applications of new technologies are often similar, so the training problems experienced at auto assembly plants, for example, may be highly relevant to those at John Deere facilities, which produce a variety of farm and industrial tractors and machinery, construction equipment, and lawn and garden equipment. It also helps, notes Paris, to share training insights with people from various corporate cultures. ''At Procter & Gamble, for instance, employee participation is taken to the limit, and we've talked about how training is done under these circumstances and the kind of management structure that is required,'' he says.

Even though the board is relatively new, there is already concrete evidence that it works as an effective market-research tool. The move to make more courses available on disks that can be used on personal computers at the plant site, as opposed to using the more expensive time-sharing system, clearly answers customers' needs to cut costs in the delivery of computer-based training. Another example is Control Data's new delivery system, which is also more economical than the time sharing. The system allows customers to operate a local area network in which multiple IBM-PC-compatible microcomputers within a plant may be connected.

The On-Site Visits

As noted earlier, the Training Advisory Board is just one part of Control Data's customer-response effort. The on-site visits and interviews with the end users represent the other critical half of what Control Data is doing. In fact, notes Johnson, one of the biggest benefits of the training board is that "it has opened the door to the plants where we can reach the people in the best position to decide about what kind of training is most appropriate." And often those interviewed include various levels of personnel, ranging from the plant manager to the shop-floor technician. In some cases, TEG consultants will accompany maintenance technicians as they go about their normal trouble-shooting and problem-solving activities in order to better understand the work process and the types of training needed.

On-site course evaluations have also been conducted. At a John Deere facility that produces the combine used in corn and wheat harvesting, Control Data representatives reviewed an industrial electronics course with the maintenance technicians who took the course, the training instructors, and other maintenance engineers and supervisors. "We talked about some of the weaknesses of the course, how we utilize the training program, and how well Control Data's product fits," notes Wayne Carter, maintenance engineer and part-time instructor. "I think it's absolutely essential that the vendor get out to the plants and survey the managers, engineers, and students. Control Data spent the whole day here canvassing many people."

Richard Hensley, a maintenance engineer at John Deere's engine-works facility, agrees that end-user input is critical to developing good training. Control Data interviewed Hensley and other engineers, technicians, and supervisors in order to evaluate two courses—one on statistical methods for quality control, offered on a pilot basis, and another on troubleshooting techniques. "Even though it is too soon to say whether all the customer input Control Data is receiving will actually lead to better products for us, I think that what they're doing is definitely a step in the right direction," says Hensley.

Need for More Equipment-Specific Training

A high-priority concern expressed by some Control Data customers is the need for more and better quality equipment-specific training in a format that can be readily utilized. Both Carter and Hensley say the training provided by the equipment manufacturers is geared more toward engineers than toward the skilled technicians who actually maintain and repair the equipment. Often, vital information concerning start-up and frequent adjustment procedures is buried in thick manuals, which can take days to sift through, notes Carter. The instruction usually consists of complex blueprints and diagrams of machine parts—information that is needed for occasional in-depth servicing but not for the daily troubleshooting and maintenance tasks that plant-floor technicians routinely perform. "We had to extract and rewrite the start-up procedures for ten different brands of machine tools," Carter notes. Most of the problems associated with machine downtime, he adds, have to do with faulty instruction or lack of information.

Computer-based training, which relies mostly on audio-visual methods of learning, would be a more effective format than the highly detailed written texts currently provided by equipment manufacturers. "The average industrial craftsmen, though highly skilled, are usually high school graduates, with varying degrees of reading ability. With a two-inch-thick manual, the learning doesn't always happen that well," says Carter. In addition, as electronically based equipment improves in reliability, technicians and engineers are less likely to trouble-shoot on a regular basis and will not remember the details of how the equipment functions. "That information needs to be readily available on a tape or disk that the maintenance operator can just pop into the computer," Carter notes.

Despite the need for equipment-specific, computer-based courses, few equipment vendors have moved in this direction because of the prohibitively high costs of developing the courseware. According to one estimate, every hour of instruction requires approximately seventy-five hours of work to develop. Though it is unlikely that any equipment vendor would undertake such a project alone, a more plausible scenario, according to Carter and Hensley, would be a cooperative arrangement, in which the customer, the equipment vendor or manufacturer, and a third party such as Control Data would share the costs of developing the training. "The equipment vendor knows the machine best and thus can provide the subject-matter expertise, while Control Data can get it into a computer-based format and then market it to other companies as well,'' says Carter.

Though not exactly equipment-specific, such courses have been codeveloped by Control Data and the Allen-Bradley Company, which produces a variety of programmable and numerical controls used in industry. So far, the companies have worked together on two courses: one on programmable controller fundamentals and the other on variable frequency drives. The course on programmable controllers includes four modules that teach the fundamentals in control circuits, hardware, programming, and troubleshooting. Allen-Bradley participated in the project because it was finding that maintenance technicians had varying entry-level skills and were thus unprepared for its highly technical, equipment-specific classroom training. While not a substitute for the hands-on experience gained from the equipment-specific classroom training, the computer-based course on programmable controllers, jointly developed by Allen-Bradley and Control Data, prepares students for the classroom training by providing them with a consistent level of knowledge. Though the same goal could be achieved by offering another introductory classroom course, that would be a more costly alternative for customers. With computer-based training, maintenance work can proceed at its normal pace, since it can be taken on an individual basis rather than pulling twenty maintenance technicians off the floor at the same time to take a class.

Moreover, the computer course relies on built-in, mastery-based training techniques, meaning that students must prove they have mastered the material in each lesson by taking a test before moving on to the next lesson. Though still considered to be a conceptual and generic course (the training is applicable to programmable controllers produced by any manufacturer, not just Allen-Bradley), the material presented goes beyond that offered in basic technology courses.

In working on the course, Allen-Bradley provided the expertise in technical content, while Control Data was responsible for the instructional approaches and strategies used. In addition, Allen-Bradley shot and produced the four video segments that accompany each module. The other course, on variable frequency drives, was codeveloped in a similar fashion, although Allen-Bradley was also involved in determining instructional strategies. Allen-Bradley is now developing computer-based courses on its own without Control Data's assistance. "And that was precisely our goal—to get Allen-Bradley self-sufficient in the computer-based training business. We learned from them and they learned from us," notes Keith Johnson. Now, he adds, Control Data has agreements with Allen-Bradley to market some of the computer-based training courses the equipment manufacturer develops.

Although Johnson characterizes the present working relationship with Allen-Bradley as a successful one for both sides, developing equipment-specific training on a cooperative basis is a more difficult prospect: "When you provide training on another vendor's equipment, you can get into all sorts of liability and certification problems, in terms of who's responsible for what. . . . Also, when customers say they want equipment-specific training, that often means training that is unique to their plant—in other words, training to understand how a programmable controller works to make a particular widget at that plant. So the training that is needed is more than just equipment-specific, it's plant-specific," says Johnson. To make such plant-specific training economically justifiable for Control Data, there would have to be enough people at the plant who needed the training to maintain the equipment. What Johnson does envision, however, is developing courses, in cooperation with other equipment manufacturers, that are more specific to typical applications of technology used in industry—for example, how a programmable controller operates a conveyor system. "It's still a generic course, but it's getting into system aspects that are commonly used across industries," Johnson explains.

Control Data has also shortened the length of some of the generic courses so that students can get to the equipment-specific training more quickly. Input from Training Advisory Board members has been very helpful in this respect, notes Johnson, since they have provided advice on which sections of a course may be redundant and which need more emphasis.

Conclusion

Canvassing customer views via an advisory board of customers and a network of end users at the plant sites is not necessarily the easiest route to developing better training products and services—a point acknowledged by both Control Data and customers alike. "Ask five different training instructors about a particular problem, and you'll get five different answers," notes engineer and training instructor Hensley. And, indeed, Johnson says that in the process of interviewing maintenance technicians, engineers, training instructors, production supervisors, and others, "you don't get a consistent view of what is needed." At this point, the Training Advisory Board becomes an especially useful device to help Control Data staff sort out the differences and to steer them in the right direction. Sometimes the training representatives who sit on the board ask another staff member from their company—usually someone closer to the plant floor—to also attend the meetings.

Asking customers to voice their opinions naturally invites some criticism of Control Data's products, which can, at times, lead to "pretty stressful board meetings," says Johnson. Nevertheless, the advantages offered by the board far outweigh any disadvantages. "I think the general feeling has been that the board experience has been useful for everyone. For Control Data, it means working with our customers to put together better training solutions," says Johnson.

12

A Proactive Approach Toward High-Technology Training: General Motors' Linden, New Jersey, Plant

Kathleen C. Hemmens

In 1984, General Motors (GM) underwent a massive reorganization, which included its Automotive Assembly Division. As part of this reorganization, GM introduced a wide range of automated production systems into a number of its facilities, including its assembly plant in Linden, New Jersey. This quarter-mile-long industrial plant had formerly manufactured Buicks, Oldsmobiles, and Cadillacs, using predominantly manual assembly methods. Under the reorganization, it became part of a newly established Chevrolet-Pontiac-Canada (CPC) Group and, with several other GM facilities, was charged with the responsibility for GM Project 25—development and manufacture of two new Chevrolet models, the Beretta and the Corsica.

The divisional reorganization and the introduction of automated, robotic systems into the Linden assembly plant mandated an extensive training effort to prepare plant personnel to operate, maintain, and repair these all-new, electronically controlled pieces of equipment and to keep the automated production system up and running. At the Linden plant, the Engineering Services Department is responsible for identifying high-technology training needs, for developing in-house training for engineering and skilled-trades personnel, and for ensuring that equipment-vendor training is tailored to meet GM's specific needs.

Over the course of approximately six years—and several unsuccessful training experiments—the high-technology training coordinator and her colleagues in the Engineering Services Department have developed what they believe is an effective, proactive method of working with high-technology equipment vendors to get what they want in the way of training. Central to their current satisfaction with contracted training is a set of training specifications that are based on the knowledge gained during those six years of trial and error. The *CPC Group Equipment Vendor Training Specifications* states unequivocally that "technical training requirements be given equal consideration (by the vendor) with equipment specification and system definition." It states further that the outcome of the training must result in: "The owner (plant) becoming self-sufficient in all phases of operation, troubleshooting, maintenance, repair, and modification of the equipment or systems being installed. The equipment vendor will be responsible for the development of effective training as an on-going part of doing business with GM."

Exactly what these specifications mean in practice and how the GM/Linden training experience led to their development are the subject of this chapter.

High-Tech Training: The Early Experiments

Lois Fortenboher, an electrical engineer and coordinator of high-technology training at the Linden plant, recounts that the Engineering Services Department's first plunge into high-tech training occurred in 1979 when a new, automated conveyor system was installed in the plant's paint shop. Training in the operation, maintenance, and repair of this "programmable logic system" was conducted by the vendor, but the training "just did not take," according to Laurence Patrusevich, plant engineer and a member of the current in-house training team. The extent to which it did not take became evident only later, when Patrusevich and chief electrician Don Knowlson found themselves spending a great deal of time troubleshooting problems with the new system because the shop electricians were not able to handle them. They began to realize that the vendor had provided adequate training about the insides—the electronics—of the "blue box" it was installing, but no training at all about how this "blue box" would function to control the conveyor system in an automobile assembly environment. The problems faced by the shop electricians, according to Patrusevich, were hook-up and synchronization problems that the vendor training had not prepared them to handle.

To remedy the situation, he and Knowlson designed an in-house training program with their best electricians, using the vendor's blueprints. But they went beyond the electronics of the circuit board (where the vendor stopped) to the crux of the in-plant problem: "getting the right information into the controlling piece of equipment and the right directions coming out." They taught the electricians how to look at the problem in the context of the whole system and how to get the conveyor moving again with the least amount of lost production time.

This experience also taught the engineering staff that many of the GM troubleshooters were "pipe, wire, and relay" electricians who were uncomfortable with the new electronic equipment and unfamiliar with some of the basic electronic concepts needed to understand and repair it.

More training was obviously needed, so in 1981 the department contracted with a Woodbridge, New Jersey, branch of the Chicago-based DeVry Technical Institute for delivery of an in-house Basic Industrial Electronics Course for twenty GM electricians. Because this was the first time the Linden plant had ever contracted with an outside educational organization for customized high-technology training, it provoked high-level management-union discussion (with United Auto Workers Local #595) and novel scheduling arrangements to enable the trainees to attend the six-hour-a-week class.

Although the training staff at Linden had reviewed the DeVry curriculum and made some changes in emphasis, they soon found that this course, like the earlier vendor training, was still too oriented to circuit board electronics and not oriented enough to training in problem diagnosis and solution. It was at this point that the in-house staff realized the importance of hands-on training as a supplement to the traditional classroom approach. Perceiving the inadequacies of the book-learning method, the training staff obtained a programmable logic machine so that the electricians could replicate maintenance problems that occurred on the floor and experiment with solutions. The introduction of this component into the training made a noticeable difference in skill attainment. According to Fortenboher, "The more they played with the machine, the better they got."

The next step in the evolution of high-technology training at Linden was the introduction of computer-based learning using Control Data's PLATO system. By the end of 1981, scheduling employees for the DeVry course had become a problem, and the engineering staff was looking for a way to continue the basic electronics course, but in a flexible mode that could more easily accommodate employee schedules. Computer-based learning appeared to be a solution to that problem. For the next two years, PLATO was used to teach not only basic electronics, but pneumatics and hydraulics as well. But the experience only served to reinforce the lessons of earlier experiments: print or console-based teaching was not as effective for the group being trained as learning by doing—solving production problems on the actual equipment in the stress-free, unhurried atmosphere of the classroom and then applying the learned skills out on the floor.

Reorganization and Plant Renovation

At this juncture, in 1984, General Motors reorganized its assembly division and simultaneously introduced a number of new automated production systems into the Linden plant in preparation for the changeover to production of Chevrolets. The training task facing the Engineering Services Department was immense, and they approached it in an unusual way that built on their earlier training experiences. The way the Linden plant chose to approach training also placed requirements on the equipment vendors that they had not been used to meeting.

The in-house training staff, working closely with the local union representatives, knew that they needed instructors familiar with automobile assembly production if the training was to be relevant and job-specific. They decided that the creation of an in-house corps of instructor-experts was the best way to meet these criteria. This instructor corps would be responsible for creating the courses and teaching their fellow workers how to operate, maintain, and repair the new systems being installed in the plant. This group would also become an in-house hot line, available to provide troubleshooting assistance when a system failed.

Nine electricians, one machine repairman, and one pipe fitter were handpicked by the plant's chief electrician to be members of the instructor corps on the basis of their competence, interest, and ability to learn, as well as the respect their peers had for them. In July 1984, the group was divided into teams, each of which was responsible for a different area of training, and sent out to the various equipment manufacturers' application schools for training. The original equipment manufacturers (OEMs) had been alerted to the need for a train-the-trainer approach, and, according to Fortenboher, most were supportive and helpful. The robotics supplier, GM-Fanuc, created a special course in teaching techniques for the Linden group, and Allen-Bradley, the programmable logic system supplier, provided instructional texts free of charge.

After completing all phases of the OEM-supplied training, the instructor teams developed courses for their co-workers based on the materials and manuals supplied by the vendors, but tailored to be job-specific and relevant to everyday maintenance and repair problems. Over the next two and one-half years, the instructors trained 200 production-oriented personnel and over 200 skilled tradespeople in operating and trouble-shooting the new systems, using a combination of classroom and hands-on training methods.

According to Fortenboher and her colleagues, the creation of this in-house instructor corps solved a number of problems previously associated with vendor and other contracted training programs:

- The development of an in-house group of instructors/experts ensured immediate assistance, which a vendor or OEM cannot provide.
- The method enabled training to be scheduled in sync with the plant's production and maintenance schedules.
- It was much less expensive than providing vendor training for all the employees who needed it.
- It was flexible; in an in-house system, instructors can pace the course according to trainee skill levels and also digress from the curriculum to deal with problems brought to class from the plant floor; it also permits the essential hands-on equipment experience.
- The trainees were comfortable—they knew one another and the instructors, and they felt freer to expose uncertainty and ask questions than they would have in an off-site vendor training situation.
- It enabled the training staff to keep ahead of equipment installation and provide basic, introductory training before equipment implementation in the plant.

Development of Vendor Training Specifications

In the training modes described above, the high-technology training staff had found a mix of elements that produced success, and they wanted these elements to be incorporated as much as possible into future training programs offered by equipment vendors. Fortenboher took the next step in this direction by committing to paper, in the form of training specifications, the lessons that she and her co-workers had learned since 1979. She developed a seven-page document that spells out the GM/

CPC/Linden training philosophy, the purpose of the specifications, alternative training scenarios, and the minimum level of response required of the vendor.

The specifications require that the vendor assign a coordinator to work in conjunction with the Linden training coordinator prior to the award of the contract, and that thirty days following the award, the vendor "shall submit instructional objectives, detailed course outlines, proposed educational delivery methods, and schedules."

The specifications also ask the vendor to propose training designs for two different training scenarios: a train-the-trainer scenario in which the vendor will train individuals selected by GM and certify these individuals as competent to teach others; and a total-population-training scenario in which the vendor delivers the training directly to the plant work force. For both scenarios, the specifications require flexible scheduling—"training may be required on any or all of a three-shift basis"—and the provision of "sufficient instruction materials and training aids (to the owner) to support future training needs."

To obtain the kind of diagnostic-oriented training that had been so difficult to come by in the past, Fortenboher spelled out in considerable detail what she and her staff wanted in the curriculum for each trainee group. Separate specifications are included for the various levels of personnel to be trained—operators, skilled tradespeople, and engineers—and the subject matter outlined in detail. The emphasis in the specifications on "failure diagnostics, troubleshooting, system interaction, review of typical field service problems, etc." is striking and is evidence of how serious the training team is about the need for diagnostic-oriented training.

The specifications further stipulate that the training shall be competency-based and "structured to assure that the student demonstrates competent performance" and that 30 to 50 percent of the total course time shall be hands-on training. The vendor must provide one training aid (equipment, models, or simulators) for every two students. Additionally, the vendor is asked to prepare troubleshooting/diagnostic aids, such as pocket cards or diagrams, that employees can use on the job; the vendor must also permit the owner to photocopy all training and service manuals for future in-house use. These latter specifications are intended to support the development of in-house expertise in maintenance and repair of the systems and independence of the vendor in the event of equipment or system breakdown.

Examples of Successful Vendor Training

The written specifications described above were first used in a solicitation requesting bids to provide and install an automated windshield and back light (rear window) application system in the glass installation area of the Linden plant. (This system uses robots to apply a urethane coating to automobile windshields and back lights.) Progressive Tool and Industries (PICO) of Southfield, Michigan, won this bid, and a cooperative training relationship was established with this company on the basis of the Linden plant's training specifications.

Jesse Harris, the director of training at PICO, provided Fortenboher with a draft of the training manual prior to printing; she reorganized the content, separated the training for the mechanical and electrical trades because separation was more time- and cost-effective, and returned her red-lined copy of the manual to Harris. They then worked together to shape the final forty-hour curriculum. PICO delivered the training on site in three sessions: the first session, eight hours long, provided an orientation to the equipment and the system and described its functioning and safety features. Sessions II and III, each sixteen hours long, concentrated on preventive general maintenance and on the electrical and computer controls of the system. System functioning and diagnostics were emphasized in the latter session, but both included on-the-floor operation of the equipment. Several instructors from the original in-house instructor corps also participated in the course. PICO prepared manuals, slides, and videotapes of the course and left them with the training group, so that the course can be taught again by in-house instructors as necessary.

Harris confirmed Fortenboher's positive evaluation of this

cooperative effort and provided additional background on the GM-vendor relationship. He indicated that GM has made it very clear to equipment vendors that they must be responsible for training and that the training must be responsive to GM's guidelines. Although Harris acknowledged that the delivery of customized training requires a substantial investment of his staff's time and energy, he finds that cooperation pays off in "greater customer satisfaction and repeat business." Prior consultation with the customer's training staff and with the maintenance supervisors who will be responsible for the new equipment enables PICO to provide "an in-depth training experience that is much more agreeable to everybody."

Harris also described how the advent of automated equipment has changed the training environment for both the customer and the vendor. In the days of high-labor, low-technology equipment, there was little emphasis on formal training; the maintenance personnel were expected to teach themselves on the job through trial and error. The introduction of high-technology equipment—and, more importantly, the configuration of many pieces of automated equipment into production systems—has made the earlier method of learning obsolete. At this point, according to Harris, it is primarily the large companies who understand the requirements of the new situation and are pressing vendors to help them meet the training challenge, but he predicts that demands for responsive, customized training by vendors will become widespread in the next ten years.

GM/Linden's relationship with Robotic Vision Systems, Inc. (RVSI) is another example of a successful cooperative training venture that incorporated the principles outlined in the specifications but implemented them in a more flexible way. The plant contracted with RVSI in late 1985 to provide an automated system that seals strategic points in the car body against water, fumes, or fire. The system's major elements are an RVSI vision-sensor machine that sights each car's position on the conveyor and a Cincinnati-Milicron T3776 robot that performs the sealing operation on the car body.

Joel Leiter, one of three electricians responsible for the sealing operation, described the installation of the equipment and the initial training as a mutual learning experience for both RVSI and the work force being trained. According to Leiter, both the vendor and the customer "learned by doing how to get the system up and running" over a six-month period, during which the in-house engineers and electricians worked side by side with RVSI's field service staff to perfect the system's operation. This training mode was necessary, in Laurence Patrusevich's view, "because this technology was so new that its documentation and manuals were being developed as the system was being installed and put into operation." Experimentation and system alteration continued during the initial six months of "working the bugs out" that took place after the equipment was in the plant.

Although the RVSI-Linden working relationship during this experimental stage did not take the customary form, it achieved very satisfactorily the training objectives GM wanted. What made it work, Lois Fortenboher contends, "was RVSI's willingness, unusual in a vendor, to permit the in-house journeymen to participate in the trial and error of getting the system operational." In the course of this hands-on training, the involved work force learned the logic of the system's programming—not only how it worked, but why. Although RVSI's training was not limited to these activities and included more formal training in robotics and sealing operations, this initial period of hands-on experience was the most important element in developing in-house competency and ability to diagnose and quickly remedy system malfunction.

Lessons Learned

GM's Linden plant has undergone a significant metamorphosis in the past six years, from a low-technology, high-labor assembly plant to a completely renovated high-technology facility. The demands placed on the internal training staff, the equipment vendors, and the work force in the course of this transformation required a reexamination of traditional ways of doing things and of traditional relationships between customer and vendor and between salaried and hourly workers in the plant.

The introduction of high technology changed not only the production system, but the social system as well.

Training is one of the first elements in the social equation to be affected by the changeover to high technology, and the response of the internal training staff and the vendor to the new situation can make a crucial difference in the work force's reaction to automation and its willingness to learn the workings of the new equipment and master its operation. At GM/ Linden, the management invested a great deal of time, energy, and money in learning how to meet the training challenge most effectively. As this chapter describes, several methods were tried, evaluated as inadequate for the plant's needs, and discarded. Each experiment increased the staff's understanding of how high-tech training needed to be structured to incorporate pedagogical techniques appropriate for a work force being trained in a production-oriented environment.

According to Fortenboher, one of the most important lessons learned was the value of providing basic training to employees prior to the equipment-specific vendor training. Employees had to become thoroughly familiar with the programmable logic system controlling the production process if they were to be able to take advantage of vendor training in the operation and maintenance of new equipment being introduced into the system.

The staff also learned that hands-on training is most effective for work-force veterans who have been away from the classroom for a long time; they learned that input about maintenance problems from the hourly workers enhanced the relevance of training sessions, and that novice learners responded more comfortably and positively to peer instructors whom they knew and respected than to equipment suppliers or outsiders from technical institutes.

These insights and others noted in this chapter have shaped the training specifications that now govern customer-vendor training relationships at Linden and at the other plants in the Chevrolet-Pontiac-Canada Group and, to a degree, they are probably specific to GM's particular circumstances and culture.

The lesson that *is* generalizable, however, to other companies contemplating the move to high technology is the demonstrated necessity to take training seriously and to be willing to experiment—and perhaps make some mistakes—before discovering the training formula that works. Further, the GM-Linden experience indicates that the customer must take the lead in identifying specific training needs and desired training scenarios, if it is to get the kind and quality of training that will produce a competent work force.

13

Goodyear Tire and Rubber Company: Building a Training Commitment into the Contract

Jocelyn F. Gutchess

At the Goodyear Tire and Rubber Company, leader in the U.S. rubber industry and the world's largest producer of tires, training "is an investment, not an expense," according to one company training director. That this claim is not just lip service to a trendy idea is made evident in the day-to-day companywide commitment to training by Goodyear management and staff at every level of the company's operations. In carrying out this commitment, Goodyear has developed several principles to which it adheres:

- Training should be, and is, fully integrated with overall management. It is not a separate activity to be coordinated on an optional basis with operational decisions, but is an integral part of such decisions, starting with the planning process and implemented on a continuing basis.

- Training should be, and is, designed to give Goodyear a multiskilled work force, with each employee able to perform a broad range of tasks as needed. It is felt that the flexibility provided by such a work force will enable the company to improve productivity and hence competitiveness.
- Training should be, and is, objective-based. All training is designed to ensure that the trainees can actually perform the tasks for which they are trained. It is not enough to attend classes; trainees must be provided with the opportunity for hands-on experience and must demonstrate competency on completion of the training.
- Training should be, and is, self-sustaining; that is, trainees become trainers, passing their training on to other employees as appropriate. Although Goodyear initially uses its vendors to train employees, the goal is to develop an independent training capacity; as Goodyear explains it, "to stand on our own feet."

During the 1970s and 1980s, Goodyear, along with the rest of the tire and rubber industry, has faced increasingly stiff competition, particularly from imports. To meet that competition, Goodyear has had to develop new technologies and to retool and modernize its manufacturing processes. New plants have been opened; old, inefficient plants have been closed. All this has required a massive training and retraining effort. This chapter will examine how the Goodyear training program is carried out, with specific attention to the relationship between the company and the vendors who have provided that training.

The Goodyear Training Function

The Goodyear Tire and Rubber Company is a diversified, multinational corporation, headquartered in Akron, Ohio. The company operates 51 manufacturing plants spread around the United States and 43 plants located abroad in twenty-seven other countries. It also owns and operates seven rubber plantations, as well as approximately 2,400 other facilities around the globe for the distribution and sale of its products. Employing about 120,000 men and women, the company manufactures tires and tubes, a large number of related rubber products for industrial and consumer use, and chemicals and plastic products. It is also engaged in various gas and petrochemical operations.

With net sales in 1986 of more than $9 billion, the company is easily the leader in the world tire market and especially in the U.S. tire market, where it holds a 30 percent share. Having successfully fought off a hostile takeover attempt in 1986, the company is undergoing a major restructuring designed to make it leaner, stronger, and more competitive. It should be noted, however, that the effort to improve competitiveness is not new but a process that has been going on for some time. In 1987, the company expected to continue that process, planning new capital investments of $1 billion. Training will continue to play an important part in the company's restructuring efforts.

Responsibility for training at Goodyear is divided between training for employees in the manufacturing side of the company's operations and training of the sales staff. The manufacturing training is essentially a decentralized system, under which each plant has its own training manager who is primarily responsible for training within the plant. The training managers are generally selected from within and, for the most part, serve in that capacity full time, although some are part time and have other responsibilities. To be a training manager, each must have had manufacturing experience and know shop-floor processes and problems first hand. A training division at the corporate level provides guidance and support to the local plant training activities. The corporate training group is located at a modern training center in Tallmadge, Ohio, near the Akron headquarters. The center, a converted elementary school, includes, in addition to classrooms, a well-equipped video production studio where new audiovisual learning materials can be produced for use in specialized Goodyear training programs.

The company estimates that approximately 7,500 Goodyear employees will attend training courses at the center this year. This number will include many plant training managers, all of whom must undergo a training course at the center before they can take on the training assignment. In addition, the center provides training for management and staff as well as for line supervisors. But training does not stop at the center. A spokesman for the company indicated that in all likelihood, each of the approximately 120,000 Goodyear employees, both in the United States and abroad, receives some kind of company training every year.

Up until the mid 1970s training at Goodyear was essentially an in-house operation, carried out as needed but without special attention or direction. When the changing market required a different approach, however, the situation became, as a member of the training center staff described it, one of "wall-to-wall training around here." To anyone observing the company's current training operations, Goodyear's commitment to training is both very strong and very clear.

Goodyear Training Principles in Action

A basic element of the Goodyear program is the integration of training into the regular operations of the company. This starts with the planning process and continues straight through. Whenever a new plant is opened, or an older plant is reconverted and modernized, the training staff is brought in as soon as planning begins to work with engineers and plant managers to determine what skills and what training will be necessary for successful operation of the new venture. The first step is a survey of the available work force—either the existing work force or the local labor market (in the case of a new plant)—to determine the existing skill, experience, and knowledge level. Along with this assessment, there is an analysis of the skills and knowledge that will be needed to operate and maintain the machinery that is being installed. When the results of these two assessments are compared, preparation of a training plan can begin. To develop an appropriate curriculum and suitable training materials when new equipment is involved, Goodyear training specialists work directly with the vendors of the equipment being installed. It is a cooperative undertaking, and by its nature it has its ups and downs. On the whole, however, working relations have been good, and vendors are generally very willing to cooperate. Goodyear is a good customer and one they do not wish to lose.

One example of this process is provided by the Goodyear tire wire cord plant in Asheboro, North Carolina. This plant, which opened in 1984, manufactures the steel wire cord that is used to make radial tires. Until the plant opened, Goodyear had only one other wire plant, located in Luxembourg, in Europe. Long before the Asheboro plant opened—in fact, even before ground was broken for the new plant—Goodyear had determined its skill needs and had decided to staff the management and technical jobs with its own skilled personnel, drawn from some of its tire plants. These people, who would eventually become trainers of the rest of the Asheboro work force, were sent to Luxembourg to learn how to operate and maintain the wire-making machinery being installed at Asheboro, and to help develop training materials that could be used once they returned home. The first group of trainees spent almost nine months in Luxembourg; a second group was there for about five months.

In the first weeks there, training took place both in the classroom and on the job. After they had become familiar with the existing equipment, the group began a series of visits to the vendors of new equipment, working with them in developing the necessary manuals and other training materials. Based on the vendor exposure, the Luxembourg trainees developed specifications for training and then asked the vendors to develop manuals with detailed drawings and extensive, step-by-step instructions on how to operate and maintain the machinery. This was not always an easy task for the vendors; language was sometimes a problem, as was adaptation to American ways of operating. However, the job was done; manuals were prepared, and the trainees became trainers. Once the plant opened, the vendors sent their own people to Asheboro to follow up on the training and to resolve any problems that might occur. One vendor, for example, continues to provide training support, sending some of its staff every year to work with the Asheboro personnel.

The integration of training with decision making does not stop with the start-up phase of a plant's operation. Training is an important element in the continuous effort to improve productivity. As every plant manager knows, new technology can help in improving the ability to compete, but only as long as the equipment is operating. Downtime becomes crucial, particularly where operations are continuous and interdependent. If some part of a computerized integrated operation breaks down, forcing the whole operation to shut down, there must be someone immediately available who can analyze the problem and set it right. For plant managers, training and retraining the work force becomes a priority problem-solving mechanism. The link with vendors becomes especially important in dealing with such problems as they arise. Sometimes representatives of the vendors can be brought into the plant to work with the technicians, providing hands-on training as necessary. In other cases, Goodyear employees may be sent to the vendor for additional training. The point is that the decision to train is an operational decision, made by the plant manager with his or her training manager, and tied directly to the solution of operational problems.

Training for a Multiskilled Work Force

At Goodyear, the emphasis on productivity and competitiveness has been translated into the principle of developing, insofar as possible, a multiskilled work force, able to operate and maintain all of the equipment in its new high-tech plants. When the Asheboro plant was opened, for example, it was decided that, at certain levels, the operating and maintenance personnel should be merged; the company would try to develop a staff able to perform a broad range of functions and tasks. To lay the foundation for such a policy, Goodyear began to recruit and hire its local work force as soon as ground was broken for the new plant. As indicated earlier, the managers and technical personnel were sent to Luxembourg, while those who were initially hired as maintenance employees were sent to Randolph Technical College in Asheboro. Goodyear not only provided the equipment on which the workers could be trained, and paid the trainees a salary while they were in training, but the company also developed its own special curriculum, working with the college's staff. This link with Randolph Technical College still continues, although the courses are now given at the plant. Motivation apparently is high, and almost all of those taking the courses pass. Further strengthening the multiskill development policy, the Asheboro plant uses a pay-for-knowledge system, in which workers are rewarded for improving and broadening their skills. Training under this policy, however, is not just a matter of taking self-improvement classes; rather, it is directly linked to the company's need for particular skills.

A similar approach was taken when the tire plant in Tyler, Texas, was modernized. The conversion to radial tire production, which took place over a two-year period, involved the installation of entirely new and different equipment and, therefore, retraining of the entire work force. As each new machine was scheduled to start up, Goodyear pulled workers out and sent them to school—operators, for a minimum of three weeks, and maintenance personnel, for several weeks of retraining. In this case, much of the training was carried out at Tyler Junior College, with the state providing the facility, instructors, and the printing of training materials, and Goodyear providing the equipment and training allowances for the trainees. Since successful completion of equipment-specific training was dependent on achievement of a certain level of literacy and numeracy skills, Goodyear also provided this basic education for those who needed it.

Training Is Objective-Based

Perhaps the most significant element of Goodyear's training program is that it is objective-based. No matter what skills are needed, the approach is always the same. Fundamental to the process is an analysis of the skills required and the development of task statements. From this follows the identification of the trainee objectives—the performance expected of a trainee at each step of the training process. And, based on these objectives, the training program is developed. This is the way it works:

As Goodyear awards contracts to a supplier for new equipment, the supplier is requested to enter into a training agreement to provide operator and maintenance training for equipment. Although the training agreement is not included in the purchase order, generally it is coordinated with the award of the equipment bid. The training agreement includes the following requirements:

- Hands-on performance training is the required method of training for operators, maintenance persons, and management. Hands-on performance training is defined as the process by which the learner is told how to do something and then shown how to do it; next he or she must demonstrate an ability to perform. The process uses diverse media, specific learner objectives, simulators, classroom time, actual equipment, and sequenced instruction. A performance checklist is used to certify the performance of the learner.
- The content of the training must be specific and to specifications.
- Training must be completed before production start-up of the equipment.
- Training must be conducted by a full-time trainer furnished by the supplier.
- Goodyear training specialists must have access to the supplier's manufacturing plant so that the necessary detailed tasks analyses can be performed and appropriate training materials prepared.

Goodyear prefers that training take place at its own installations, but if there are insufficient numbers to make this practical, training sometimes takes place at the vendor's locale. The length of the training period varies, naturally, depending on its complexity, but it is bounded only by achievement of the training objectives. For example, some of the Tyler, Texas, plant sessions lasted only five days. One, however, was around forty days. Sometimes training is carried out on an intermittent basis, involving the supplier in repeated visits to the Goodyear facility.

The Tyler plant conversion involved more than fifty vendors, considerably more than the typical thirty to forty vendors per plant. Training agreements were entered into with most of these vendors. One of these was a company that makes solid state motor controls for the Goodyear production line. As the training program was described by a Goodyear training expert, the vendor's training representative "knew the equipment; we knew instructional system design." Working together, they decided exactly what a maintenance person needed to know and do to operate and maintain the control system. These decisions led to the development of task statements, leading in turn to written descriptions of the trainee's objectives. Based on these descriptions, they decided what training aids were needed, such as simulators, guides, manuals, and/or video materials. The vendor then went ahead and developed these materials. The training took place in Texas at the Goodyear plant over a period of several months. At its completion, the Goodyear workers had achieved the training objectives, were certified to handle the equipment, and were able to troubleshoot problems that arose.

Although the Goodyear training agreements require that trainees demonstrate an ability to perform, the vendor is not penalized for individual failure beyond his control. There is no question that Goodyear will pay a vendor, even though a trainee, upon completion of training, cannot demonstrate achievement of agreed-upon objectives. There is a relationship of trust between the two parties, so that if, for example, a learner appears unable to learn, the situation is brought to the attention of Goodyear, which then takes whatever corrective action is appropriate.

Currently, the Goodyear training staff is giving attention to the problem of recertification, to keep up with changes that are constantly being made in the technology. At Asheboro, for example, annual recertification of maintenance personnel is a long-range goal that Goodyear is aiming for; indeed, it is currently experimenting with some self-recertification. Recertification requires, however, a continual update of performance checklists, and this is a task to which not all of Goodyear's vendors give a high priority. The company often finds it necessary to push its suppliers in this direction.

Training Is Self-Sustaining

The fourth notable element of the Goodyear training effort is that training is designed to be self-sustaining. Once training begins, former trainees become future trainers. That this policy is followed assiduously, and that it succeeds, is proven in the numbers. At Asheboro, with a work force of approximately 460 employees, about 110 are labor trainers. This number can be compared to the original group of 20 managers and technicians who were sent to Luxembourg for training before the plant opened three years ago. At the Tyler, Texas, plant, there are 84 labor trainers. The Goodyear train-the-trainer policy is not merely window dressing; it is not a "buddy" system, with one person simply providing informal on-the-job training to his or her co-worker. Each job has been subjected to a thorough task analysis. Each trainer has been certified for the job and is able to ensure that the trainees for whom he or she is responsible also achieve the objectives demanded by the curriculum.

Some of the training program conducted at the Tallmadge training center are classes for persons selected to be trainers. To be selected, each person must have (1) had work experience in Goodyear, and (2) met all the performance objectives relevant to the particular job. In addition, no one becomes a trainer without going through the center's trainer certification program.

Maintenance training has a special place in the company's operations. The Goodyear training staff has developed a maintenance training system, which at the present time is being used in seventy-eight locations both in the United States and abroad. The system provides skill training on a needs basis, encompassing more than 1,000 tasks, each of which has been subjected to task analysis. In addition, each trainee must meet established performance objectives. To meet the practical realities of day-to-day manufacturing operations, this generic skill training is coupled with a certain amount of machine-specific training, sometimes provided initially by the equipment vendor. The system is working. For example, Goodyear's Lawton, Oklahoma, tire plant, which formerly relied on some contract maintenance, today has no such contracts. All maintenance is provided by Goodyear-trained personnel. The vendors, too, apparently accept the new system and have been willing to work with Goodyear in training their own staffs as part of good customer relations.

Conclusion

There is no doubt that Goodyear has had to get through a difficult period in the last decade. Tied as it is to the automotive industry, the going has not always been easy. The company's commitment to training, however, remains strong—perhaps even stronger than before. By insisting on objective-based training, even—in fact, particularly—from its vendors, Goodyear is developing a work force that is both productive and competitive. Its training policies, particularly its self-sustaining training approach, are meeting their objective—to help the company both build a multiskilled work force and fulfill its mission to continue as the world leader in the industry.

14

Ford Sharonville:
An Emphasis on
User-Vendor Cooperation

Joan L. Sickler

During the first quarter of 1986, the Ford Motor Company announced that a new product would be produced by its Sharonville transmission plant in suburban Cincinnati, Ohio. The new product—the E4OD—is a four-speed, automatic, electronically controlled truck transmission, and it represents a twenty-five-year leap in technology compared to the other transmission being manufactured at the plant—the popular C6 rear-wheel-drive transmission. The C6, which was developed in the early 1960s, will continue to be manufactured at Sharonville, along with the E4OD, because of its best-in-class quality rating.

The twelve-month retooling of the plant for the new product included the introduction of 119 new machines from forty different vendors. Among the generic new skills required of the work force were a knowledge of metrics and blueprint reading, computer awareness and keyboard skills, new forms of gauging, the fundamentals of *computerized numerical control* (CNC) and statistical process control, and geometric dimensioning and tolerancing. In addition, specialized skills were called for in the operation of a number of the new pieces of equipment, specifically the 200 programmable logic controllers which have been purchased for the launch.

Faced with the introduction of a new product, the Sharonville plant had the option to select from among three methods for providing training in the new technology: request the services of a launch team from corporate headquarters, contract out the business to an independent training firm, or use in-house staff to design and administer the training. At Sharonville, the choice was clear: to create an internal joint labor-management Launch Training Team.

The Sharonville approach to training its work force for the new technology springs from its own unique history of worker involvement in decision making at the plant. A strong, progressive union leadership, committed to the long-term employment security of its members through new skill acquisition, and an innovative and cooperative management have merged at Sharonville to produce a forceful team effort in training. The decision to establish the joint Launch Training Team grew out of the earlier successes achieved at the plant by the joint Technical Training Committee (TTC), a volunteer group of eight hourly and five salaried workers that has been in place since 1982. The TTC, in turn, has been successful because its members are, first and foremost, technical experts in their fields, according to Charles Guy, currently the union health and safety representative at the plant and the driving force behind the early union involvement in training. Also, the TTC members come from both management and labor and represent each of the major job categories in the plant, a level of cooperation characteristic of the Sharonville facility since the early 1980s.

An Environment of Cooperation and Involvement

Briefly, the cooperation between the United Auto Workers (UAW) Local 863 and the Ford Motor Company management at the Sharonville plant was initiated in 1979 under a negotiated contractual process between the national UAW and Ford Motor

Company to encourage labor-management cooperation and increase employee involvement in work-related issues. The 1982 national agreement between the two parties called for the establishment of a jointly administered Employee Development and Training Program (EDTP) that provides substantial training, retraining, and development opportunities for UAW-represented employees. In addition, the 1984 agreement introduced a provision for jointly administered local training funds for broad-based skills development and training for the workers.

The first pilot Employee Involvement (EI) groups at Sharonville were created in 1980 on the shop floor and followed by a similar process in the salaried ranks. In 1981, two full-time EI coordinators were appointed—one drawn from labor and one from management. Today, 30 percent of the employees are involved in the weekly problem-solving groups, and the plant has also initiated a pilot project to establish Natural Work Teams of production workers ("manufacturing technicians") who will operate the new product manufacturing process as their own business. Prior to this, the plant manager had taken a number of significant steps to reorganize and reduce management layers—from seven to four—and to make all types of cost information widely and easily available to facilitate problem solving and action by the EI groups.

Both labor and management at the plant credit the employee involvement process with the significant improvements achieved since 1980. Sharonville has risen from the lowest- to the highest-ranked in quality and cost among the seven plants in the Transmission and Chassis Division. Yet, despite its gains, the plant has also experienced the effects of competitive pressures on its ability to retain jobs. In March of 1985, after one of its two products—the outmoded rear-wheel-drive C5 transmission—was discontinued and before the announcement that it had won the new E4OD transmission, Sharonville underwent a significant reduction, from 3,500 to around 1,900 people. Thus, the current Sharonville work force is highly motivated to provide and take advantage of training that upgrades skills and improves employability. Within this environment of an established employee involvement process, and backed by a union and management commitment to cooperation generally and training in particular, the Sharonville plant was poised to take the reins of its own training program when the new product launch was announced.

The Joint Launch Training Team

The launch training organization at Sharonville consists of a staff of five hourly and seven salaried workers, including the plant training coordinator. The salaried staff coordinate engineering training, line supervisor training, training in statistical process control (SPC) and dimensional control planning (DCP), and ongoing management and communications training. Two members, one hourly and one salaried, address the nontechnical training (communication, problem solving, motivation, and leadership styles) needed by the Natural Work Teams. Other hourly employees, most of whom are also members of the plant's Technical Training Committee, are responsible for developing and delivering all technical training and for training coordination with equipment vendors.

Since the equipment for the launch of the new product represents a dramatic leap in technology for the plant's work force, preparation through basic skills training was a clear need. Before attempting equipment-specific training in areas totally new to the workers, the technical training members of the Launch Training Team first set out to design their own two-week, eighty-hour curriculum of basic machine skills training for skilled tradespeople and production workers. The first priority was to bring some of the skilled trades instructors in the plant up to speed on the new technology. Between the summer of 1986 and March 1987, 280 of the plant's 320 skilled tradespeople completed the eighty-hour curriculum.

Through stand-up teaching, hands-on training, and the use of interactive video training programs, the curriculum covers metrics, blueprint reading, geometric dimensioning and tolerancing, gauging, computer awareness and keyboarding skills, generic troubleshooting and lubrication, statistical process control, and the fundamentals of CNC. In groups of twelve to sixteen, the skilled tradespeople and, later, the manufacturing technicians assigned to the new product launch go through the machine-skills curriculum. For the manufacturing technicians (production workers), the hard-skills training is followed by a forty-hour set of courses covering the "soft" human relations skills needed for teamwork, as well as by an overview of basic finance, accounting, and engineering skills and a discussion of the corporate and plant-level structures of the UAW and Ford Motor Company.

"It's not a vendor's job to give you the basic skills," says Larry Morrow, a machine repairman and member of the launch technical training group. "The engineers and vendors generally want to run through the sequence of operations (on the new equipment), and they feel that is adequate *if* you have the start-up skills."

As one of the workers who designed the eighty-hour basic-skills curriculum, Morrow noted a number of the principles behind the design of the courses that also guide the development of equipment-specific training with vendors. The method of course delivery, for example, was specially designed for the needs of the older Sharonville work force, which has an average age of forty-eight to fifty years. The standard high school or college courses were too heavily weighted toward theory, without the hands-on, experiential approach more appropriate for an older worker. "People this age who work in auto plants want to touch things," Morrow notes. "We got the talking down to three hours and the doing up to sixteen hours." Acknowledging the workers' emotional barriers against learning has been another key element in the training. "Getting them to relax and feel good about themselves is our primary goal," Morrow says. And peer teachers drawn from the work force are the best way to do that. "Hourly workers are good role models," he says. "We could have found technically more competent people, but they wouldn't have related as well."

Vendor Relations

At Sharonville, the basic steps in developing training with the equipment vendors include the following:

• *Visit to the vendor.* Members of the technical training group (part of the launch team), along with one or two designated skilled tradespeople and manufacturing technicians who will be working on the equipment, make a preliminary visit to the vendor to examine the new equipment and determine what aspects of its operation are, in fact, new to the work force. This contact helps to set the parameters for the training. "We're learning that we don't always know what we want to know," notes one member of the technical training group. This first step differs markedly from traditional practice. "In the past, the engineer would go by himself," remarks Robert Kuhl, training coordinator at Sharonville. "The first time the operator would see the equipment would be on the floor." Today, however, Kuhl notes, "more than ever we're sending people on the road." While these and later visits to the vendor translate into higher travel costs, Kuhl states that there is a real payoff: The operator has "buy-in and ownership" of the equipment at an early stage.

• *Establishment of performance objectives.* The technical training group members return to the plant to develop written performance objectives specific to that piece of equipment. They will share them with the vendor and explain in detail where their special concerns lie in developing training based on their knowledge of the current skills of the plant work force. "In most cases with a vendor, you've got to dictate training to them," Robert Klette, a pipe fitter and member of both the joint Launch Training Team and the TTC, points out. "You've got to be specific on what you want people to be able to do." Most vendors do not have a separate training department, according to the technical training group, and the Sharonville approach is to take an aggressive stand on training with the vendor early on. "We try to get them involved as early as possible in the training," one member says.

• *Operator participation in machine run-offs.* The skilled tradespeople or manufacturing technicians who are designated to become the subject-matter experts on the equipment then return to the vendor to participate in the final test runs of the machine and to become specialized in its operation, keeping in mind their later responsibility to serve as peer trainers on the equipment at the plant. All workers who volunteer and are accepted for the new positions as manufacturing technicians on the Natural Work Teams agree as part of the job to share their skills and knowledge with their co-workers.

• *Development and delivery of training at the plant.* The vendor, technical training group members, and subject-matter experts jointly decide on the length, design, content, and mode of delivery for the training to be delivered at the plant. Those package courses offered by the vendor that are judged appropriate for the Sharonville workers are accepted as is; others are modified to meet the plant's special needs. Where appropriate, trainers from the vendor will deliver courses; in other cases, textbook packages will be taught by the subject-matter experts at the plant.

• *Certification of learning.* The Sharonville technical training group has set a high priority on evaluating the effectiveness of the training—whether it be in-house generic skills training or vendor-delivered, equipment-specific training. The certification process generally takes the form of hands-on demonstrations of ability to operate the equipment and troubleshoot problems when they arise. Members of the technical training group have constructed simulated equipment—often using parts from the plant floor—to certify trainees on the content learned both from the basic skills curriculum and from equipment-specific training. For example, technical training group members constructed a CNC lab in the training department consisting of twelve computers and a small CNC lathe and mill. Klette used existing plant components to build a lubrication simulator to certify the trainees who had completed the basic skills course in lubrication. Two other members of the technical training group constructed a certification procedure for the programmable logic controllers, using units from the vendor interfaced with pneumatic machine circuit simulators. Faults are introduced into the system, and the electricians trained on the controllers are required to troubleshoot the problems. When the vendor delivers the training, the Sharonville team requires them to show that learning has taken place. "We insist that they include a form of demonstration of achievement," Klette says. The trainees must be able to demonstrate after a defined number of hours of training that they can achieve the performance objectives.

Vendor Relations: Two Examples

Gould, Inc. Industrial automation manufacturer Gould, Inc., is supplying 200 Modicon programmable logic controllers for the new product manufacturing process at Sharonville. Gould representatives were first brought to the plant by the Ford Transmission and Chassis Division engineer in charge of the equipment purchase to discuss training. Gould had previously received a copy of the revised training specifications developed by the division, and under the contract with Ford, had agreed to provide fifteen weeks of training to the plant and to have two full-time service representatives in residence at the plant for the period of the launch, or between one and two years. The other pieces of the training package included "retrievables," or interactive video training programs and the standard written instruction manuals and troubleshooting guides.

Prior to the initial meeting with Gould, two electricians from Sharonville were sent by the Launch Training Team to another Ford plant, where Gould programmable logic controllers (PLCs) were already in use. They spent one week familiarizing themselves with the equipment and observing a Gould PLC training session under way at that facility. Their feedback to the team was basically positive, with some recommendations for changes. These recommendations were discussed with Gould and the course of instruction reviewed. Members of the Sharonville technical training group prepared a five-point list of performance objectives for the training, setting out very defined tasks to be learned and specifying how the learning must be demonstrated. For example:

- Identify and describe the functions of various boards to include understanding of fault lights. Electrician will demonstrate this by locating and eliminating prebugged faults.
- Understand the method of solving logic (method of scan). Electrician will demonstrate this procedure by troubleshooting a predesigned circuit.

Gould reviewed the objectives and modified the course content to suit Sharonville's needs. The plant also called for adjustments in the timing of the training—requesting that half be delivered early and half six months later, closer to the time of the launch and after the equipment was installed on the floor. The Launch Team also insisted on personally meeting with and approving the Gould training representatives who would be working at the plant to ensure that they would be accepted by the Sharonville work force. A number of other factors—large and small—were negotiated and renegotiated between the plant and Gould, and both parties are pleased with the results.

John Akerley, central region education manager for Gould, describes the relationship with Sharonville as "very unique," noting that only an estimated 2 percent of Gould users call for customized training. Instead, nearly all of them attend established, scheduled courses delivered by Gould. In the case of Sharonville, the training "was customized to their special needs," Akerley says. "We had left some things out and they restored some of these and added others." Training that is tailored to the user's needs pays off in the end. "Only they know what is important for them to cover," he says. And when the training is over, Gould gets feedback from the user "that they finally did it right; they got trained people who didn't have to go to the engineering folks to run the equipment, and application skills increased." Akerley notes that the company is experiencing an increase in requests for modifications in on-site training programs. "Customizing training is not a hassle if the customer is willing to pay for that," he notes, adding that the company "needs to advertise to our customers that the option to design tailored programs is available."

Lamb Technicon. A Litton Industries subsidiary, Lamb Technicon in Warren, Michigan, is the supplier to Sharonville of the transmission case machining line, a multimillion-dollar line of equipment with five major transfer machine sections, each with the equivalent of thirty individual machine tools. The company has a training department and routinely offers standard textbook/classroom training packages. In the case of Sharonville, limited formal training was requested, so it was up to the plant launch team to negotiate an appropriate training component. After examining the standard package, the Sharonville technical training group judged it more practical for them to take a hands-on approach to training its own core of subject-matter experts.

The approach fit well with one of Lamb's own philosophies of user relations, according to Michael Farrell, Lamb vice-president for sales. ''We generally encourage the customer as soon as practical to assign people to the machine, and we bring them into our plant so they can become totally familiar with the machine.'' Lamb sees a payoff down the line once the equipment is installed and in operation. ''The more familiar the technicians are, the better equipped they are to troubleshoot and maintain the machinery,'' Farrell says. And that, in turn, will affect overall reliability and performance of the equipment. Also, Farrell notes, early involvement creates a ''pride in ownership'' on the part of the operators, ''because they have been involved in the building phase.''

Since March 1987, eight skilled tradespeople and manufacturing technicians from Sharonville who have completed the plant's basic-skills curriculum have been working with the equipment on site at Lamb, operating the machines prior to the acceptance of the equipment by the Ford engineers. They are scheduled to work at Lamb through July and they represent the ''retrievable training'' for the plant, according to Klette. As the subject-matter experts, they will help design and deliver the training for the other workers at the plant.

The cooperative relationship with Lamb has had an immediate payoff as well: Two of the Sharonville machine repairmen participating in the on-site operation identified two immediate problems on the equipment—with the spindle guard and lubrication—and showed the Lamb engineers how to correct them. ''They point out a problem we may have overlooked, and a correction is made,'' Farrell acknowledges. And workers won't have to face the problem on the Sharonville production floor.

In addition, in a process Farrell describes as ''simultaneous engineering,'' Lamb has maintained an ongoing relationship with Ford through its design phase as well. In the case of the Sharonville transmission caseline, all groups from the user and vendor—including Ford production engineers and manufacturing engineers and Lamb personnel—have met together bi-weekly since the order was first placed in April 1986 to discuss the ongoing design parameters and functional description of the equipment. "Continuous improvement is a way of life at Lamb," Farrell says.

Training Specifications

Of the forty equipment vendors supplying Sharonville with the new technology for the E4OD launch, nineteen have been categorized by the Launch Training Team as high priority for the development of equipment-specific training. Each of these vendors has received the formal document of training specifications drawn up for the Ford Transmission and Chassis Division. Originally a complex and cumbersome twenty-three-page document, according to Kuhl, the training specifications were rewritten in 1985 by all the division training coordinators and trimmed to a little over three pages with accompanying data sheets. The stated purpose of the document is "to ensure the efficient operation, maintenance, and troubleshooting of the equipment purchased for the mutual benefit of the Ford Motor Company and the supplier." Many of the factors that the Sharonville team consider critical to a worthwhile training program are included, among them:

- Request for a "detailed equipment description, so that the training activity can evaluate the organizational training needs."
- A training format requirement that "the vendor is specifically prohibited from developing only lecture style, noninteractive training sessions. Equipment demonstration and hands-on training for all participants is required."
- A validation section that calls for evaluation of the training package by "one or more of the following criteria: pre- and post-test, hands-on demonstration, task certification, or other."

Existence of the training specifications does not, of course, ensure that the vendor will use them, and their impact generally is far greater before the purchase is agreed to than it is once the machines are already built and on their way to the plant. "Once the ship has already sailed, we have no real clout," Kuhl says. Training specifications "should go out with the purchase orders. They must be part of the original contract." The efforts by Kuhl and the other division training coordinators focus on getting the engineers—often those at the division level who negotiate purchase contracts—to present the training specifications to vendors at the earliest contact. "Those engineers buying the equipment need to have their training hats on," Kuhl says. "If we don't negotiate it up front in the purchase, it's hard to hold the vendor to the training specs." Still, Kuhl points out that an aggressive local training committee often can get "as much on a personal level" as through formal negotiations. "What they lack in management clout, they make up for in know-how and the ability to get things done outside of the system," he says.

The Sharonville approach to training—like its approach to business as a whole—is structured to draw on the expertise in the work force at whatever level and in whatever department it may exist. "We're crazy not to tap into anybody who has a specific skill that we need," Kuhl notes. "There's so much unexplored and untapped talent out on the floor."

15

The Vendor's Role in Training to Support Computer Integrated Manufacturing: Caterpillar Inc.

Russell W. Scalpone

Much has been written about the importance of factory automation in the "reindustrialization" of America. Corporate strategic planners have long hoped that the falling cost of computer memory and related devices would offset the rising cost of almost every other resource, especially human labor. Unfortunately, the simplistic portrayal of robot armies displacing human workers has understated both the potential contribution of factory automation to a business and the need for human involvement in automation to make it work. A brief overview of what is encompassed by the automated "factory of the future" will illustrate.

The Importance of Automation and Computer Integrated Manufacturing

The earliest form of modern automation was the numerically controlled machine tool. Through the use of instructions preprogrammed onto punched or magnetic tapes, a machine tool could be guided so as to make parts with a high degree of accuracy and reliability. Later, machine tools that could be guided directly by a computer or programmable logic controller (PLC) were developed. Another kind of computer-aided machine is the robot, which replaces human labor on repetitive or dangerous tasks, such as picking, placing, and assembling parts; welding; or painting. PLCs not only allow machine instructions to be changed rapidly, but also permit the actions of many machines and robots to be networked and hence coordinated, like a basketball team, as the product passes from one stage of production to another.

Computer-guided machines, however, are only one aspect of factory automation, albeit the most visible aspect. An equally important aspect is streamlining the flow of information that runs the factory. This entails using computers in designing and testing new products, processing customer orders, scheduling production, planning material requirements, and keeping track of inventory.

The greatest benefit, and also the greatest challenge, in applying automation to manufacturing comes from using the computers in all areas of the business at the same time. This is because manufacturing benefits the most when the computers used by design engineers, order clerks, inventory planners, production schedulers, and the production machines themselves are all linked together, speaking the same computer language and referring to the same data bases. When the various parts of the business are tied together in this fashion, they are said to be "integrated" and the end result is known as computer integrated manufacturing (CIM). Thus, CIM is the marriage of information and action in the factory of the future.

The Importance of Training in Implementing CIM

Implementing CIM on a companywide basis is a complicated undertaking; computerizing the company's accounting system is simple by comparison. All departments affecting manufacturing operations must work together in a closely coordinated fashion to design and develop CIM systems and compatible data bases. Most companies are unaccustomed to such intense coordination and hence find CIM products extremely difficult.

Much has been written about the importance of education and training in making CIM technology workable and reliable (for example, Scalpone, 1984; Thompson and Scalpone, 1985), as well as the relative value of various outside sources of CIM training (Scalpone, 1984). These sources include: training firms, equipment and system vendors, universities, professional organizations, and consultants. This chapter describes how a vendor worked closely with a customer in providing training to support a major CIM project.

The Caterpillar–Allen-Bradley CIM Training Program

Caterpillar Inc. is a multinational company that designs, manufactures, and markets a wide variety of heavy equipment and vehicles. Its products include earthmoving, construction, and material-handling equipment and engines for heavy equipment vehicles as well as marine, petroleum, agricultural, industrial, and other applications encompassing diesel, natural gas, and turbine power. Caterpillar has fifteen plants in the United States and fifteen other plants strategically located in approximately a dozen countries. It employs over 50,000 people and is headquartered in Peoria, Illinois. Its annual sales in 1986 were $7.3 billion.

In the early 1980s, like many manufacturers of durable goods, Caterpillar felt the double body blows of intensified foreign competition and a dramatic downturn in industrywide demand. These problems caused the company to lose almost $1 billion from 1982 to 1984.

In 1985, the company returned to profitability with a commitment to pursue a carefully planned business strategy intended to ensure that these losses would not recur. An important part of the company's strategy was a plan called Plant with a Future (PWAF). PWAF is a plan aimed at reducing manufacturing cost while retaining the company's position as the top-of-the-line, quality producer in its markets. PWAF contains detailed plans for the progressive upgrading of manufacturing facilities through a four-step process:

1. Simplifying and streamlining operations to improve efficiency.
2. Consolidating operations by forming related manufacturing activities into "cells." Each cell would embody a particular product or process, such as machining cell, assembly cell, engine-making cell, or transmission-housing cell. Workers in each cell could then be responsible for controlling their own process and inventory.
3. Automating the cells by installing state-of-the-art, computer-guided manufacturing equipment.
4. Integrating the cells by tying them together with a computerized planning and control network, with all cells operating from a common manufacturing data base. The PWAF plan describes the "architecture" for tying together product planning, process planning, business planning, and production planning with day-to-day operations, and indicates how customer orders will be executed by applying Caterpillar's version of just-in-time production scheduling.

Needless to say, the PWAF plan has important implications for Caterpillar's U.S. manufacturing installations and their employees. Therefore, another planning group was assembled by Caterpillar to create a human resource plan to prepare employees at all levels to support the company's strategy and related changes in operations. The human resource plan was an exhaustive document covering such things as the Caterpillar human resource philosophy, desired management and communications environment, the strategy for designing new jobs and qualifying people for them, and related reward systems.

Training to aid in the implementation of PWAF figures prominently among the projects and programs in the human resource plan. Therefore, in 1985, Caterpillar's technical training team identified behavioral training objectives for a survey course that would cover fundamentals of CIM most likely to affect plant management and staff personnel. This survey course was entitled "CIM Electronic Concepts and Terminology."

The CIM Electronic Concepts and Terminology Course

In mid 1985, the technical training team at Caterpillar's Corporate General Office prepared an outline for the survey course in CIM, specifying between five and nine behavioral objectives for each of eight course sessions. The intent was to use the training to enable participants to recognize and, wherever possible, have hands-on experience with various components of a CIM installation with an emphasis on manufacturing hardware. The course would, therefore, have to cover an extremely wide range of technical topics, from sensors and machine control devices on and up through business planning systems. Major topics to be covered included:

- Hierarchical design of CIM systems
- Computer-aided engineering and downloading of engineering data directly into the computers that control production
- Sensors and coding systems that permit tracking of the product as it moves through the various stages of production, providing feedback as to whether or not correct operations/processes have been performed
- Logic systems, control devices, and computer devices—such as PLCs—that monitor and control individual motors, production machines, or groups of machines in the plant
- Robots, robot programming, and operation
- Data transmission, communication, and control systems
- Flexible manufacturing systems
- Business planning considerations in the purchase and installation of computerized manufacturing systems

In the course of planning, the need for outside support in conducting the training became immediately apparent to the technical training team. Subject-matter experts would be needed to cover a wide variety of technical topics. The Caterpillar people investigated a wide variety of sources for this expertise before discovering the capabilities of one of their vendors, Allen-Bradley.

Allen-Bradley, a subsidiary of Rockwell International Corporation, is an eighty-year-old company, headquartered in Milwaukee, Wisconsin. It was originally famous as the manufacturer of control boxes and panels with large green and red "start" and "stop" push buttons. In addition to industrial controls and systems, it has major groups that specialize in electronics and industrial computers. Within the industrial control and systems group, start and stop push buttons have evolved into a wide array of products:

- Electrical and electronic contacts, sensors, and switches
- Motor controls
- Computerized control devices, such as PLCs and computerized work stations that govern automated equipment
- Computerized communications networks to connect automated machines with computer work stations and central host computers
- Software to coordinate and orchestrate interaction in a factory full of production equipment through both local and centralized control systems that pass information along "data highways"

The Allen-Bradley customer coordinator (sales engineer) responded enthusiastically to Caterpillar's request for assistance in the development of the CIM course, and course development began.

Pilot Version of CIM Course

The pilot course was launched in October 1985 with substantial assistance from Allen-Bradley. Allen-Bradley provided a total of seven instructors who were customer support people from the Allen-Bradley groups making the products or components featured in the various course sessions. Allen-Bradley technical writers and support people produced training materials and supplied videotapes, product information, and specifications, as well as equipment set-ups and demonstrations for use in the hands-on portion of the course.

A central feature of the course was Allen-Bradley's conceptual model of how CIM is planned, organized, and managed. This conceptual model was based upon the organization of responsibility for various CIM-related products within Allen-Bradley's experience with CIM projects in its own manufacturing facilities.

Participants for the workshop were solicited by sending letters to key management people in six major manufacturing facilities throughout the central United States. Actual attendees were two groups of twenty-four Caterpillar management people, drawn from a wide variety of jobs and facilities throughout the United States. The forty-eight participants represented manufacturing systems engineers, manufacturing planning supervisors and planning personnel from the plants, training personnel, and management and technical people from the general office involved in developing standards and documentation to implement PWAF.

Each of the two course groups attended five four-hour sessions and, at the conclusion of their participation, completed detailed feedback sheets. Oral and written feedback from participants revealed the following overall results:

- Reaction to course content was enthusiastically positive, and the course appeared to be effective in accomplishing its written objectives.
- Participants could not absorb enough content in twenty hours and needed more time.
- Greater subject matter continuity between sessions was needed.
- Sessions should be shortened and spread out over a longer time period to allow participants sufficient opportunity to absorb the content and get through the assigned reading material.

Revisions of the CIM Course

As a result of feedback, the decision was made to proceed with an expanded and modified version of the course:

- The course was lengthened to eight sessions, but each session was shortened to three hours. Only two sessions were scheduled per week, so that the total course could be spread out over four weeks.
- Greater continuity in subject matter was written into the course content.
- More detailed information dictated by Caterpillar's PWAF was developed and incorporated into the course, making it more relevant to the company's strategic plans.
- Class size was reduced from twenty-four to twelve participants. (This was later increased to sixteen when more equipment set-ups and demonstrations became available.)
- A broader range of people was invited from the plants, again using a solicitation letter.

In soliciting participants for the revised course, a broader group was contacted; pains were taken to ensure that the decision to send a participant was made as close as possible to the level of the participant. The new crop of attendees included plant engineers, plant managers, data-processing managers, and a diversity of people from plant staff functions. However, the difficulty of recruiting upper-level management and executive people for the new twenty-four-hour course convinced the technical training team to prepare an eight-hour overview version of the course.

The revised twenty-four-hour version of the course and the eight-hour overview course were launched in January 1986. By April 1987, approximately 900 management and staff people had been through the long course, and 180 managers had been through the overview course.

Participation of Production Supervisors, Hourly Personnel, and Union Representatives

Production supervisors and hourly personnel were scheduled to participate in the CIM course starting in the third quarter of 1987. The decision to schedule them to attend at that time, rather than sooner, was based upon the feeling that training would be most effective if it were timed to coincide with the participants' first contact with actual CIM applications on their jobs. This first contact was earliest for plant management, engineering, and planning people who were developing these systems, software, and standards, as well as purchasing actual equipment. These salaried people were designing and implementing CIM applications in concert with the PWAF and were deemed to have the greatest "need to know." CIM applications were expected to arrive on the plant floor in late 1987, and hence the exposure of supervisory and hourly people was planned for that time frame.

The involvement of union representatives in the CIM training was influenced by the timing considerations mentioned above, as well as the nature of other topics under discussion with the union when training was started. These topics included the streamlining of operations based upon Caterpillar's cost-reduction commitment and a program for increasing employee involvement in decision making.

A major breakthrough in the employee involvement issue occurred in March 1986, when an agreement was reached to launch the Employee Satisfaction Program. It was felt that this agreement would be a good foundation upon which to build additional employee involvement in CIM training. Subsequently, union officials in one entire local participated in the eight-hour overview CIM course in November 1986. Reactions of the group were predominantly positive, and the participation of more bargaining-unit personnel was scheduled to take place in the third quarter of 1987.

Results of the CIM Course

While no formal, quantitative assessment has yet been performed to determine the impact of the course on the business, interviews with training management and a cross section of participants support management's earlier conclusion that the training was achieving its purpose: it was facilitating implementation of the PWAF and related CIM steps. Moreover, feedback from the participants indicated that both the structure and manner of presentation of the course were having beneficial effects:

1. The depth of coverage for each area of CIM was felt to be good, and the emphasis on programming and using actual equipment in the course conveyed an understanding of both technical terms and the objects to which they referred. The course provided visualization of the various technologies encompassed by CIM and gave participants a sense of familiarity with equipment by permitting them to experiment with hardware.

2. Participants reported that they were able to apply a wider range of technical disciplines to their work as a result of the course. For example, engineers saw how their work affected production planners, and production planners grasped how the availability of new technology would affect the planning function. Learning the technical components of an automated machine control system, along with related physical principles of operation, gave planners an understanding of how equipment maintenance requirements were likely to affect production scheduling.

3. Participants felt that they now better understood the benefits of the new manufacturing technology, and hence the reasoning behind its purchase. Their perception of how CIM technology was likely to affect them in the plant was, therefore, more realistic than it was prior to the course, and thus they were better prepared to accept and work with the equipment planned for installation in their plant.

In addition to enhancing knowledge, it appeared as though the training program may well have had certain psychological effects upon the participants. One of these effects is similar to the psychological concept of "desensitization." The desensitization concept has been used not only by psychotherapists but also by trainers in teaching people to overcome unwarranted fears. Desensitization reduces fear by exposing a person first to the least scary aspects of the feared situation under positive circumstances, then gradually working up to progressively more scary aspects of the feared situation, thereby enabling the person to grow accustomed to the source of fear. For example, in training people who are afraid of public speaking, the trainee might first present a speech to one other person, then to an empty auditorium, finally to a filled auditorium, and so forth. The CIM course used this principle by first exposing participants to simple relays and sensors, then gradually working up to the more complex systems that tie these components together.

Another psychological effect that may well have been engendered by the course was that of reducing the perceived complexity of CIM by increasing the participant's familiarity with the concept. Research in the field of attitude change (Scalpone, 1974) has shown that very complex and unfamiliar stimulus situations tend to be unpleasant for a person. With repeated exposure under certain conditions, however, familiarity not only breeds greater comfort with the stimulus, but also leads a person to judge the stimulus as less complicated or complex than before.

Based upon the reports of participants, it appears as though the opportunity to actually touch and work with the various types of automation equipment in the CIM sessions had "demystified" factory automation, and participants were now able to visualize complex, automated systems as collections of similar components linked by computerized controls.

The capacity of training to produce beneficial psychological effects in a short period of time through gradual exposure of participants to complex automation technology is something that could have major implications for implementing industrial modernization and deserves further exploration.

A major criticism of the CIM course was that its pace was too fast for individuals with no background in electrical or electronic work; many had to attend make-up sessions, especially if they had missed one of the class meetings. This problem could be attributed to the "building block" structure of the course content, which required the trainee to have knowledge of earlier sessions in order to fully comprehend later content. Course structure, however, was probably not the only factor that necessitated a high level of effort to keep up. Participants had a wide range of job functions and backgrounds, and those with less exposure to mechanical and electronic devices were mixed in with more technology-literate individuals. Moreover, the fact that the training was conducted within the work environment during working hours meant that many people were subject to demands upon their time that impeded efforts to attend the sessions; hence the need for make-up work.

Participants also noted that a great deal of outside reading was required to keep up with the classroom sessions. The readings were mostly product information and specifications relating to the devices discussed in class as well as background articles covering such topics as CIM, flexible manufacturing systems, and production scheduling. Judgments of the amount of reading effort were probably influenced by the participant's previous experience: most management training courses do not require extensive outside reading. In this respect, the CIM course resembles a university-level laboratory course more than a typical management training seminar, and the reading requirements and pace of the course are both likely to become more of a problem if the same format is used with lower-level participants.

What Can Be Learned

The Caterpillar–Allen-Bradley CIM course is a lesson in training design at two levels. At one level, it is an example of how to present what may be the most complex and technically difficult subject ever taught to managers. The successful recruitment of so many voluntary participants, the positive reactions of those participants, and the related positive effects on such a diverse audience suggest that it was a logical and effective way to build support within management ranks for a major technological change. The course's hands-on format and building block structure appear to be well suited to the job of fostering understanding and acceptance of novel and complex manufacturing technology. Moreover, given the rapid pace of technological change in manufacturing and data-processing technology, this type of training is likely to be needed in many, if not most, businesses that intend to survive into the twenty-first century.

At another level, we can learn something from this case study of how a vendor company can position itself to provide "value added" to customers through the use of training as a service that empowers the customer in the use of technology.

Several factors positioned Allen-Bradley as a vendor to support Caterpillar in the CIM training project. First, Allen-

Bradley was organized into a series of product groups responsible for various types of CIM components. Allen-Bradley's customer coordinator represented all these component product groups and, therefore, possessed some knowledge regarding each. He could also directly access a knowledgeable product engineer or product support center when the customer needed additional technical support. In this way, the customer coordinator served as an information middleman or resource locator, a type of organizational position deemed vital by Paul Strassman in his book on the requirements for successful application of advanced information processing technology in the workplace (Strassman, 1985). Furthermore, Allen-Bradley's practice of freeing product support people for use by the customer in training enabled Caterpillar to have access to a large number of diverse specialists from a single source to assist in course preparation and instruction.

Second, Allen-Bradley is a company that emphasizes training as an aspect of its customer support services. This emphasis was reflected in such capabilities as a production studio, technical writers, videotaping capabilities, and a catalogue of over fifty multiday training sessions in CIM-related topics, for which continuing education units were offered.

Providing this kind of support is a trend among progressive manufacturers: they are not only selling products, but also offering services that enhance the capability of the customer organization to use the product. Allen-Bradley's motivation for providing training support services cannot be construed as purely altruistic: such services are becoming as important as product features, price and delivery terms, and product quality in their effect upon the customer's decision regarding whom to buy from on a long-term basis. Moreover, the practice of helping customers benefit from a multimillion-dollar CIM investment is a good way to ensure the survival and growth of a customer base.

Future Directions

A good way to conclude a case study is to ask "Where do we go from here?" One thing is certain: as the training moves lower in the organization, more time and care will be needed to cover the same training content with supervisory and hourly personnel. The educational level and overall literacy level of participants will be lower. The backgrounds of these later participants will also be narrower in terms of their exposure to management systems and equipment and, consequently, their capacity for dealing with abstract concepts will be reduced. As a result, the training will have to make an even more concrete connection between each concept and the thing to which it refers. Training will need to be targeted to specific job duties with the accuracy of a rifle rather than the coverage of a shotgun. For example, maintenance people will need a wider range of working skills, since in highly automated plants, mechanical, electrical, electronic, and software problems become increasingly difficult to separate. Maintenance people must know something about each of these areas if they are to troubleshoot the cause of a breakdown and get the equipment running again.

The job of the machine operator will change most profoundly, since operating a machine will become more the job of programming it, setting it up, observing and testing it to see that it is working properly, and responding to the various automatic error messages that occur. Thus the dividing line between maintenance and operations will begin to dissolve as CIM hits the plant floor, and the technical training mission will be one of preparing both maintenance and operating people for their new, more complex, and less specialized role. Therefore, it would not be surprising to see the CIM survey course evolve into a carefully structured curriculum of technical training, covering all important knowledge and skills areas.

Vendors will have an important role in ensuring that all vital skills and knowledge areas in the technical training curriculum are covered with professionally developed and effective training. But more vital to the change program will be the role of administering the training and linking it to the job progression structure of the hourly work force. In this way, technical training will become a way of life rather than a singular event that empowers people to participate in making the new technology successful.

16

Miller Brewing Company and Amatrol: A Successful Partnership in Training for New Technology

Jocelyn F. Gutchess

A unique blend of talent, expertise, and experience in the relationship between the Miller Brewing Company and an outside training vendor—Amatrol—is helping Miller, the second-largest beer manufacturer in the United States, take full advantage of, and adjust to, technological advances in the industry. The keys to the successful collaboration between the two companies appear to be (1) the "bottom-up" planning process that preceded the establishment of the training program; (2) the willingness and ability of both parties to work together to maximize program effectiveness; (3) Amatrol's flexibility in adapting to the special requirements of Miller Brewing; and (4) the strong corporate support given to the program.

Meeting the Competition

Miller Brewing, an established beer manufacturing company with headquarters in Milwaukee, Wisconsin, is a wholly owned subsidiary of Philip Morris Companies, Inc., the tobacco and food processing conglomerate. With 1986 sales of over $3 billion and about 11,000 employees, Miller is second only to Anheuser-Busch in the American beer industry. With a more than 20 percent share of the U.S. market, Miller makes Miller High Life, Miller Genuine Draft, Meister Brau, Miller Lite, Milwaukee's Best, and Lowenbrau. Its Lite beer is the leader among the American light beers and is the second-largest-selling beer in the world. Currently, the company is having considerable success with its bottled draft beer as demand for that product increases. In addition to its Milwaukee plant, the company owns and operates five other breweries, located in Eden, North Carolina; Fort Worth, Texas; Albany, Georgia; Fulton, New York; and Irwindale, California. Miller also has five aluminum can manufacturing plants located near the breweries, as well as a glass plant in Auburn, New York. The can plants provide about one-half of the requirements for the breweries, with the balance provided by outside container companies. The Milwaukee plant, now over 100 years old, is the oldest of the breweries; it spreads out in over 70 old buildings. The newest brewery is the Irwindale plant—a modern facility of seven production lines, all concentrated in one vast but efficiently organized building.

In the past twenty-five years, the American beer industry has undergone significant changes, not only in the technology involved in the manufacture of beer but also in the structure of the industry itself. From a relatively open industry in the 1960s, characterized by many small and medium-sized local brewers, the industry has consolidated and is now dominated by a few big national companies. In 1960, the top five brewers controlled only 30 percent of the total national market. Today, almost 90 percent of the market is under the control of the top five. That is not to say that competition does not exist in the industry—it does. These top five companies, as well as the smaller companies, fight hard for market share, and, therefore, production cost is an important element. Competition is particularly tough at the present time, since the per capita consumption of beer in the United States appears to have declined, or at least to have stalled in recent years. This slackening of demand can be explained by several factors, including demographic trends (the slowdown in population growth), the fitness boom, and the raising of the legal drinking age in many states. Whatever the causes, one result must certainly be increased emphasis by the brewers on cost efficiency and, along with that, full utilization of the most efficient, usually the most advanced, technology.

The Need for Technological Training

A beer manufacturing plant consists basically of three operations: making the beer, packaging it for distribution and resale, and shipping. Since the packaging costs represent approximately one-half of sales revenues, it is clear that this is an area where efficiency is at a premium. At Miller Brewing, new technology has been introduced in recent years into all phases of the manufacturing process (for example, the brewing process is now completely automated), but particularly in moving the beer through the packaging production line. A production line at Miller Brewing starts with a "de-palletizer," a machine that takes the empty containers off the pallets on which they are brought into the plant and puts them on a conveyor through a rinser, ready to receive beer. They then go to a "filler," where they are pressure-filled with the beer and then either crowned (bottles) or sealed (cans). The next step is a pasteurizer, where the contents are, in effect, sterilized; then to a labeler and, finally, to the packaging machines, which put the containers into holders and the holders into cartons, ready for direct loading into either trucks or railroad cars.

The machinery that is used today on these production lines is driven by hydraulic or pneumatic pressure or is electrical. Hydraulic pressure is used when a steady, smooth, rigid delivery of power is necessary; pneumatic, when speed and flexibility are more important. All the machinery currently in use is controlled by microprocessors using specially designed electronic systems. Each of the production lines (from seven to thirteen per plant) requires from four to six operators, with the higher number being necessary for bottle production lines. (Before the introduction of the new technology, each line required from ten to twelve people.) In addition, there is a maintenance crew of several workers, who are responsible for keeping the machinery going, repairing it as necessary, and maintaining it in optimum working condition.

The extent of operational improvement resulting from the introduction of new technology is significant. Whereas the older filler machines could process only about 1,000 cans per minute, the machines currently in use can handle from 1,500 to 1,800 cans per minute—and a new one is expected to be introduced in the near future that will be able to fill up to 2,200 cans per minute.

Responsibility for training at Miller Brewing is a shared one. Generally speaking, training of hourly workers is left to the management of the local plants. Typically, it has been the production supervisors who have been responsible for training operators and maintenance personnel under their supervision. In addition, the manufacturers, the suppliers of the machinery and equipment used in each plant—and there may be as many as thirty or more manufacturers in each situation—generally provide some sort of training for workers using their equipment.

Responsibility for management training and development is assumed by the corporation. Gerald E. Poggi is the manager of the unit that fulfills this function. In addition, he is also responsible for oversight of the technical training that is carried out by the company in its various plants to assure that it meets the needs of the company. To help him in that task, he recruited Joseph A. Benkowski, then technical trainer for the company's Milwaukee plant, as the company's corporate technical training coordinator. Benkowski, with broad experience in vocational training and skill development, started out as a tool and die maker. As a result, not only is he thoroughly familiar with the world of training and vocational skill development, but he also knows and understands shop-floor problems first hand. It is through the efforts of Poggi and Benkowski that the highly successful training program with Amatrol has been developed and carried out.

The first step in developing the present corporate technical training program was a survey—in fact, two surveys, one in 1982 and another in 1984—to assess the company's existing technical training and to identify specific training needs of the breweries and container plants. Perhaps the major finding was that the training being provided by equipment suppliers tended to hamper rather than promote the development of a flexible work force. This vendor training was very specific, related only to the machine, or even limited to particular components of a machine provided by this or that supplier. Flexibility, particularly among the maintenance personnel, was sacrificed. When something went wrong with a machine, typically only two options were open to the maintenance personnel: either to undertake a trial-and-error replacement of machine parts until the trouble was corrected, or to go back to the machine manufacturer for advice and assistance. Clearly, either option is both time consuming and costly.

In both the 1982 and 1984 surveys, studies were made of every brewery and container plant to determine which training needs were common to all facilities and to identify the areas where a corporate training initiative, rather than a local program, would be desirable and appropriate. The answer was maintenance training for both hourly and supervisory personnel in the packaging and brewing areas. Specific courses identified in the appraisal were hydraulics, pneumatics, electronics, microprocessors, welding, centrifuge, filtration, Sankey CO_2 systems (to fill beer kegs), continental seamer (to seal the cans), and microbiology.

In addition, certain principles or guidelines for the training were developed. These are:

- When feasible, new technical training programs should be developed so that the supervisory personnel can do the training in-house. The objective here is to overcome the problems that exist when the training is manufacturer- or vendor-based, specifically the lack of continuity and ongoing availability of expert knowledge and technical assistance when needed. Trainers representing the equipment manufacturers leave when the training is completed and are not generally immediately available to help when things go wrong. In the past, training courses of maintenance personnel have taken as little as two or three hours, augmenting the manual left behind by the trainer. This amount of training has proved not to be enough.

- Training programs should provide hands-on training. The surveys clearly demonstrated that pure classroom training without hands-on experience is not effective.
- Training programs should be systems-oriented. Again, to develop a flexible work force that is able to respond quickly and effectively to production problems, it is necessary to develop generalized courses that give trainees a broad knowledge base rather than machine-specific courses. For example, hydraulics should be taught in a way that gives the trainee a sound basic knowledge of the theory of hydraulics as well as practical application, thus enabling him or her to troubleshoot any hydraulic system, and not just a specific machine. This type of training, it is believed, will provide for greater transfer of skills to other pieces of equipment.

As a result of the surveys, a long-range corporate technical training plan was developed and, after presentation to the resident plant managers for their review, adopted by corporate training for implementation. It perceives the technical training program as a pyramid (see Table 1). At the base are the more general subjects required of most, if not all, personnel, moving up to increasingly specialized knowledge areas, required by a decreasing proportion of the work force. Each level is built on the skills and training availability at the lower level. The final product will, of course, be a highly skilled, very flexible, and very efficient work force.

It is useful here to mention how the survey-studies were carried out. These were not simply questionnaires distributed by the corporate office to managers of the breweries and can plants. Nor was an outside consultant called in to carry out the assessment. Instead, this was a systematic, bottom-up review of current training practices and future needs. Each plant was visited by Benkowski; training programs and practices were observed; and probing discussions were held with managers,

Table 1. Automated Manufacturing
Technical Training System.

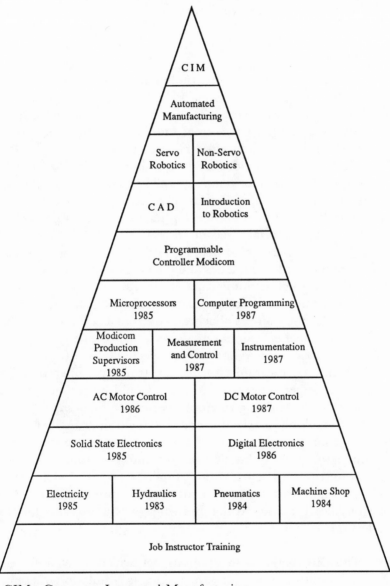

CIM = Computer Integrated Manufacturing
CAD = Computer-Aided Design
Source: Miller Brewing Company

supervisors, and plant hourly workers. It was from these studies and observations that the training principles were derived and the long-range plan developed.

The Search for a Trainer

Since knowledge of hydraulics and pneumatics is essential to the operation of a brewery production line—and since this is an area in which maintenance is frequently a problem—it was decided that these two areas should be the first courses offered under the new program. In conformity with the new guidelines, a decision was made that the training materials would have to be developed in a format that would permit company supervisors to do the training. Essentially, that meant that the company itself would have to develop its own curriculum and its own training materials. Second, it was important to find a suitable trainer capable of providing both the theoretical aspects of hydraulics and pneumatics and the necessary hands-on training. Such a bench-training capability would, of course, require that the trainer have the necessary equipment and machinery available for the trainees. The trainer would also have to be able to adapt his or her training methods to the company-prepared training curriculum. Whoever was selected for the training job would, in fact, be training trainers—training Miller Brewing Company supervisors who, in turn, would be responsible for passing on the training to employees under their supervision.

In making its selection of a suitable trainer, Miller's corporate training unit surveyed the field, looking at about ten manufacturers of hydraulic bench-training equipment around the country. The bench trainer finally selected was Amatrol, Inc., a small training equipment manufacturer located in Jeffersonville, Indiana. Miller Brewing gives as reasons for the selection:

• The construction of the training unit, which is well designed, well built, and provides an acceptable simulation of equipment actually used in Miller plants.

- The ability of Amatrol to perform realistic industrial systems training, that is, generalized training applicable to all hydraulics and pneumatics machines.
- The quality of training materials that were provided with the training equipment.
- The quality of the training program provided with the bench trainer.
- The willingness of Amatrol, and particularly of its president, Don Perkins, to work with Miller's corporate training unit in fashioning a complete training program, tailored specifically to Miller's needs.

In addition, it is clear that the price was right.

Amatrol, Inc.

Amatrol, Inc., is a successful, family-owned and -operated business dedicated to helping U.S. industry move into the high-tech era and thus strengthen its ability to compete in world markets. Starting with an engineering background, Perkins, the president and founder of the company, established the first enterprise in 1965. This company, now called Dynafluid Systems, Inc., was a manufacturer and installer of dedicated industrial automated systems, as well as a distributor of fluid power equipment. Installations for clients may be found throughout this country and overseas. Dynafluid Systems is now a regional automated manufacturing systems and component house, offering consultation, software, and hardware (with a full line of flexible high-technology equipment) to industry.

The company's interest and involvement in training and education have been an evolutionary development, begun soon after the first manufacturing company was established, when Perkins and his associates realized that training was essential to the continued growth and success of the company. Use of Dynafluid's products and services was, and is, dependent on the technological sophistication of the company's customers. However, when Perkins looked around the country to locate trainers and training programs for his clients, he found it was "just barely there, or too commercial," not relevant to current needs and the particular requirements of individual customers. Nor could he find the desired level of technological training in the schools—neither in the vocational schools, nor in the community colleges, nor even in higher-level technical or engineering schools.

Hoping to fill the gap, Perkins first added an education division to the Dynafluid company to train industry personnel in the latest industrial systems. However, the demand for both training and training equipment grew. Thus, in 1981, Perkins established Amatrol, Inc., as a separate and independent company, dedicated entirely to technological training and education. The name (chosen by one of Perkins's sons—a partner in the business) is an acronym for *automated machine control*. For Perkins, who worries about the competitive ability of U.S. industry, 1980 was a watershed year—"the year we woke up," as he puts it, to the need to adapt to and utilize technological advances if American industry is to survive.

His early involvement in technological training, plus his familiarity with industrial automation, led Perkins to develop training systems equipment and materials that have proven highly effective. He points to several elements that he believes are essential to successful training.

- Trainees must be given an opportunity to become fully involved in their own training, with plenty of opportunity for hands-on experience.
- To maintain a high level of interest, the training day is divided into relatively short time periods, with the program changed every twenty to thirty minutes so that there is not a drop-off in attention.
- The focus of training is on problem solving on the machine. Diagnostics and troubleshooting are at the core of the program.
- All instructors are industry-experienced personnel, familiar with theory and applications as well as with training techniques.

Over the past six years, Amatrol has gradually evolved from a regional company to a national, even international, business. Just recently the company—currently employing about sixty people—moved into a new building, which houses all aspects of its operations: classrooms equipped with training simulators; a manufacturing facility, where both the training equipment and tailor-made automated factory machines are constructed; a library; offices for the experts responsible for writing the training materials; and production facilities, where these materials can be reproduced. Combining its industrial and educational experience, the company designs and builds the training equipment, writes the courseware, and trains the trainers. Amatrol includes among its customers many top U.S. corporations, such as General Electric, General Motors, Chrysler, Eastman Kodak, Weyerhaeuser, Coca-Cola, and Martin Marietta. It also works closely with many school systems, training instructors so that they can effectively teach high-tech courses. In addition to hydraulics and pneumatics, the training courses now available from the company include microprocessor control, air logic control, servo control, robotics, and computer integrated manufacturing (CIM). Future plans call for increased attention to CIM.

The Training Program

At the present time, four train-the-trainer cycles have been completed by Amatrol for the Miller Brewing Company—three in hydraulics and one in pneumatics. Each cycle has accommodated from fifteen to sixteen trainees, selected by the local breweries and can manufacturing plants to take part in the program. Each session lasts one week and, according to Perkins, it is a very intensive week, with long days at the training facility and required homework. Perkins says that he gives the trainees brochures and literature describing the pleasures awaiting a visitor to the Louisville area, but that they barely have time to make use of the information. Instructor-trainee ratios are high, with plenty of opportunity for individualized instruction. Trainees get to know both Perkins and his instructors and are encouraged to keep in touch with Amatrol after they leave, particularly when and if they run into hard-to-solve problems.

Each Miller plant is responsible for paying travel and subsistence costs of the employees it sends to the training program. All other costs—tuition, training materials, curriculum development, and so on—are paid by the corporation. Miller Brewing does not use an open-ended contract, but negotiates a per capita price with Amatrol for each training session.

Both companies, Miller Brewing and Amatrol, are very satisfied with the way the program has been carried out. They are particularly proud of the smooth working relationships that have been developed between them. Perkins describes Miller as "unique in their approach," and reports: "The system works fine. Pretty smooth." Benkowski, commenting on Amatrol's commitment to Miller's training needs, says, "What I feel is more important is the rapport that has developed between Amatrol and the Miller Brewing Company. On many occasions, supervisors have called Don Perkins for his help and he has always been helpful. The feedback from the supervisors who have attended the hydraulics training program has been nothing but excellent."

Of particular interest is the cooperative approach to the development of the course material, including a leader's guide for use by the trainees when they return to their plants and become trainers of maintenance personnel under their supervision. The guide was developed by the corporate training unit, but with ongoing technical assistance and input from Perkins and the Amatrol staff. Amatrol uses this guide in its training sessions, along with its own training exercises. The result is that Miller now has a leader's guide that is not only familiar to the supervisors who have undergone training by Amatrol, but is also easy for them to follow and teach from when they are conducting hydraulics training in the Miller plants.

Apparently the hoped-for pass-through of the training program is taking place. Miller supervisors trained by Amatrol have become involved in setting up second generation training programs within the various plants to begin to develop the broader knowledge base and flexibility in the work force that are envisaged by the corporate training unit. The Fort Worth brewery, for example, which formerly relied entirely on its own resources for technical training, is reported to be enthusiastic about sending its supervisors to the Amatrol program, in the expectation that then they will be better able to meet the plant's training needs.

The success of the hydraulics program has encouraged Miller to expand its use of Amatrol, and a new course in microprocessor machine control is being planned.

Amatrol is not the only third-party trainer used by Miller Brewing. A good working relationship has also been established with a Chicago-based training company, Energy Concepts, Inc., to develop and carry out a train-the-trainer program in electrical technology. In this case, the course materials used will be those developed by Energy Concepts. As with Amatrol, however, Miller has worked with the training company to ensure that the program will be a good fit, directly addressing Miller's needs.

Keys to a Successful Partnership

As Miller moves to implement its long-range technological training plan, its goal remains the same—that is, to develop a flexible, highly skilled, competent work force able to take full advantage of new technology as it is developed and introduced. Miller is convinced that it is no longer enough to have people who know only this or that machine. The knowledge and skills of the work force must be broad-based and systems-oriented, but at the same time they must be geared to practical applications and problem solving on the shop floor. Reliance for training on the manufacturers and suppliers of the machinery used in the breweries and can plants—as in the past—does not meet this need. Nor can the company rely on established vocational and technical schools to meet their training needs. It might be possible for the company to send its staff to such schools, but, generally speaking, these schools do not have machinery and equipment similar to those used in the company's plants and therefore cannot provide adequate hands-on experience for

Miller personnel. Moreover, the schools must gear their courses to a generally lower level of experience than that of the Miller supervisors; the training is simply not appropriate. A third-party trainer can overcome all of these problems.

Why has the Miller Brewing–Amatrol training program worked so well? Several explanations can be offered:

- Miller Brewing knows exactly what it wants. Its training needs were specifically identified through two companywide, in-depth surveys, carried out by an in-house corporate training staff that knew the industry and knew training. Careful planning, from the bottom up, resulted in a well-designed overall training program.
- Amatrol knows what it can do and how to do it. Combining its industrial experience with a significant exposure to education, Amatrol was and is in a strong position to give Miller technical assistance as needed and to adapt its training program to Miller's specific needs. This it has done.
- Strong working relationships have been established and maintained by the two companies. There is good communication between the two parties, a real sense of being in this together and pooling efforts to solve a common problem.
- Throughout the development and implementation of the program, it has enjoyed strong corporate support from the top management of the company. The budget proposals of the corporate training unit have not been squeezed; decentralization is encouraged. Apparently, there is a recognition by top management that technological training is an essential element in the ability of the company to compete. This has allowed corporate training to move ahead, both energetically and confidently, with its program.

As Miller Brewing continues to work toward its training goal, it will be interesting to see whether the company will continue to rely on third-party trainers such as Amatrol to provide the necessary technological training. At the present time, there is every reason to believe the company will stay on this track, certainly as long as companies like Amatrol can be found to meet its needs.

PART FOUR

DESIGNING AND DELIVERING TRAINING COST-EFFECTIVELY

The American Society for Training and Development estimates that employers in the United States spend roughly $30 billion a year on formal education and training, not counting informal on-the-job training or wage and benefit costs. By 1990 that figure is expected to increase 25 to 30 percent, much of this amount prompted by rapidly changing technology, intensified competition, and skill obsolescence in the work force. Yet, despite this trend toward more spending on training, few employers have seriously assessed the value of their training dollars.

This part examines some of the innovative approaches taken by companies that have carefully analyzed the costs and benefits of training. Their experiences suggest that, while there is no formula that guarantees low-cost, consistently high-quality training, there are systematic methods that can help companies in the design and delivery of more cost-effective training. The methods used have allowed managers to better determine training needs and thus maximize the investment in training.

Designing cost-effective training in today's corporate environment takes careful planning and coordination at various stages of the training process. Critical decision making includes such concerns as: selection of project management, training

251

timetables, performance goals, comparative costs and benefits, in-house versus outside resources, instructional design, delivery methods, and evaluation standards. Three noteworthy approaches to cost-effective training are highlighted here: a "systems approach" for managing the educational process, cooperation with community colleges, and the use of satellite communications.

The Systems Approach

In many large corporations, the training process has become more complex than ever before, requiring the talents of various educational specialists—career development specialists, project managers, instructional designers, subject-matter experts, writers, computer programmers, and audio-video experts—who work together as a team to ensure the availability of training throughout the organization. The wide range of delivery methods available—particularly the most advanced computer-based training or interactive videodisc—multiplies the options for cost-effective training but also adds to the complexity.

The IBM case study describes how a systems approach to training and education, devised by the corporate training department, breaks down the educational process into more manageable steps and improves decision making and budget planning at each stage. The systems approach organizes the process into four steps: curriculum design, based on defined business requirements; instructional design for each course; course development led by interdisciplinary professional teams; and delivery through the most advanced techniques available. Integrated within all four steps are provisions for measurement and evaluation to ensure ongoing feedback for improvements and modifications. While each of the phases has a direct bearing on the quality and costs of training, IBM has found that the key to cost-effectiveness is the method of delivery used. The company has begun to decentralize education through such job-site training systems as computer-based training, interactive videodisc with personal computer, and other self-study methods using workbooks or videos. Despite the often high development costs of the more advanced methods, some IBM divisions have cut costs by 25 to 50 percent and saved millions by closing educational centers and eliminating travel and living expenses.

Similar systematic approaches toward training, which link design and delivery methods to business and performance objectives, are described in two other case studies. The first involves the training of temporary word-processor operators with Manpower, Inc.'s SKILLWARE system, and the successful application of SKILLWARE at three major companies: Miller Brewing, Xerox, and Vista Chemical. The SKILLWARE disk-based computer program has helped Manpower to reduce training costs and, at the same time, assure the supply of highly qualified operators.

The second case illustrates a training program in place at a high-tech manufacturing facility of Travenol Laboratories, Inc. A major objective of the program was to develop a common vocabulary between the maintenance and production departments and ultimately cut maintenance costs. Results of the program are impressive: Direct cost savings amounted to $250,000, and the channels of communication between these two groups were strengthened due to the maintenance department's better understanding of financial and productivity-related issues and production's increased awareness of the technical functioning of equipment.

Cooperation with Community Colleges

A major consideration in the design and delivery of cost-effective training is whether to use in-house or outside expertise. More and more companies are forming training partnerships with community and junior colleges because they find that this arrangement is more cost-effective than training solely with in-house resources. This type of cooperation is likely to spread even further, as community colleges become increasingly flexible in terms of course schedules and locations. One particularly promising development has been the organization of consortia of community colleges, which join with one or more employers to conduct large-scale training programs. The largest reported consortium is General Motors' Automotive Service Educational Program (ASEP), described in Chapter Twenty. In place at thirty-nine colleges, this program provides training for technicians who will service General Motors automobiles, which increasingly are equipped with computer-controlled engines, braking systems, and transmissions.

Satellite Communications

Among the most exciting developments in the corporate educational field is the use of satellite communications to bring graduate-level engineering courses to the work site. With the high rate of obsolescence in the engineering field (now estimated to occur in five-year cycles—three and one-half for software-related areas), the need for continuing education of engineers is especially acute. Described in depth are the efforts of the National Technological University (NTU), a nonprofit group that links faculty members at some of the nation's leading universities to working engineers via a national satellite television network. The experiences of three principal NTU clients are examined: Hewlett-Packard, Digital Equipment Corporation, and Eastman Kodak.

17

Achieving Cost Savings and Quality Through Education: IBM's Systems Approach

Jill Casner-Lotto

IBM, the world's largest manufacturer of information systems, spends some $700 million annually to educate its employees in locations around the world; it employs approximately four thousand people who work full time within six major areas of education; and each year it delivers about five million student-days of education to its employees. As impressive as these numbers are, they only begin to tell the story of IBM's deep commitment to the education and growth of its employees. Equally important is the company's innovative approach to managing a dynamic educational process that, in recent years, has led to significant cost savings without sacrificing quality.

Known as the Systems Approach to Education, it actually encompasses several innovations that have been developed at IBM during the past ten to fifteen years. Three years ago, however, concurrent with the creation of a new corporate department of education, the various elements were combined in order to gain executive support and communicate the concepts and strategies throughout the corporation.

Basically, the approach consists of four major steps: (1) a detailed curriculum design for every major job category, based upon defined business requirements; (2) instructional design for each course; (3) course development led by an interdisciplinary professional development team; and (4) delivery of education through a variety of methods, ranging from the traditional classroom to more advanced technological means, such as computer-based training or interactive videodisc, combined with a personal computer. A fifth—but by no means a final—step is measurement and evaluation of training. These activities are not considered separately, since measurement of costs and effectiveness of training begins at step one, with curriculum design, and is built into the systems approach at each successive stage.

The simple philosophy behind IBM's systems approach is that "education can be managed like any other part of the business," notes Jack Bowsher, IBM's corporate director of education systems. In a presentation he made to the company's division presidents, Bowsher acknowledged that the resources for education are always in competition with the resources for new manufacturing facilities, new products, and new services. Education "is not something you do only if you have a profitable year," he states. "On the other hand, no company becomes the most profitable organization in the world by wasting money on 'nice to do' education programs. . . . This pressure to reduce the cost of education, plus the pressure to have education more available, has led to the many innovations covered under the Systems Approach to Education."

IBM's Emphasis on Education

IBM's varied product line includes information processing products and systems, telecommunications systems, office systems, typewriters, copiers, educational testing materials, and related supplies and services. Product excellence is equated with a well-trained work force. Though several corporations have only recently recognized the value of education and its link to corporate success, IBM's commitment is as old as the company itself.

The emphasis on education was originated and shaped by its founder, Thomas J. Watson, who became president of the company in 1914. Despite his own limited educational background—a high school diploma supplemented by some commercial business training—Watson believed that the profitability and growth of the corporation depended upon the knowledge and skills of its employees. Two quotations on education are attributed to him: "There is no saturation point in education" and "Progress today in business depends on education." He made the latter statement in 1933—in the midst of the Depression and declining revenues at IBM—the same year he built IBM's first education center in Endicott, New York, directly across from the corporation's only major manufacturing plant.

These same principles—that education is a necessity for growth and is a key to productivity, quality, and profitability—are very much a part of IBM's corporate culture today. Indeed, several of its model personnel policies would not be possible without a strong education and training program. Education is considered essential for maintaining IBM's practices of full employment and promotion from within. Additionally, the increasing pace of technological change in recent years has intensified the need for continuous retraining of IBM employees.

"Education is a given in our business," remarks William M. Ouweneel, a program manager in the Corporate Education Department. "The question here is never *if* we should train— it's *how* do we train?"

Why a Systems Approach to Education?

The ever-increasing demand for readily available, low-cost, yet consistently high-quality education is the prime factor behind the use of IBM's systems approach. "Every fifteen minutes (of education) must be outstanding" is one of the simply stated goals of IBM's Corporate Education Department. The major way to achieve that goal, says Bowsher, is through a process that ensures full instructional design and documentation, course development led by a professional team of experts, and selection of the most cost-effective delivery systems. Implementing the systems approach throughout the organization will take about five to ten years, Bowsher estimates. And certain elements of the approach are already being practiced in some divisions. "They may not know it as a systems approach to education," he says, "but the basic ideas and principles which the approach is based upon are gradually gaining acceptance."

Having a systems approach in place also helps to clarify and structure the educational process. While widening the range of choices available to educators, new delivery methods—particularly those based on state-of-the-art technology—have also made course design, development, and delivery an increasingly complicated process. It is a process that requires the talents not only of the instructor, who, in the past, might have been solely responsible for creating and teaching a course, but also of a team of highly trained educational specialists who must pool their energies and expertise. The systems approach breaks down that process into more manageable steps and facilitates careful decision making and budget planning at each stage.

"Recentralizing" Education

Communicating the systems approach, as well as IBM's general educational guidelines, is the job of the Corporate Education Department. Located at IBM's Management Development Center, in Armonk, New York, the department oversees the educational process, providing direction, consistency, tools, and guidance to the corporation's vast educational organization. There are six major areas of education, including technical education, which covers training of engineers, programmers, and manufacturing personnel; service education for IBM's customer engineers; marketing and product information for marketing representatives and systems engineers; finance and planning education; information and office systems education; and management development training. Each major area is headed by a director of education, who reports directly to a new corporate vice-president of education.

Education and training were centralized functions at IBM until the mid 1950s, when a strategic reorganization decentralized the business, including education. However, several forces have caused a gradual "recentralization" of educational systems, according to Bowsher. The need to "off-load" or convert centrally located classroom education to more available, site-based delivery methods required coordination of course development and delivery, as well as planning of education curricula. In addition, by the mid 1970s, there was no focal point of education on the corporate staff. "You had the potential of developing courses in at least twelve areas of education at more than 450 IBM locations," explains Bowsher. "That costs a lot of money, and there's bound to be a lot of redundancy, since many courses are repeated at various locations."

The challenge, he adds, is to provide some degree of consistency, or standardization, through the centralized development of courses and instructional materials, and then to deliver the education on a decentralized basis, adapting the curricula to meet the needs of a particular location. "Frankly, it is not easy to do, and most organizations never made it happen," Bowsher states.

Describing the Systems Approach

As noted earlier, the systems approach entails four major steps: curriculum design, instructional design, course development, and delivery. But to think of these as totally independent, consecutive stages misses the point. "Education is a dynamic process," states Ouweneel. "As soon as you start designing the curriculum, you're already considering the various delivery systems for specific courses. And once you've reached the course-development stage, the choices concerning delivery are becoming more finalized." Furthermore, measurement and evaluation are integrated within all four stages—particularly within curriculum design and course development—so that the results of evaluation offer continuous feedback for improvements and modifications.

Described below are the major steps in the process as well as the progress made and problems experienced along the way.

Curriculum Design. IBM's goal is to ensure that each job within the organization has a matching curriculum that clearly spells out the educational and training requirements needed at various points within the employee's career. Four specific levels are acknowledged:

1. Entry education for basic orientation.
2. Training on how to do the job.
3. Training that permits a person to grow within his or her job.
4. Advanced education that allows an individual to move into a job of greater responsibility. This step supports the practice of promotion from within.

Allowing flexibility in the curriculum design is important so that employees may tailor the educational program to meet personal needs.

A well-designed curriculum represents the "coordination of learning events," Ouweneel observes. "The challenge is not just knowing what employee skills are needed—but *when* they are needed. That's a key point." The design of curricula at IBM is based upon "people-performance" requirements that are outlined in the corporation's strategic business plan. Thus, educational objectives, from the start, are directly tied to business goals.

So far, detailed curricula exist for many major positions within the organization, including programmer, systems engineer, marketing representative, computer operator, and customer service representative. Still, Bowsher sees more work ahead, since there are many courses and curricula that are not always matched against the educational requirements of each job. Another area that needs work is the development of educational and training programs to facilitate the introduction of IBM's new products and services. "If executives are seeking a major directional change to support that product or service, the message on how to make that happen can be built into the educational system," Bowsher explains. "We couldn't possibly announce all the new products and services each year without the education programs to drive the messages on what to do." The Corporate Education Department is currently improving the needs-analysis procedures that determine the content of these programs. Bowsher cites four key issues to be considered when new products or services are announced:

Who must be aware?
What does the company want the employee to remember?
What references must be available?
What skills are required?

Instructional Design. A crucial step in IBM's systems approach, instructional design has the most direct impact on quality. With good instructional design and documentation, says Bowsher, "there will almost always be a high-quality course, no matter what delivery method is used." A relatively new field in the corporate educational environment, instructional design concentrates on the overall course objectives plus detailed teaching and learning points—that is, what motivates people to learn, how and why to design certain learning objectives, what makes lessons "stick" on the job, how to teach information faster and more effectively, and so on. Instructional designers are considered the "architects of education," providing the course structure and working closely with subject-matter experts who fill in the content. Instructional designers are also responsible for the design of workbooks and other instructional materials used throughout a course and for providing remedial lessons to students who need some review.

Course Development. So-called traditional course development—in which an instructor spends a few days creating a course—is a thing of the past in high-volume courses at IBM. That method has become obsolete, since courses often required several months or years of improvements by other instructors—a costly effort that was never really measured, Bowsher points out. Today, courses are developed by professional teams, reflecting the full spectrum of educational expertise. A professional development team usually includes a project manager, instructional designers, professional writers, audio/video specialists, print/

layout experts, and computer programmers and authors.

Bowsher recommends the use of a clearly outlined and simple management system to keep course development projects under control and to assure high-quality courses developed on time and within budget. A typical management system might include the following phases:

- Needs analysis and requirements
- Design of course
- Development
- Validation test prior to production
- Production of course materials
- Pilot classes
- Reproduction of materials
- Training of the trainers
- Evaluation and enhancement

The important point, Bowsher stresses, is not the number of phases in the system, but having the system itself—and keeping it simple so that all levels of management can understand it.

Up until ten years ago, IBM relied strictly on company professionals to design and develop courses. Now, while subject-matter experts are almost always company employees, both outside education development companies and in-house personnel are called upon to develop courses, depending upon the volume of work required. "If we're dealing with especially large volume, it pays to have the job done on the outside. It just makes better business sense," says Ouweneel. He adds that the hiring of outside companies for big assignments is not unique to the education department but is commonly practiced in many areas of IBM.

Nonetheless, maintaining a highly talented, well-trained inner core of professional educators is crucial, and one of IBM's goals for education is to develop more specialists in a variety of fields, including instructional design, audio and video, writing, authoring, layout, and project management. "The key message is that if the company education department is going to do this type of work, it must have talented people with creative management, because that is what you buy with outside education development companies," Bowsher states.

Delivery of Education. IBM officials point to the delivery
system as the key to achieving cost-effectiveness in education.
The push to decentralize the delivery of education through advanced technological systems such as on-site video/computer systems or interactive television is a relatively recent phenomenon.
In fact, despite the new technology, about 75 to 80 percent of all
education at IBM today is still conducted within the traditional
classroom. Nevertheless, education that is readily available at
or near the employee's work site, as opposed to a centralized
educational facility, is clearly the wave of the future at IBM.
Bowsher estimates that over the next ten years, about half of
the company's education and training will take place in the
classroom, and half will be delivered by "student-driven, learn-
ing-center-based" systems—mainly, computer-based training,
interactive videodisc with personal computer, or other self-study
methods, using either workbooks or videos.

In an undated publication entitled "Systems Approach
to Education at IBM," Bowsher provides an excellent overview
of the various delivery systems in use at IBM and their major
educational characteristics.

• *Traditional classroom.* This proven method is usually used
when there is a low-volume course or the course material changes
frequently. Courses requiring a great deal of discussion, such
as case studies, also use the traditional classroom.

• *Multimedia classroom.* Classrooms were designed around
1970 that have rear-screen projection for slides, foils, movies,
videotapes, audio tapes, and so on, and that permit the lights
to remain on while the instructor uses a mixture of media. The
instructor teaches at the "executive presentation pace," using
handouts rather than expecting the students to take notes. The
result is more instruction per hour, with a higher retention level,
plus a very motivational class environment. Research is currently being conducted on the use of personal computers with
keypads to provide instant feedback on the level of training.

• *Tutored video classroom.* The expert is either on videotape
or is being taped as he or she teaches. The students are in remote
classrooms with a tutor who helps to facilitate the class, including
questions and answers. This is a proven method when it is not
feasible to have the master teacher in every classroom.

- *Interactive television classroom.* The master teacher is in a studio or classroom. The students are in remote classrooms (a few feet away or hundreds of miles away) watching one or two monitors. The students are able to ask questions, and all students hear the answer from the master teacher. This approach is more expensive than the tutored video classroom, but the students are in direct contact with the master teacher.

- *Self-study.* The course materials usually consist of workbooks, videotapes or videodiscs, and possibly audio tapes. There may also be local computer exercises. There is no instructor, which makes this an inexpensive delivery system, but some form of monitoring, such as computer-managed instruction, is required to be certain the students spend a sufficient amount of time to really learn the lessons of the course.

- *Guided Learning Center.* This is supervised self-study. The students go to an IBM Guided Learning Center, which will have from six to thirty study areas. Here they receive a new module of the course each hour. Most of the learning takes place within the workbook. The videodisc and the computer exercises provide motivation and reinforcement. Again, there is no instructor.

- *Computer-based training (CBT).* The students will use either a personal computer or a terminal connected to a large remote computer. There is no instructor, which makes for an inexpensive delivery system. CBT and self-study courses are often prerequisites to classroom courses. The facts are taught with self-study or CBT, and the lessons are applied in the classroom.

- *Interactive videodisc with personal computer.* Research projects are currently using this system, because it has the cost advantage of no instructor plus the advantage of video, in addition to the full power of a personal computer. The students must learn chapter one before they go on to chapter two. There are many exercises to test the learning, and remedial teaching is available if the students do not do well with exercises. The system is very motivational. The system provides individual learning and is easily available on a local basis.

A key strategy to reduce costs and increase accessibility is to off-load large-volume classroom courses to self-study, computer-based training, or interactive videodisc training. Despite the steep up-front development costs, company officials believe the benefits far outweigh the costs. Some divisions within IBM have off-loaded 50 percent of their courses and cut costs by 25 to 50 percent, mainly by closing educational centers and eliminating travel and living expenses. Bowsher sees the potential for off-loading 50 to 60 percent of all student days.

IBM has carefully itemized the costs of education, including planning, delivery, travel, and living expenses. Based on these factors, three average figures are cited to reflect the cost of IBM's educational programs: $50 per day for self-study, computer-based training, or interactive videodisc training; $150 per day for classroom education within commuting distance from home; and $300 per day for classroom education at a centralized training facility.

Another advantage of the newer delivery systems is that the same amount of learning can occur in less time, with some courses reduced to half the length of the classroom version. In general, IBM estimates that learning occurs 25 percent faster with the new delivery methods and is equally effective as traditional classroom education. "At $50 a day per student, this is a cost and productivity breakthrough," Bowsher states.

None of this means, however, that the classroom has become obsolete. On the contrary, self-study modes combined with classroom learning often provide the most appropriate training. "Just about any subject matter contains certain basic information—documented facts and theories—which can easily be put into some kind of self-study or computer-based training," Bowsher notes. "But how that information or those theories are applied is best taught in the classroom, where interaction and guidance are provided by an instructor." For example, a marketing course on the "logical selling process" is offered through self-study, but how that process relates to IBM's most recent product can only be taught in the classroom. Similarly, typical customer-service questions can easily be learned by sitting in front of the computer. Actual practice in responding to questions, however, takes place in group role-playing sessions.

The self-study/classroom combination actually enhances the role of the instructor, since students often ask better and more challenging questions in class once they have absorbed the basic facts through a self-study course. IBM is currently designing a training and development curriculum for instructors, which includes about fifty modules to improve instructional effectiveness. "Today's instructor is much more than a dispenser of education; he or she is an active manager of the learning process," observes Ouweneel.

Measurement and Evaluation. Four sources of data are considered in the evaluation process: (1) post-training surveys to determine reactions of trainees, (2) knowledge and skill tests administered before and after training, (3) interviews with trainees and observations on the job to determine the application of training in the workplace, and (4) impact on business results. Not all courses are easily measured and evaluated, and Bowsher believes not enough has been done in measurement. It is particularly difficult to measure the effects of training on the business. However, IBM is making headway in certain job categories that have established performance standards. For example, the effectiveness of training for IBM's customer service engineers can be measured by considering the amount of time it takes to repair machines in customer locations and the period of time the equipment remains maintenance-free.

While training department managers are primarily responsible for evaluation, the line manager plays a key role in this function. Without the right "climate of expectations" to facilitate the student's use of training on the job, says Ouweneel, the training may be worthless. Training departments work closely with line managers, either by providing guidance on ways to apply training or by making sure the managers are trained in the same techniques as the trainees so that they are able to judge whether or not the training is being practiced on the job. "We listen a great deal to our line managers," Bowsher adds.

The Systems Approach in Action: IBM's National Service Division

IBM's customer service engineers are responsible for the installation, maintenance, and repair of the company's products.

"Their training needs to be outstanding because no one else can fix the machine or program," says Bowsher. Nowhere is the systems approach more evident than in IBM's National Service Division, headquartered in Franklin Lakes, New Jersey. Mike Negrelli, manager for education planning and operations, says the division has used a systems approach to education for the past twenty years and explains why: "The biggest advantage is that a systems approach ensures a standardization of course quality because of its various checks and balances, such as job task analysis and measurement techniques, which can be reviewed by management," says Negrelli. "Thus, no matter in what geographic location the course is offered, similar patterns of quality are repeated."

The National Service Division offers more than 400 computer-based training courses and many self-study and classroom programs. On average, each year customer engineers receive eight days of computer-based or some other form of self-study training, plus eight days of classroom education. Typically, entry-level employees have a two-year technical degree from a community college or equivalent technical training and experience. Thus, customer service education consists basically of applied technical knowledge. Curricula are designed directly around IBM products, covering such subjects as installation, maintenance and repair, troubleshooting, writing and analysis of diagnostic reports, and upgrading equipment.

The education department constantly off-loads classroom courses by phasing in the lecture portion to a computer-based mode. Over the years, several educational centers have been closed, reducing classroom, living, and travel costs substantially. Two major training facilities have been retained, however— one in Chicago and one in Atlanta. According to Negrelli, the more complex a product, the greater the need for some hands-on instruction, conducted in a laboratory or classroom situation. "The training is complete only after students show they can assemble, take apart, troubleshoot, and repair equipment under the guidance of lab instructors who are experts in the products," he explains.

The availability of computer-based education for the factual material, however, enhances training in several ways. The service division operates a computer-based training network, with all the courses stored in a mainframe computer. Thus, students at any of the branch offices can take a course simply by signing on to the network and interacting with the mainframe computer.

No critical mass of students is needed to justify a course offering—one or more people could take a computer-based course at any time. The computer system can be geared to accommodate either the slow or fast learner, since many of the computer training programs are self-paced, featuring quizzes to test knowledge and remedial exercises to correct problems. Another important advantage, Negrelli adds, is that the trainee spends less time away from the job. "You don't lose people's services on the job the way you would if they were trained in the classroom. A person might work six hours and take two hours of a computer-based course or even work four hours and take four hours of training, thus allowing for the continuity of work responsibilities," he points out.

Computer-based training does require a higher level of skill to develop course programs when compared to classroom delivery or instruction, Negrelli believes, and it also demands a greater degree of creativity to maintain student interest. Having a systems approach provides a framework for addressing the more complex aspects of developing computer-based training. "Based on our tests of trainees, the quality and effectiveness of learning with computer-based courses is equal to that of classroom education," he says. Those who complete computer-based training are also found to perform as well and, in some cases, to retain material longer.

As part of the systems approach, evaluation is an ongoing process. It consists of various techniques to measure training effectiveness: pilot testing of new programs and reworking of courses; skill- and knowledge-based performance tests, with the results compared against performance standards defined by the original course objectives; interviews with trainees; and posttraining surveys. Supervisors of trainees cooperate with the training department in monitoring the application of training on the job.

In general, Negrelli finds no disadvantages to using a systems approach. Though it takes time and resources to train course developers in the various steps and in how best to implement the approach, "we don't think of that as a disadvantage—in fact, doing it in a less disciplined way would be considered a disadvantage because of the impact of poorly designed training on the organization," Negrelli adds, citing high costs and poor job performance.

Concluding Thoughts

When Jack Bowsher explains IBM's Systems Approach to Education to other companies, he often gets a standard reaction: "What you're doing is unique to IBM—IBM is high-tech and profitable. We simply couldn't afford such an elaborate systems approach." To Bowsher, however, quite the opposite is true. "What we're doing is not unique to IBM at all. It can be applied in any organization that has people who need training," he says. As to the high costs involved in developing and carrying out the systems approach, Bowsher points to the millions saved through off-loading classroom courses, the consistent quality reflected in its courses, and the fact that minimum time is spent on each course. On the other hand, the greatest cost to any company, Bowsher believes, is an "employee not fully trained to do an outstanding job."

"Our biggest challenge is managing through a change process," he says. Education is changing and no longer consists simply of classroom lectures, notes, and tests. Getting that message across is not always easy. "People don't immediately embrace changes," Bowsher adds.

Nevertheless, there are signs that the systems approach—with all the changes and innovations it brings to the educational process—is taking hold. Eight months after they were hired, IBM trainees who were college graduates were asked to compare the learning environment of their universities with that of IBM. The majority said they found the IBM system more structured and challenging. The fact that there were choices available in the methods of learning—classroom, self-study, interactive television, computer-based training—was an important reason for their preference. Bowsher believes there is another underlying factor. "Our system communicates the message 'We want you to learn,' as opposed to 'You better not fail,' which, unfortunately, does prevail in many schools and universities. Once we take people in, we don't want them to fail and our system is geared to that," he states.

Among IBM's top executives, the systems approach is finding favor as well. What is especially impressive, says Bowsher, is that "we're not just talking about theories. We've had in-depth experience with just about every major delivery system. We're measuring the cost of education. We can point to a piece of the business that is actually doing these things and is getting results."

18

Manpower Temporary Services: Keeping Ahead of the Competition

Sandra Kessler Hamburg

In 1981, Mitchell S. Fromstein, president of Manpower, Inc., the world's largest supplier of temporary office workers, realized that the high-tech office revolution posed a significant threat to the viability of Manpower's product in the marketplace. The more complex automated office equipment becomes, the less inclined companies may be to use temporary workers who have not been specifically trained to operate their in-house word-processing or other computer equipment.

For Fromstein, the key question was "How are we going to supply ourselves with good workers in a high-technology society?" He sees the answer in plain terms: "If we can't produce that type of worker, we'll go out of business." Fromstein's—and Manpower's—response was to make a major strategic investment in training and state-of-the-art office equipment in order to keep Manpower's customers supplied with people who were up to date on the skills needed to operate a full range of word processors or other computer equipment.

271

Not long ago, the typical secretary or typist could jump from one brand of electric typewriter to another with little loss of efficiency or skill. The proliferation of dedicated word processors, personal computers, and the like has significantly altered that situation. A secretary or typist walking into a new office cannot be expected to flip the *on* button, roll in a fresh sheet of letterhead, and go. Each work station or electronic typewriter requires a significant amount of training investment before an operator is proficient enough to work independently.

Many large or even small companies are understandably reluctant to have a temporary worker fill in for a vacationing secretary if that person needs to be trained on special equipment. Many companies would rather make do with existing personnel than go through the time and expense of training someone who would need greater supervision and would not be there long enough to make that training pay off.

Another problem for Manpower is that a significant proportion of its work force is made up of women returning to the labor pool after having raised families. These somewhat older re-entry workers are often prone to ''technology phobia,'' the fear that learning to master a complicated computer terminal is an impossibility. For many of them, the most electronically advanced piece of office equipment they were likely to have last come into contact with was an IBM Correcting Selectric typewriter.

General Background

In a typical year, Manpower's 1,350 offices in thirty-three countries employ approximately 700,000 people on a temporary basis to provide short-term support to over 300,000 business firms worldwide. Each year, Manpower interviews and tests over 1,500,000 potential temporary workers. By its very nature, temporary work is short term. Manpower's turnover rate—like that of other temporary-help firms—is as high as 35 percent a year.

With such a large and constantly changing pool of human resources, Fromstein saw that drastic steps had to be taken to preserve Manpower's market. But he also saw that what might be a threat could also be an opportunity for Manpower to take the lead in the office-temporary business.

Like any business, Manpower needs to be able to respond to the market. It has to have a product customers want. It needs a reputation for credibility and reliability. Most of all, it needs to keep an eye on changes in the market. "Office automation surfaced over six years ago in our strategic planning. When we realized what was going to happen, it made our blood run cold. We were sitting there with a work force of close to a million, and the closest most of them came to office automation was an electric typewriter," Fromstein said.

The obvious answer to Manpower's problem of keeping its work force up to date was providing training on automated office equipment. Unfortunately, the more obvious training solutions, which might include classroom sessions or vendor-supplied manuals, would not be cost-effective or time-efficient for Manpower. According to Fromstein, "the investment in training needed to be amortized over a short period of time," largely because of Manpower's high turnover rate and fluid employment roster. In regard to costs, Manpower faced two choices: either the cost had to be absorbable or the trainees had to pay for their training. Manpower, as a matter of policy, ruled out the latter solution. The costs of training, it decided, would have to be kept to a minimum.

Traditional training solutions were rejected as too time consuming, too expensive, and too technical. Among the training strategies Manpower considered were traditional classroom settings using Manpower trainers, vendor-sponsored classes, vendor-supplied manuals, and the buddy system of learning, but all of these proved inefficient, ineffective, and much too costly.

Fromstein estimates that Manpower is now spending in excess of $100 per person for training. He hopes that in several years that cost can be brought down to about $35 per person, as the costs of equipment and research and development are amortized. However, if major purchases of new equipment are made in the future, costs may remain near the current level.

"But even at $100 per person," Fromstein says, "this training cost is substantially lower than any teacher-driven classroom environment."

What Is SKILLWARE?

The disappointment with traditional training approaches led Manpower to develop its own unique training system, called SKILLWARE.

SKILLWARE is a disk-based training method, which involves no teachers, classrooms, or technical manuals. For each new piece of office equipment or software package—such as Lotus 1-2-3—Manpower's in-house group of specialists, headed by Melanie Cosgrove Holmes, director of Manpower's Special Projects Group, develops a new SKILLWARE diskette.

SKILLWARE is specific to each type of equipment and is used only on that equipment. Trainees are led through each step of a word-processing program on the actual equipment they can expect to find in an office. One of SKILLWARE's great strengths is that it is a real-life document—rather than a computer program—that allows operators to make mistakes and learn from their errors. "To our knowledge, Manpower is the only temporary-help firm that is utilizing the actual equipment—personal computers, dedicated word processors, and multifunction, multiuser computer systems—as the trainer, rather than applying any kind of simulation system," says Sharon Canter, information specialist. "We also have the only training system that takes a novice every step of the way, from disk insertion through printing a document. The companies using simulators omit this last step, which we feel is crucial," she adds.

SKILLWARE leads the trainee through the basic and more advanced word-processing functions in step-by-step fashion, using operator-to-operator language. Holmes notes that one of the defects of most vendor-supplied training manuals is the "technospeak" generally used and the unnecessary technical detail built into most manuals. "Vendors assume a certain amount of technical expertise on the part of computer operators. Most operators, however, are not technically adept. Neither is it important for them to know technical data or how to service the machines. The only important criterion is whether an operator can sit down at a terminal and create, edit, and print a document," Holmes adds.

SKILLWARE lessons are grouped according to activity, such as cursor movement, centering and underlining, word wrap, indenting, tab setting, global search, and so on. Each step builds upon previous information and, as the program proceeds, there is less and less prompting for simple tasks, such as the need to press *enter* to complete a function.

The training diskettes are leavened with humor, both to break up any monotony that might ensue from spending six straight hours at a terminal and to reinforce concepts. While SKILLWARE developer Holmes admits that the humor can sometimes get corny, trainees consistently note that it adds appeal to the program and keeps their attention at a high level. Each lesson ends with a summary and a quiz or, sometimes, an additional practice exercise.

Time Effectiveness

SKILLWARE provides two major advantages over classroom training. It is self-paced. Trainees can complete a course in as little as six hours or as much as two days, depending on their level of expertise and familiarity with automated equipment. Each SKILLWARE diskette is similar. Trainees tend to spend less and less time with each new training diskette as they train on different equipment or software packages. The similarity allows them to skip over those areas that tend not to vary from word processor to word processor. The more different programs they work on, the faster they tend to complete them.

SKILLWARE requires no third-party instructor, although each site has a facilitator who is accessible to trainees to answer any questions that might arise. Trainees can therefore start and finish the training on their own schedule, depending only on availability of equipment at different Manpower office sites. Trainees like this flexibility. They can also brush up if need be without interrupting the flow of others' progress, and they gain a sense of control over the learning process. Fromstein considers this essential for a successful training program. "Most Manpower employees have been out of the classroom for years, perhaps decades. They tend to be uncomfortable in a classroom setting and prefer the interactive software," Fromstein says.

SKILLWARE is also a hands-on learning experience. Each operator sits at his or her own terminal and creates a document, from blank screen to printed page. The end-program quiz for trainees requires them to write a letter to Mitchell Fromstein about their experiences with SKILLWARE. Reactions run the gamut from that of a housewife returning to work after a hiatus of decades who is astonished at her facility with word processing to the pleasant surprise of a Xerox sales manager who learned the skills he needed with SKILLWARE to enable him to talk knowledgeably to his work-station customers.

Not only do these letters provide an important sense of accomplishment for the trainees, they also represent valuable feedback for the company. According to Canter, "these letters have at times been used to make improvements in the training system."

The first SKILLWARE training appeared in 1983, backed by a $5 million investment in research, development, and equipment. The first diskettes were developed for the popular dedicated word processors sold by IBM, Wang, Xerox, Digital Equipment, NBI, CPTK, Lanier, and Micom. Subsequent SKILLWARE has been designed for the IBM 5520 Shared Logic System and a variety of software for the IBM PC, including Lotus 1-2-3, Visicalc, Multimate, DisplayWrite 2 and 3, Wordstar 2000, and dBase III. In addition to English, SKILLWARE has been translated into French, Spanish, German, Danish, Norwegian, and Dutch, for Manpower's international offices. It is also in the process of being translated into Hebrew.

Manpower's latest large-scale investment is in the IBM System/36 equipment and the SKILLWARE to go with it. Fromstein has called this commitment "a major move to the next rung on the ladder." Manpower strongly feels that the System/36 will soon become a major force in office automation, and the company wants to be prepared by providing experienced operators. The System/36 has as many as nineteen optional keyboards, he pointed out, and three or four for word processing alone. He has equipped the Manpower offices with three of those keyboards so far.

Manpower is also guarding its investment in training against skill decay through post-training support. Recognizing that its employees don't always get the opportunity to utilize their training right away on the job, Manpower has developed small, colorful, pocket-sized operator support manuals for each piece of hardware and software on which Manpower trains. As employees finish training, they receive a manual that can then become part of their personal library. When a word-processing job comes up on equipment that an operator has been trained for, the Manpower employee can brush up on his or her skills using the minimanual and take it to the job for quick and easy reference. The manuals use everyday language and reproduce in print the screens of the SKILLWARE training.

In addition to providing the manuals, Manpower also allows its employees to come in at any time to brush up with the SKILLWARE itself.

Fromstein notes that the operator-to-operator language in which both the SKILLWARE diskettes and the operator support manuals are written is an essential element in the success of the training system. According to Fromstein, "The communication gap between managers and end users of automated office equipment is the biggest stumbling block to the productive use of that equipment. Most training is directed at top management by systems people." However, he adds, most of the equipment is subject to "task migration. As soon as the manager understands how to use the equipment day to day, its actual use generally falls to a staff person."

SKILLWARE diskettes are also used for "cross-training" purposes for operators who already know how to operate one piece of equipment and who want to learn additional systems. Because Manpower offers training opportunities on such a wide range of hardware and software, about one-half of the operators who come to the company already have some experience on equipment or software and are looking to broaden their repertoire of skills through Manpower's training.

Assessing the Skills of Experienced Operators

In addition to developing its own skilled operators through SKILLWARE training, Manpower also needs to critically assess the clerical and mechanical skills of those who come to the company with prior experience so that they can be properly assigned and placed. As a result, Manpower devised the first office automation selection system of its type—and it does just that.

Called ULTRASKILL, this hands-on test evaluates an operator's skills on any word processor and word-processing software for the personal computer. ULTRASKILL measures an operator's ability to create an actual document in an office environment.

According to Fromstein, "The only true method of testing lies in assessing an operator's ability to apply skills and knowledge to a realistic work sample. Measuring automation skills is more than measuring the ability to do a number of separate tasks. The evaluation must include a measure of how well an individual performs those tasks as a complete unit in a job-related situation."

ULTRASKILL requires the applicant to create a document from a handwritten rough draft or from dictation, edit it, and print it. The finished product must be a perfect final copy. Although speed is measured in terms of total document production time, Manpower has found that for the productive operation of automated office equipment, the word-per-minute measurement of traditional typing tests no longer provides a relevant assessment. Among the many skills that have emerged as critical in the operation of this new technology is the ability to proofread accurately and to correct errors.

Manpower introduced ULTRASKILL after an extensive research and development project, which spanned several years and involved testing 600 full-time operators at 120 firms in thirty-seven cities and three countries. Scores of word-processing supervisors were also interviewed. Results, compiled over a three-year period, were statistically analyzed to establish standards and cut-off scores based on the performance of permanent, full-time operators.

ULTRASKILL is the only test in the field that is statistically valid, as defined by the Equal Employment Opportunity Commission and the American Psychological Association. The extensive validation process was crucial to ensure that ULTRASKILL actually measured those skills needed to operate word-processing equipment.

The need for testing office-automation skills has grown dramatically. A survey commissioned by Manpower revealed that 12 percent of the *Fortune* 1000 companies currently test for automated keyboard skills. However, nearly three times as many expect to be testing for those skills within the next year.

Until now, Fromstein noted, a comprehensive method of testing for automation skills did not exist. "Even the largest, most prestigious employer did not have a satisfactory method for testing permanent employees. The high degree of interest among the major companies who participated in the validation of ULTRASKILL demonstrated a critical need for such a test," Fromstein said. The test measures thirty individual skills, using a single sample of work that can be done on any piece of equipment. Not only does ULTRASKILL measure automated mechanical skills, but it also assesses the important clerical skills. "Although the sophistication and complexity of the hardware have received the attention, it's the basics that are essential when talking about operator skills. ULTRASKILL is the only test that assesses the basic clerical skills as they relate to automation," says Fromstein.

Eight clerical skills are individually measured. "Automation has created a different order of priority in the clerical skills required to create a perfect document," Fromstein explains. Proofreading and the ability to follow format patterns have emerged as critical and are now being assessed by a testing instrument for the first time. In addition, spelling, punctuation, following instructions, editing, machine transcription, and speed are measured.

The test identifies the specific clerical weaknesses that can affect an operator's productivity. Once deficiencies are pinpointed, Manpower uses brush-up programs that it has developed, called skill development modules, to correct the problems.

In this way, operators have an opportunity to improve in the specific areas in which they demonstrate weak skills.

ULTRASKILL is used in conjunction with Manpower's recognition and proficiency tests, which assess a person's knowledge of functions on the most popular word processors. "In using a comprehensive battery to measure both skills and knowledge, we've applied the most professional testing principles to our approach," Fromstein says. The two-pronged evaluation system is used, along with a specially designed interview that identifies elements unique to the automated office. This sophisticated system for precise matchmaking is so successful that it is now being translated for use in the company's 1,350 offices in thirty-three countries. The largest firm in the temporary-help field, Manpower sales approached the $2 billion mark in fiscal 1986–87.

Building a Unique Relationship with Corporate Clients

Manpower's SKILLWARE training system is considered so unique that many companies have enlisted Manpower's help in solving their own in-house training problems. Following are the stories of three of these companies—Miller Brewing Company, Xerox Corporation, and Vista Chemical Company—that have worked successfully with Manpower to develop specific applications of SKILLWARE for their unique training needs.

Miller Brewing Company. According to Thomas J. Waller, director of export sales, Miller Brewing Company decided "to bring itself into the modern age with respect to information processing" by installing the IBM System/36 in its field sales offices. Waller, who at the time was manager of corporate sales administration for the Milwaukee-based brewery, comments that "the beer business overflows with an incredible amount of information." According to Waller, Miller's twin goals were to make that mountain of information usable both to the company and its sales staff and to find more productive in-field time for its regional sales people.

"Beer is a street-intensive business," Waller says, "with battles won or lost in the street by making retailers and consumers more aware of the product. Miller recognized that it needed to increase the ability of its field sales people to report information back to the sales office, without becoming bogged down with paperwork and taking time away from selling beer.''

In addition to facilitating more in-field time, the second objective of computerizing the sales operation was to deal more productively overall with information on sales and marketing, and not just rely on electric typewriters.

Miller found some hesitancy among field office staff in regard to word processing and automation, according to Waller. ''We got the backlash of 'Oh, I'll never learn that high-tech stuff.''' Despite this resistance, it was obvious to Miller that they needed to overcome the sales staff's initial reluctance in order to ensure the company's long-range competitive position. Waller acted as project facilitator and liaison between the ''MIS [management information systems] technocrats and the sales office staffs.'' The close involvement of the sales group with the MIS group provided a sense of urgency for the project.

Waller's main problem, in addition to overcoming the reluctance of the sales people to ''the high-tech stuff,'' was to put the new computer system into operation fast. ''We were looking for a hybrid way to get where we needed to be. We couldn't take eighteen months to do this. We didn't have the luxury of taking the sales offices off-line and bringing them into corporate headquarters for training. We would have to force-feed the training if necessary.''

Miller structured the training to take place in the field offices with IBM people. The training seminar for each office was scheduled for two and a half days. Manpower provided its SKILLWARE training to about half of the Miller field sales offices.

The Manpower SKILLWARE system was brought to Waller's attention by one of the people in Miller's MIS department. He had recalled it as being very user-friendly and highly interactive. He felt it would disarm the fear of technology harbored by many of the field staff.

At the field offices where SKILLWARE was used, the Manpower training took place before the in-house training and was coordinated with the local Manpower office. A hot line was set up to connect the Miller sales office and the local Manpower office so that any questions that came up could be answered right away.

As far as return on investment is concerned, Waller concedes that it will take time to evaluate how much the SKILL-WARE training may have saved Miller. However, Waller adds that "the group of sales people who went through the Manpower training seemed to get more out of the in-house training. Without qualification, Manpower's SKILLWARE added value to the training."

Both Waller and Manpower see the arrangement as mutually beneficial. From Miller's point of view, Manpower overextended itself to help them out of a problematic situation. As for Manpower, it has established a special relationship between itself and each of Miller's field sales offices; most likely, it would now be a top choice for supplying temporary operators for the IBM equipment Miller uses.

Manpower's Fromstein concurs: "What we get out of these special arrangements with corporate clients is a great deal of good will. Because of their positive experience with our SKILL-WARE, they are more likely to use Manpower when they have a temporary position to fill."

Xerox Corporation. Perhaps the most surprising relationship Manpower has established is with the Xerox Corporation, one of the world's leading manufacturers of automated office equipment.

Two years ago, Xerox faced a training problem in the marketing of its new Xerox 860 word-processor work stations. According to Lee Klepinger, manager of system sales training, Xerox already had a small, trained work force dedicated to marketing the 860. But the company realized that if it were to grow, it would have to engage its entire general line sales force to market this and subsequent office automation products. This meant reorienting 4,000 sales people who were for the most part total novices in the word-processing field, to enable them to sell work stations and other automated equipment in addition to the copiers they were used to marketing.

Like Miller Brewing, Xerox needed to minimize the time its sales people were out of the field and in a classroom. In addition, it wanted to complete the entire training process in less than two months.

Klepinger notes that its eventual team-up with Manpower was "something of a fluke." He had seen an article in one of the computer magazines with a quote from Fromstein. Caught in a time bind, Klepinger decided to call Manpower, which "was kind enough to share the technology" with Xerox. Klepinger was attracted to Manpower's SKILLWARE because it was "instructor proof" and had "excellent documentation for students and instructors alike."

The Xerox training program was arranged in three tiers, eventually involving its entire sales force. The initial training sessions involved twenty-eight Xerox trainers who went to the company's main training facility in Leesburg, Virginia, to learn from the Manpower team how to act as SKILLWARE facilitators. Manpower's Fromstein took part in this initial training phase.

Each regional trainer went to his or her respective region, and from then on only Xerox personnel were involved in the training program. The complete training program took place during the spring and summer of 1984.

The feedback from the Xerox regional managers and sales force was entirely positive. According to Klepinger, SKILLWARE "made the instructors feel like pros and the pupils feel as though they could master the equipment." Klepinger claims that the SKILLWARE training helped lay the foundation for the subsequent introduction of a whole series of products, including new keyboards, document management software, and word-processing software. Reaction to SKILLWARE was that it provided positive feedback, high personal involvement, and a creative approach and was fun. SKILLWARE developer Holmes, who helped facilitate the initial training phase, notes that the reaction Manpower received from sales managers was general "amazement that they have created and printed a letter."

Holmes notes that Manpower is using the diskette-based training as a means to leverage business. She says, "We use it to get higher visibility among companies we don't normally do business with and use it to increase business with our regular customers. Xerox understands that there is someone who can supply well-trained workers, and that's a plus for Manpower.'' Klepinger agrees that Manpower achieved its objective with Xerox, noting that Manpower derived excellent public relations and increased visibility, and received ''tremendous goodwill'' from its endeavor. ''Every Xerox sales representative talking to clients had positive things to say about Manpower,'' Klepinger notes.

Vista Chemical. Symbiotic is the word that best describes Manpower's relationship with Vista Chemical Company. Headquartered in Houston, Vista was formed when an investment group led by key managers of Conoco Chemicals bought that company's assets in a leveraged buyout from Du Pont. According to Cheryl Parker, the systems administrator responsible for training for Vista's Houston headquarters, four regional sales offices, and seven plants, Manpower made the right sales pitch at just the right time—when she was searching for a more cost-effective and time-efficient method of training Vista's employees as word-processor and work-station operators.

For Manpower, persistence paid off. The sales representative for Manpower in Houston had tried unsuccessfully for about a year to court Vista as a large-scale customer for Manpower's services. According to Parker, Vista had been reluctant to change temporary services because it wasn't worth the time or trouble it took to train word-processing operators.

However, when Manpower unveiled its SKILLWARE diskette for the IBM 5520 in late 1984, it felt that it had more to offer Vista, which had recently installed the system in its Houston headquarters. With a large number of work stations, Manpower reasoned, Vista would always need trained people, and Manpower now had the means to train them. Vista also utilizes IBM Displaywriter and Xerox 860 word processors, for which Manpower had already developed SKILLWARE.

The confluence of needs did not end there. Manpower did not have a 5520 set-up in its Houston office, primarily because it was too expensive a system for Manpower to install in its local offices. Parker suggested that Vista and Manpower try to cross-train their employees. Manpower would train Vista's new or current employees with SKILLWARE at Vista's office and, in exchange, Vista would allow Manpower the use of its 5520 system so that Manpower could train its temporary workers.

This arrangement provided clear benefits for both parties. Previously Parker would have had to set aside three or four days of her own time for one-on-one training with a new employee. In addition to the expenditure of time, Parker was also frustrated by the highly technical manuals that she would have had to pore through during the training process to cull the relevant material for her employees. With Manpower doing the training, Parker's time was freed up considerably. Although she generally would remain in the office to be available to answer any questions that were specific to the way Vista's internal systems work, she found that she could plan and coordinate her employees' training better.

As the relationship developed, Vista integrated Manpower's SKILLWARE into their permanent training system. Today, whenever Vista needs to train a permanent employee, Claudette Hilliard of Manpower's Houston office brings the SKILLWARE to the Vista site. In exchange, when Vista does not have new hires, it provides computer time on the 5520 system for Manpower to use to train its own employees.

This positive experience has led to an expanded role for Manpower in filling Vista's personnel needs. Whenever Vista needs a trained word-processor operator, Manpower gets first priority in fulfilling the request. Parker notes that "word processing is easy to bluff. They can use buzz words and convince you they know how to operate a machine." But by using Manpower, Parker does not have to worry about being sent a temporary worker who isn't adequately trained. She says that "every time we've called Manpower and said we needed an intermediate or advanced word-processor operator, each of their people has met the qualifications." As a result, Manpower receives first call on requests for temporary workers from Vista and has become Vista's primary supplier of trained temporary personnel.

The Vista-Manpower relationship in Houston has broadened to include other Vista offices around the country. In the past, Parker often had to travel long distances to one of the many Vista regional sales offices whose training needs she is responsible for. She now has a "nice network" of local Manpower offices around the country which she can call on to take care of her training needs in many localities.

One of the features of Manpower's training system that Parker is most impressed with is the operator support manuals Manpower supplies to each Vista employee trained on SKILL-WARE. She finds them "great for quickie questions" and accurate for the most part; in addition, they usually are more up to date than the vendor-supplied technical manuals.

Parker is clearly enthusiastic about Manpower's SKILL-WARE. If she had to, Parker would willingly pay for the training services, noting that it is not unusual to spend between $400 and $700 to train a single employee. Manpower's system—and the arrangement it maintains with Vista—eliminates that expense and also provides the flexibility to train employees thoroughly and inexpensively.

Vista also took part in the validation of Manpower's Recognition and Proficiency Test for the IBM 5520. Parker served as a member of Manpower's expert panel, which helps to design, select, and review test questions.

Manpower's Future

Manpower recently entered its first formal venture in the training field. Through an agreement with IBM, Manpower provides its training capability to support IBM's marketing effort for the System/36, System/38, and 9370 computers. SKILL-WARE training is provided to the permanent employees of IBM customers at customer sites. The portability of SKILLWARE makes it ideal for this purpose.

Manpower's Fromstein, however, still sees the future in terms of supplying highly trained temporary office workers to business. In entering the agreement with IBM, Manpower was not looking for training revenue, but for further strengthening of its core business of supplying temporary help. It's logical that businesses with SKILLWARE-trained permanent employees will look to Manpower's SKILLWARE-trained workers when temporary help is needed.

There is a definable and measurable change in employees who have trained with SKILLWARE, says Fromstein—the training helps them take an even greater interest in their work. "Our workers produce better because of the training and the sense of attachment to Manpower that it gives them. Our training gives them a sense of belonging and changes attitudes toward the job. Permanent workers can experience a similar change in attitude."

19

Reducing Maintenance Costs Through Supervisory Education and Involvement: Travenol Laboratories, Inc.

Russell W. Scalpone

Plant maintenance is one of the greatest sources of cost in a modern, high-technology manufacturing facility. At 10 to 40 percent of the cost of goods manufactured, maintenance has a major impact on the price of doing business, especially for manufacturers with highly automated equipment. Moreover, for many types of operations, maintenance costs have risen more dramatically in recent years than other sources of cost, such as direct production labor, inventory costs, or fixed costs. Thus, an effective program for maintenance-cost containment can make the difference between staying competitive and losing the benefits associated with automation and high technology. This chapter will describe the rationale and approach for a unique kind of developmental program aimed at reducing the cost of maintaining a high-technology manufacturing facility. The approach is unique and differs from traditional manufacturing cost-reduction programs in three respects:

1. The program focuses primarily on the plant maintenance function, and particularly on the first- and second-level maintenance supervisor.
2. The program seeks to expand the financial vocabulary of maintenance people and hence their ability to communicate with production people in financial terms and to solve cost-related problems.
3. The program uses participative management and employee involvement techniques in its design, educational content, and approach to conducting workshop sessions.

The approach was designed for the plant maintenance function and will be highlighted in a case study of a successful program in the maintenance department at a major manufacturing facility of Travenol Laboratories, Inc.

Rationale for the Program: Why Plant Maintenance?

Because plant maintenance accounts for such a large share of manufacturing expense and, hence, product cost, and because of the relentless growth of maintenance cost in recent years, maintenance has come under increasing pressure to improve efficiency and work smarter.

Moreover, simple solutions for controlling cost by limiting the staffing or budget for maintenance activities have been largely unsuccessful. True, one can budget for maintenance as a ratio of the manufacturing budget or apply an *indirect ratio* formula for setting staffing levels, but these approaches have not been satisfactory. Staffing cutbacks may only incur additional expense for contract maintenance, and the problem of finding, recruiting, training, and retaining experienced craft workers is already tough enough without creating cyclical layoffs. Thus, determining the ideal size of a maintenance department remains a complex issue, depending upon such things as the manufacturing technology in question, the cyclical nature of demand for maintenance work, and the types of problems one can live with.

Another reason for the importance of maintenance is the accelerated pace of technological change in manufacturing. Initially, firms sought increases in productivity and output along with the elimination of direct labor expense through automation. More recently, however, the need for product quality (which translates into process control) has become a driving force. This fact, coupled with the falling cost of microprocessors, has encouraged manufacturers to buy and install computer-aided equipment, programmable controllers, robots, and automated material handling systems, or "smart" tools with adaptive controls and sophisticated process sensors.

At the same time, these investments affect and are affected by the maintenance department in a profound way. There is tremendous pressure to prevent downtime on this expensive equipment. The primary role of human workers in the highly automated environment, therefore, shifts from making the product to minimizing disruptions and solving problems. Moreover, equipment problems become more difficult to solve in automated equipment because of the interrelationship of mechanical, electrical, electronic, and logic systems. Mechanics in highly automated facilities frequently can spend 60 to 90 percent of their time diagnosing the cause of a problem, and relatively little time in actual repair. In effect, they become "knowledge workers," and the entire enterprise becomes dependent upon their ability to keep the equipment operational.

Maintenance Improvement Through Supervisory Education and Involvement

The North Cove plant of Travenol Laboratories is located in the foothills of the Blue Ridge Mountains of North Carolina about two hours north of Charlotte by car. The plant manufactures and packages parenteral solutions, such as the intravenous dextrose and water solutions one sees hanging at the bedside of hospital patients. The plant employs a large work force, 160 of whom are in maintenance.

The plant is unusual not only because of its size but also because of the nature of its products and production processes. The parenteral solutions are enclosed in a plastic package that confers certain product advantages (not the least of which is lighter weight) over conventional glass solution containers. The making, filling, and sealing of these plastic containers, however, require a unique production technology and exacting process standards.

Computers and microprocessors control the product through the various stages of production, and much of the production equipment involves complex pneumatics, hydraulics, electronics, and computer logic. Many production areas are maintained as controlled environments with precise parameters for temperature, humidity, air pressure, and particulate matter. Quality-control personnel monitor process and environmental conditions on a continuous basis, and maintenance technicians are frequently called to make necessary adjustments.

Demands upon maintenance people in the plant are also unusual. Mechanics and technicians, like production workers, must wear special "clean-room" protective gowns, caps, and even face coverings to enter production areas. Work on certain pieces of production equipment requires extensive paperwork to document that proper procedures were followed, per requirements of the U.S. Food and Drug Administration. The plant is spread out over many acres, requiring maintenance supervisory people to be in constant walkie-talkie communication with one another and with a base station in the machine shop. In a sense, the maintenance department functions as a large commando force working constantly in both preventive and corrective modes to keep a large and varied assortment of sophisticated equipment in delicate balance.

Background of the Program. During the late 1970s and early 1980s, output of the North Cove plant fluctuated up and down as happens in many businesses with changing market conditions. During this same period, the plant work force, including many support functions, grew and shrank in concert with these peaks and valleys in production. What concerned management, however, was the fact that maintenance costs and staffing were climbing steadily across this five-year period independent of changes in production or other variable costs. Thus, regardless of what the rest of the plant was doing, demand for both maintenance support and maintenance expense was escalating relentlessly.

In response to this trend, the plant engineer (the manager in charge of maintenance) in early 1984 reorganized his department along functional lines, creating new second-level supervisory positions in order to gain better control over maintenance planning and scheduling, project work, coverage (unplanned work), facilities work, and completion of required documentation. Appointing a new third-level maintenance manager also aided coordination between various maintenance activities and freed the plant engineer to spend more of his time interfacing directly with production and engineering on longer-term plans and projects. Along with creation of new management positions, the maintenance work-order system and planning process were also strengthened, permitting better measurement and control of maintenance costs.

By mid 1984, these changes had proven successful in reducing costs and improving control over maintenance activities. Yet, there were indications that maintenance supervisors, while not unsatisfactory in their performance, were as yet unprepared to make full use of their new management systems and responsibilities. These supervisors (most of whom had previously worked as mechanics or technicians) frequently performed the work of the mechanics, had not yet cross-trained their people to the extent desired, had not achieved the proportion of preventive work desired by management, and, most important, were not using the newly strengthened planning and cost-reporting system to full advantage in their decision making. In short, they were not yet working as managers.

The plant training department was at this time investigating the problems of all supervisors and, in the same year, conducted a survey to assess supervisory training needs throughout the plant. As a result of this survey, a number of new training programs were made available to all supervisory personnel, including basic supervisory training for new supervisors and interpersonal communications workshops.

Yet, the plant engineer and maintenance manager believed that needs of maintenance supervisors were tied to the demands of the maintenance environment and the supervisors' career development within that environment. Thus, they requested that an outside consultant (the author) conduct a training-needs analysis specifically for maintenance supervisors.

In September 1985, the consultant interviewed twelve managers and supervisors and completed the training-needs analysis. The analysis confirmed perceptions of the changes occurring within maintenance and of the needs of maintenance supervisors for management skills.

The report further recommended:

- Forming a committee to oversee and approve all training and development within the maintenance department
- Establishing a more structured program to maintain the skills of mechanics and cross-train mechanics to a greater degree in key areas
- A training curriculum for maintenance supervisors

The recommended supervisory curriculum included sixteen courses, together with course-content outlines. Four of these sixteen courses were a reaffirmation of needs uncovered by the plant training department's earlier study: basic supervisory training and interpersonal communications workshops. The remaining twelve courses recommended in the consultant's analysis covered the following areas:

- preparation of supervisors to train mechanics
- time management
- delegation
- performance appraisal skills
- managing interpersonal conflict
- administration procedures
- technical management (the courses would be specific to technical functions managed by a given supervisor)
- diagnostic problem solving for maintenance
- fundamentals of business and asset productivity for maintenance
- defining practical skill requirements for mechanics
- improving maintenance work methods

One important point is that these recommendations were not aimed at improving poor performance (since performance was not substandard) but at recommending ways of enhancing the supervisor's ability to manage resources and further develop the performance of his or her subordinates.

In October of 1984, the plant manager communicated by letter to the consultant his decisions regarding training recommendations. On the one hand, all basic supervisory courses (a term applied to the first five areas above) would be conducted by the Travenol plant training department. Administrative and technical courses (the next two areas) would be given by selected management and technical resource persons. Courses in all seven of these areas would be handled on an as-needed basis.

On the other hand, courses in the last four areas, covering problem solving, business and asset productivity, practical skills development, and improving work methods, would be designed by the consultant as part of a high-priority program to upgrade management skills of supervisors in maintenance.

A proposal was submitted. However, owing to the holiday season and other factors (a plantwide program in statistical quality control was under way at this time), start-up of the maintenance development program was delayed until March 1985.

Working Philosophy and Start-up. At the outset, the consultant expressed the belief that the expense of custom-designed training would be justified only if Travenol management and program participants were actively involved at several stages of the program:

- Course development, to ensure relevance of course content
- Selection of actual projects, to apply course concepts
- Follow-up, to ensure project success and holding of any resulting gains

Maintenance management was receptive to these ideas and committed to the investment of the time despite the fact that everyone had a heavy work schedule and time was a scarce commodity. Consequently, a program steering committee was established, consisting of the maintenance manager, the administrative supervisor responsible for maintenance planning (who also served as program coordinator), and the plant training director. This committee reviewed training outlines and training materials, recommended follow-up actions, and made numerous suggestions to improve the program. It was agreed that courses would be offered in the form of small workshops to encourage participation.

Further steps were agreed upon to enhance the participants' sense of ownership, so they would not perceive the training as a "consultant's program."

- The training director, maintenance manager, and consultant would each conduct workshop sessions.
- The participants would name the program.
- There would be a kickoff session for all participants to identify and respond to any participant concerns.

The program was launched with a general orientation meeting for the total group of sixteen supervisory people. In the meeting, each steering committee member spoke before the group, the content and approach for the training workshops were presented, and concerns were voiced by the group. These concerns were subsequently addressed in the design of the program.

Workshop Sessions for Maintenance Supervisors. The format of the workshop sessions was planned with the dual objectives of education and involvement. Maintenance supervisors were divided into two groups of approximately eight each to keep the number of people in each session small and to facilitate discussion. Each session lasted about four hours and was conducted as a working meeting with an agenda.

The sessions typically started with a review and discussion of current improvement projects, barriers to solving problems, additional information or support needed to move a project forward, strategies for obtaining resources, and so forth. A portion of each session was directed to presentation of educational/training material. However, even this portion was characterized by discussion and group problem solving. At times, group brainstorming and problem solving were aided by collecting ideas or suggestions on flip-chart sheets or index cards. Often these contributions were subsequently typed and distributed to the group after the meeting.

Near the end of each session, time was provided for planning projects, activities, or meetings with people in other departments to be carried out during the two- to four-week interval prior to the next session. During this intervening period, the program coordinator or maintenance manager would follow up with the supervisors and provide help to those who needed it. This follow-up proved to be one of the most beneficial aspects of the program, since it established continuity for the program, reinforced work on projects, and fostered supportive working relationships within the maintenance management team. Participants completed reactions questionnaires at the end of each workshop session. These questionnaires were summarized and reviewed either with the steering committee prior to the next session, or in some cases with the participant group, to identify ways of improving subsequent sessions.

This more formal evaluative feedback was supplemented ad lib by frequent informal evaluation, debriefing, and discussion sessions between the consultant and various participants and steering committee members over coffee or lunch in the plant cafeteria. And since other maintenance personnel (project engineers, mechanics, and so on) frequented the same large tables in the cafeteria, it is possible that virtually everyone in the department could know how the program was going at a given point in time.

Session 1 consisted of a general orientation to the program. Sessions 2 and 3 were presented by the plant training director and covered the fundamentals of business and asset productivity for maintenance. Session 2 covered the nature of profit; the relation of expense to profit; the income statement; and the use of budgets for planning, control, evaluation, and problem solving. Actual company and plant financial information was used for illustration. Applications included exercises in using budgets and making investment decisions, as well as in selecting actual cost-reduction projects.

Session 3 focused on the working capital cycle, the balance sheet, and the concept of asset productivity. This session built on session 2 and expanded the concept of the financial impact of maintenance. Whereas session 2 addressed how maintenance affects expense and, consequently, profit on sales, session 3 showed how maintenance affects return on gross assets and the productivity of capital investment. As in session 2, actual company financial information was used for illustration. Applications for this session included exercises in diagnosing causes of equipment downtime and in identifying opportunities for improving the productivity of resources.

Sessions 4 and 5 covered diagnostic problem solving for maintenance and were aimed at providing participants with skills and methodologies for attacking their improvement projects. Session 4 presented a six-step problem-solving method that could be memorized easily and applied to any problem encountered on the job.

"Fish-bone" charts (cause-and-effect diagrams or Ishikawa diagrams) and Pareto charts were also presented as ways of listing and sorting major and minor causes for a problem. The techniques were demonstrated by working through problems suggested by the group and by presenting charts developed from available maintenance data. Applications included more problem-solving exercises as well as ranking and selection of problems to work on outside the session.

Session 5 showed how the six-step problem-solving method could be extended to the special case of equipment troubleshooting and the value of using a "working theory" in diagnosis. In addition to principles and methods, however, the session also dealt with human problems and limitations: mental and emotional barriers to effective troubleshooting and the statistical odds against success with the familiar trial-and-error approaches. Applications in this session followed the theme of overcoming human barriers to problem solving by (1) identifying ways of obtaining the cooperation of others, such as production people, in situations where their help was needed, (2) applying previously learned problem-solving techniques to a list of common maintenance problems (prepared by the consultant), and (3) developing troubleshooting aids, such as troubleshooting charts, checklists,

and diagnostic guides for use by production operators or mechanics. Individuals and two-person teams took on the task of
developing troubleshooting aids for key pieces of equipment
as outside projects. These projects collected input from both
mechanics (the term *mechanic* is used to refer to all skilled maintenance workers, including electricians) and operators, and
resulted in the creation of a wide variety of troubleshooting
tools.

Sessions 6, 7, and 8 covered techniques for developing
and cross-training mechanics and established the importance
of skill development as a management objective. The first of
these three meetings, session 6, established the interconnection
between mechanic skill, labor cost, and equipment uptime as
justification for mechanic skill development. The reason for this
approach was not that the supervisors rejected training and
development as a prudent and humanistic thing to do, but rather
that the needs analysis revealed that they, like many other supervisors, saw an inherent conflict between developing people and
assigning them where current skills were needed most to accomplish business objectives. Applications for this session included identifying current ''skill bottlenecks'' (work bottlenecks
due to skill deficiencies) and recommending improvements to
the current skill inventory form and mechanic evaluation process used in guiding mechanic development.

The aim of session 7 was to build the supervisor's skill
in assessing mechanic skill, completing the skill inventory form,
and planning for development of the mechanic. Within a high-
technology plant environment, the problems of managing and
developing mechanics resemble the problems of managing and
developing other kinds of professional knowledge workers. These
problems were reviewed and discussed, along with techniques
for observing work behavior and making appropriate inferences
regarding job knowledge and skill proficiency. Applications
focused on fine tuning of the skill inventory form and preparing for an actual developmental interview with a mechanic.

Session 8 concluded the series on mechanic skill development. In this session, the forms prepared by supervisors were
reviewed and discussed, along with procedures for the developmental interview. Applications for this session included finaliz-

ing forms and meeting with one's supervisor to rehearse the interview prior to meeting with a mechanic. The approach of having a supervisor rehearse the mechanic interview with his or her own (second-level) supervisor was chosen for skill practice instead of role-play exercises in the session because the second-level supervisor had previously mentioned dislike of role play. The rehearsal had the added benefit of a quality-control check on the whole developmental interview process. Session 8 was conducted by the maintenance manager.

Cost Reduction/Methods Improvement Projects. Improvement projects undertaken by participants during the course of the program were many and varied. Moreover, pinpointing the actual number of projects was difficult, because, although some were activities with a beginning and an end, others were ideas or suggestions for changes in work procedures or responsibilities, uses of training to reduce cost, or applications of cost-justification analyses to requests for additional maintenance staffing. In some cases, an improvement project may have consisted of merely providing certain kinds of information (cost data, informal training, troubleshooting aids, and so on) to a mechanic, engineer, or production person.

Based upon records maintained by the program coordinator and oral project reports during the sessions, the number of discrete projects would be estimated in the range of thirty to forty, with an approximately equal number of improvement ideas that participants attempted to implement. Many of these improvements involve proprietary equipment or production processes and cannot be described in detail, but representative examples are provided below, by category.

1. Reduction of cost associated with specific maintenance activities. These projects emerged from the mechanical, electrical/electronic, and materials expertise of the participants and their subordinates. This category was the most prolific source of ideas and projects:

- install electrical controllers on battery packs of electric truck fleet to prevent overuse and consequent frequent replacement of the battery packs

- fabricate modified slide bearings to avoid frequent replacement of original equipment bearings
- replace Boston ball bushing (purchased from outside) with Nylatron bushing made in-house
- fabricate in-house the small pins used in key packaging device

2. Equipment and production-related projects. These projects drew upon participants' knowledge of equipment, but were aimed at improving production processes and hence often involved production people:

- investigate addition of machines for in-house (as opposed to vendor-supplied) filter sterilization
- investigate installation of production line to manufacture packaging material in-house

3. Change in responsibilities or procedures. These items were more ideas or suggestions than projects but, nonetheless, resulted in significant improvements:

- include maintenance supervision in monthly or quarterly budget analysis process; conduct meetings to brainstorm cost-reduction ideas and investigate high-cost, high-usage items first
- take parts and materials that are entering stockroom to stock location rather than to a staging area
- make designated mechanics responsible for stockroom inventory for their own area or areas
- improve preparation for shutdown work by performing inspections to determine parts needed

4. Training. These items, like the responsibility or procedural changes listed above, were often ideas or suggestions pursued on an informal basis:

- provide training for mechanics to improve troubleshooting
- train mechanics in use of computerized work-order system
- require the engineering department to provide better training and technical information on new equipment

5. Organization and personnel. These items were requests for staffing and/or facilities changes based upon estimated cost impact:

- organize facilities to do in-house insulation work that is presently contracted
- add machinist to improve equipment utilization on third shift

While program participants tended to be "prime movers" for these projects, ideas, and suggestions, it would be a mistake to say that participants were solely responsible for the results achieved. Frequently, participants drew mechanics or people from personnel, production, training, purchasing, or engineering into their projects by requesting information, time, or other resources. Thus, the number and source of actual participants in a project varied widely.

Session 9: The Joint Production Workshop. The original plan for the final workshop was to conduct a workshop entitled Improving Maintenance Work Methods, which would have extended problem-solving methods into work simplification. Developments in the latter half of the program, however, took the program in a different direction. In the project review discussions, participants were commenting that results of maintenance work could be improved to a greater degree through more active involvement of production supervision. Maintenance procedures could be fine-tuned by maintenance, but without cooperation from the user, substantive progress would not be made. The program steering committee agreed with this view, and so the emphasis of the last workshop was shifted to focus on the production-maintenance relationship.

In order to lay the necessary groundwork, the consultant interviewed twelve production managers and supervisors, reinterviewed thirteen maintenance supervisors, and distributed a questionnaire. The questionnaire asked supervisors for rating judgments in such areas as the following:

- proportion of preventive versus corrective maintenance
- cost of maintenance work

- current level of support provided and received
- perceived level of teamwork between the two departments
- agreement on timing of equipment shutdowns

Fill-in questions were also provided to ask about the respondent's goals for a joint production-maintenance workshop. The overall goals of the questionnaire and interview process were stated as (1) defining the present situation, (2) identifying topics and issues of concern, and (3) suggesting items for further investigation and problem solving.

The total group of twenty-five production and maintenance people interviewed was divided into two mixed groups, each including both production and maintenance supervisors. This arrangement was intended to keep the groups small and facilitate problem-solving discussions.

The workshop session for each group included interview and questionnaire results as well as a description of core problem areas from an outsider's perspective. Through a discussion and ranking process, the group selected problems for joint attack and conducted joint problem-solving discussions. As the workshop concluded, participants planned follow-up action, and an information packet with interview and questionnaire results was distributed to all participants.

Results of the Program. The dollar impact of the program was not easy to determine in a precise way, since some of the cost savings achieved by the supervisors in maintenance were also aided by organizational and systems changes made in maintenance prior to the program. Moreover, not all projects or ideas were implemented in a conclusive way. Some were extended indefinitely, and others were modified or evolved into different projects. Still others had nonquantifiable benefits. Those projects tied to savings in specific maintenance expense items were most accurately measured, and other forms of cost saving were less accurately measured.

Nonetheless, total cost savings resulting directly from the education and involvement program were estimated by the coordinator and plant engineer at approximately $250,000. Most of these savings resulted from projects that reduced consumption of parts, materials, or supplies; devised ways to make parts internally; or otherwise eliminated the need to make purchases from outside vendors. Many of these savings were annualized costs based upon established usage rates per year and will thus generate recurring savings from year to year.

The behavior of people in the plant is another way of gauging results, possibly a better one than estimated total cost savings. Attendance of the maintenance supervisors at the sessions was high even during periods of record production, when excuses for nonattendance were readily available. The supervisors searched out and discovered new sources of financial and productivity-related information in such areas as purchasing, personnel, and accounting. Moreover, many of the supervisors began to seek information from these sources on their own time, to share it with one another in their day-to-day conversations, and to use it in problem solving. In short, the use of financial and productivity information became part of the culture and value system of supervision in the maintenance department.

Finally, the program opened and strengthened channels of communication. Follow-up sessions on projects created a framework for communication within the maintenance supervisory group, and the projects themselves stimulated supervisory communications with mechanics and production people. Moreover, the joint sessions with the production department established a foundation upon which to build an improved working relationship.

Following the workshop, the production department requested that the maintenance department provide it with briefings on the technical functioning of production equipment. To date, over 200 production people have participated in these briefings, which cover such topics as operation and maintenance of hydraulic, pneumatic, electrical, and electronic systems. Furthermore, steps have subsequently been taken to increase the production operator's involvement in the care and maintenance of production equipment.

Conclusions: What Has Been Learned? The most important thing learned from the program is that education coupled with involvement can have significant, even strategic, value for an organization.

Education alone can improve the quality of decision making, but it is involvement that provides the opportunity to make informed decisions. Moreover, involvement need not be limited to selecting projects and making suggestions. It can also allow program participants to ensure the relevance of educational content by contributing to the design and ongoing modification of the program.

Another lesson learned is the value of personal commitment to an objective. The plant engineer and maintenance manager were committed to the program as a vital stage of development for the maintenance department. The steering committee reflected this commitment by investing extensive time in working with the consultant to plan course content and follow-up on the job. And commitment to discovering the best possible program approach further enabled Travenol to broaden the group of committed ''stakeholders'' and to take advantage of opportunities that emerged late in the game.

Lastly, a conclusion can be drawn about the maintenance function: it cannot be ignored. Powerful economic forces are driving American business toward a high fixed-cost investment in automation to achieve competitive levels of quality and cost. Some companies will go gradually, others swiftly. But as the ''factory of the future'' draws nearer, the knowledge and skills of the maintenance work force will loom larger as the means of achieving a return on these expensive capital assets.

20

A Training Consortium:
General Motors'
Automotive Service
Educational Program

Jocelyn F. Gutchess

Combining the technological and management strengths of the company with the educational resources of communities, General Motors' Automotive Service Educational Program (ASEP) is an interesting and apparently successful effort to help ensure a continuing supply of competent service technicians trained to deal with the state-of-the-art technologies in the company's products. General Motors did not reach its position as the number one industrial company in the world by accident. The attention that the company pays to service at the end of its production, distribution, and sales line is one of the reasons for its success. The revolutionary changes that have recently taken place and that are continuing to occur in the manufacture of cars and trucks require technicians at the consumer end of the line who have been trained in the new technologies so that they can maintain and repair the new vehicles. These technicians must be trained differently from those who preceded them. ASEP is one way in which General Motors is dealing with this problem.

ASEP encompasses four principal elements: the company, its dealers, local community colleges, and the young men and women who will become trained technicians. How these four elements are brought together to meet the technological needs of today and tomorrow is the subject of this chapter.

Keeping Up with Technology

In 1986, General Motors (GM) moved once again into the number one position on the *Fortune* 500 list. With sales of $102.8 billion and 811,000 employees, GM is the biggest company not only in the United States but in the world. In 1986, the company sold 8.8 million passenger cars and trucks worldwide. GM manufactures Chevrolets, Pontiacs, Oldsmobiles, GM trucks, Buicks, and Cadillacs—and has announced the development of an entirely new kind of car, the Saturn, which will be produced by a newly established wholly owned subsidiary. In 1986, 38.5 percent of all new cars and trucks sold in the United States were GM products, distributed through a network of approximately 10,400 dealers. This network is extremely important to GM. More than 80 percent of the company's sales and revenues come from U.S. operations. GM makes most of the major components of its vehicles but also uses outside firms for materials and supplies as well as for some important parts. Although the primary focus of the company is on automotive vehicle manufacture, GM also makes nonautomotive diesel-electric and electric products, including diesel engines, aircraft engines, railroad locomotive engines, ordnance, and navigational and guidance systems.

In 1984, the company acquired the Electronic Data Systems Corporation, which develops and produces data and information systems for all sorts of industries, including manufacturing industries. In the next few years, General Motors significantly increased its technological capacity in several additional ways. In 1985, it acquired Hughes Aircraft Company, a world leader in advanced electronics, systems engineering, and high-speed computer software, which it currently operates as an independently managed, wholly owned subsidiary—the Hughes Electronics Corporation. Also in 1985, it combined the principal automotive electronics operations of GM and a portion of GM's defense operations into another wholly owned subsidiary, the Delco Electronics Corporation. Hughes and Delco were teamed together in a major new business unit for GM's high-tech defense and electronics activities. In another move to assert its technological leadership, GM signed an agreement with Etak, Inc., of Sunnyvale, California, giving GM exclusive rights to use Etak's technology in the manufacture of navigational systems in cars and trucks in the United States and Canada.

As the company has moved into the high-tech era, one of its problems has been how to keep its work force up to speed with new fast-paced technological developments. The problem concerns not only workers on the production lines, but also white-collar workers, including managers. Also involved are the employees of GM dealers across the country, especially the technicians who must service, maintain, and repair GM cars and trucks. ASEP is attempting to meet that need.

Beginnings of the Automotive Service Educational Program

General Motors had traditionally been involved in the training of its personnel, including training of its dealers' staffs. The long-established GM Institute, located in Flint, Michigan, is well known, especially for its engineering training programs—at one time it even provided free training to the sons and daughters of GM dealers. For many years, changes in GM's training programs were more or less evolutionary in nature, but in the early 1970s several things happened that forced more drastic changes. Burck E. Grosse, national director of technical service for GM, points to two events that triggered the establishment of the ASEP. One was the government requirement for the installation of emission controls. The second was the oil crisis induced by the economic and pricing controls of OPEC, the cartel of oil-producing and exporting countries. Emission controls had the effect of decreasing the fuel efficiency of automotive engines, while, at the same time, the actions of OPEC made it imperative that fuel efficiency be improved. A third factor in the equation certainly was increasing competition from foreign-made cars. Something had to happen to enable GM to hang on to or increase its share of the U.S. automotive market. That something was, of course, the introduction of the computer into the mechanical systems of today's automobile.

The first computers appeared in GM products in 1979; today, there is at least one computer in all GM cars and light trucks, and as many as six under the hood of some GM cars. That's not all; more changes are on the way. For example, GM is in the process of developing new diagnostic devices, such as the TECH 1, to accurately and quickly determine what is wrong with your car. This hand-held scan tool with plug-in software will require someone especially trained to use it. GM is also looking forward to the paperless repair shop, where each mechanic will have his or her own terminal and a shop without a part window, where all parts will be ordered by electronic communication and delivered by overhead conveyors. Within the next few years, major new engines will be introduced, as well as significantly changed braking systems and transmissions. All of these advances have meant that the lessons being taught to fledgling mechanics in high school and community college automotive courses are no longer adequate and often not even relevant to today's automotive vehicles, let alone tomorrow's. GM has found that the automotive training that young men and women receive in community colleges lags from seven to ten years behind current technology. For high school programs, the gap is as much as fifteen years. Through ASEP, GM hopes to close that gap.

Computers first appeared in GM cars in 1979—which was also the year that the first ASEP was inaugurated. Delta College, a community college serving Bay, Saginaw, and Midland counties in Michigan, was the site of the first program. Another, located in Dallas, soon followed, and then a third in Chicago. By December 1986, thirty-nine schools had been started, well down the road to the company's goal of establishing fifty programs or more. This network is expected to bring an up-to-date training potential within reach of every GM dealer in the country (see appendix at the end of this chapter).

How the Automotive Service Educational Program Works

ASEP is basically a cooperative program in which local community colleges are enlisted to help train automotive technicians who are employed from the outset of the program by GM dealers. The concept starts with the needs of dealers for highly trained and motivated technicians who, they have discovered, are increasingly hard to find and to retain. It ends with the students placed in jobs and launched on satisfying, rewarding careers. In between are two years of training and education at a community college, leading to an associate in arts degree, an associate in science degree, or occasionally, an associate in applied science degree. The training, however, is shared by the colleges and the dealers. The college provides the classroom aspect of training. The dealer provides the hands-on, on-the-job training. For one period—varying from five and a half to eight weeks, depending on the program design adopted by the particular college—the student is on campus full time, carrying a full course load of both academic and technical subjects. During the next period, the student is back home, working as a full-time paid service employee of the dealer who sponsored him or her and receiving carefully supervised on-the-job training. This cycle is repeated—usually six times—through the two-year period, at the end of which the successful students graduate and receive a degree.

One of the most unique features is the preprogram employment of the student participants. The applicants actually secure an employment agreement or understanding before they begin the two-year course of study. They then go through the training as employees rather than as students. Unlike most college programs, they get the job first; then they go through the program. The advantages of doing so are clear. Not only has the dealer made an investment in the trainee, but with competition for trained technicians as tough as it is today (because of concern about service efficiency and profitability), the dealer will certainly hire the new graduate, if possible. What the dealer is getting is not just a well-trained technician but someone who is launched on a career and who has acquired the foundation for further professional growth. The expectation is that in the future supervisory and service manager positions will very likely be filled from the ranks of ASEP graduates. The relationship that is built up over the two-year period between the dealer and the student is very important. By involving the dealer both with the recruitment of the student before entry to the program and with the student's training throughout the period, a strong foundation is laid for a continuing association that is beneficial to both parties.

GM makes it easy for interested dealers to participate. Sponsoring dealers must be willing to provide work experience, accounting for as much as 50 percent of training. And they are asked to pledge sponsorship for the full two-year period. They are also expected to provide their trainees with uniforms. However, except for the wage that is paid to trainees during the on-the-job training phases of the program—a wage that is gradually increased as trainees acquire more skills—there is no other cost to the dealer. Some dealers do assume, in addition, part or all of the tuition and/or housing costs. As a general rule, though, these are paid by the trainees themselves. Further, the dealer knows that the trainees will be able to work on GM cars and trucks, since they will be trained by GM-trained faculty on GM equipment, using GM-prepared manuals. All this will help make the trainee more productive and, hence, more profitable.

From conversations with dealers who have participated in the program, and with program administrators, dealers are apparently satisfied with the results. Typically, dealers who have sponsored one or more trainees continue their participation in succeeding years. Most sponsor at least two trainees at a time—so that they will always have at least one working in the shop while the other is at college. However, there is no requirement for double sponsorship. Some dealers, such as one large Chevrolet dealer in the Washington, D.C., area, sponsor as many as six trainees at a time. Dealers who typically have a hard time getting their regular employees back into a classroom to update their skills find that ASEP can give them the technical expertise and productivity they need. The relatively low investment required and early involvement in training enable them to develop incentives for loyalty and productivity that, even in the short run, can improve profitability.

Selection of Students

Naturally, the selection of the students who participate in the program has a great deal to do with its success. Like other aspects of the program, the selection process is a cooperative one, involving all three of the main actors: dealers, the college, and GM. Selection is rigorous; students are carefully screened. They must be literate, endowed with mechanical aptitude, and motivated, and must have demonstrated the potential to successfully complete the two-year program. Students can be and are recruited by the dealers, who then introduce them to the college. In other instances, they are recruited by the college, which then looks for a suitable dealer (usually with the help of the company), either through the community college's program coordinator or through the staff of a GM training center serving the area. (The role of the training centers will be more fully described later.)

The community colleges that are involved in the program must also offer ongoing automotive technician programs as part of their curriculum. If a prospective student comes to the college looking for automotive training and appears particularly suited for ASEP, the college can seek GM's help in linking him or her with an appropriate dealer-sponsor. Testing of prospective students for admittance is performed by the college. For example, Northern Virginia Community College tests potential enrollees for reading ability, math proficiency, reasoning, and mechanical aptitude. In addition, the student is interviewed twice, both by the director of the program and by a counselor in the office of cooperative education. They want to be sure that the student has what it takes to manage and stick with the two-year program.

Recruitment is generally directed toward local secondary schools. The Virginia program is probably typical. In that program, each year the ASEP director goes into area secondary schools with vocational programs and meets with both interested students and their teachers to tell them about ASEP. As the dealers in the area have come to know the program better, they have increasingly done more of their own recruiting. Not surprisingly, recruits are sometimes drawn from the GM family itself—relatives of individuals currently working for or associated with GM or a GM dealership.

By and large, trainees enrolled in the program are recent high school graduates. But there is no age limit, and there are many instances of older students who have had some work experience and who are eager to upgrade their knowledge and skills. At least one student, in his forties, felt he got so much from the program that he continued his education and is now serving as an instructor. Program instructors report that motivation and enthusiasm generally run higher among the ASEP students than among those in the regular college automotive technician classes. They credit the difference to the fact that the ASEP students have jobs while they are in college. Classes vary in size from one community college to the next, the largest ranging from thirty to thirty-two students and the smallest from sixteen to eighteen.

Program Content

The ASEP program is no snap course, but a rigorous educational and technical training program designed to produce topflight automotive technicians who not only meet the needs of today but will continue their career advancement in the future. Although the instructional program in the participating community college will differ in some details, all include three basic elements: a general liberal arts education, state-of-the-art automotive theory, and practical training. The liberal arts curriculum generally includes English, mathematics, history, psychology, and courses sharpening communications and reasoning skills. Automotive theory and practice are taught in courses that include such topics as automotive heating and air conditioning systems, automotive drive train and body components, brake and suspension systems, electrical and electronic systems, transmissions, and engines. Students who have difficulty with the academic aspects of the program—and some do—are usually offered a chance to improve their records with remedial courses provided by the colleges. The students must accumulate sufficient credits for graduation, and since they spend at least half of their time away from the college campus, this can mean that the pace of classroom instruction must be accelerated. At Northern Virginia, where the traditional periods are of five and a half weeks' duration, students have an eight-hour academic day in the first year, starting at 7:30 each morning with two hours of math. They seem to like it, however—no complaints were heard.

Obviously, the training given by the dealers is an important element of the total program and, indeed, academic credit is given for this training. If the program is to have real meaning, the work done by the trainee while under the supervision of the dealer must be relevant to the training received in the classroom at the college. It is the responsibility of the ASEP coordinator at the community college to see that this occurs. When the trainee reports to the dealer for the on-the-job training cycle, the dealer is provided with specific information as to what the trainee has been studying in the most recent classroom cycle and is asked to make sure that the student is exposed for a significant part of the time to work that is related to that training. At the end of the period the sponsor is asked to rate the trainee's performance. Specific evaluation sheets are sometimes provided. This rating, then, becomes part of the student's grade for the course. To assure that the linkage is made, and to resolve problems as they arise, the program coordinator must visit the work sites on a regular basis.

This attention to the linkage between classroom and the job, plus the rigorous selection process, has served to keep the

ASEP dropout rate very low. Students do leave, of course—
primarily for financial reasons, but also because of changes in
their personal lives (for example, the family moves away); some
leave because they cannot make the grade. Moreover, not every
student who completes the two-year program will pass and
receive a degree. It is not at all unusual to have eighteen in a
class finish of the twenty who started out. Whenever a student
does leave the program, GM and the college conduct an exit
interview to determine the nature of the problem and to enable
corrective action to be taken as appropriate. Students are offered counseling to help them overcome barriers to successful
completion. In addition, the program administrators try to follow
up with these students to encourage them to return to the program if they are able to do so.

Undoubtedly, the fact that the student has a job and is
being paid while going to school contributes a great deal to the
low dropout rate. One other factor should be mentioned, and
that is the group spirit—the feeling of being part of something
special—that the program engenders. Whether it is deliberately
cultivated (and in some cases, apparently, that is the case) or
develops on its own is not important. The fact is, it does exist.
This group élan not only helps to reduce the dropout rate during the training period, but can lead to the development of an
informal support network. After program graduates leave, they
appear to keep in touch with each other and can and do help
each other solve problems they meet in their own work.

Costs

Going to college costs money, and this is just as true for
ASEP students as for anyone else. For the most part, the students
themselves pay for tuition and books. Costs differ among the
participating colleges but, on average, an ASEP student can
expect to pay from $400 to $500 per semester. With six semes-
ters, completion of the program will cost from $2,400 to $3,000.
This is the rate for students who are residents of the area served
by the community or state college. Rates for nonresidents are
usually double that for residents, and in some instances this can

cause a problem. For example, the ASEP being offered at the Catonsville Community College outside of Baltimore is designed to serve GM dealers throughout the state of Maryland. But only residents of Baltimore County are eligible for the regular tuition rates. However, GM and the colleges have worked out reciprocal arrangements to solve this problem in many of the participating colleges, and, so far, it does not seem to be a major deterrent to student participation.

Most colleges can help students with financial aid or at least help them get it. Some have also introduced special financial incentive programs. At Northern Virginia, for example, the student receiving the highest grade for the first year's work receives a scholarship worth one quarter of the next year's tuition. The fact that the student is employed by the dealer-sponsor for at least half the time, of course, helps meet the college costs. Most participants will be able to earn that much and more. Furthermore, in some cases, the dealer-sponsor assumes responsibility for tuition expenses.

Students may also have to pay for room and board, especially if they live in areas outside commuting distance from the college. But, in this respect, they are not different from other college students, and indeed it is reported that they have been very inventive in arranging low-cost housing for themselves. Dealers may see it as a problem, but the students do not. ASEP students do have to shoulder one cost that most other college students do not: the cost of their own tools. Traditionally, auto mechanics own and use their own tools on the job, and since ASEP students are working at a job for part of their time, they must buy their own tools. An initial set—bought at a discount through the college—will probably cost a minimum of $800; most are about $1,000. (Experienced mechanics can have as much as $8,000 to $10,000 invested in tools.)

While the community college provides the faculty, curriculum, physical space, and administrative expenses for the program, GM provides the equipment and materials that are used in the program. This includes new cars, shop manuals, parts, and so on. In addition, the company provides training for the faculty involved in the program at no cost to the individual.

Although there are no exact data available on the total costs of the ASEP program, GM estimates that of the approximately $22 million in material and equipment donations that were made by GM in 1986 to all community colleges—and this includes non-ASEP automotive programs currently in operation throughout the country—approximately $4.5 million went to the ASEP programs.

Role of General Motors Corporation

ASEP is basically a college program, run by community colleges, which trains automotive technicians for employment with auto dealers. Since the technicians will not be GM employees, how does GM fit in? The answer is: from start to finish. The connection is substantial and continuous. First, GM is the instigator of the program. The company is responsible for starting new programs, for identifying community colleges that will be able to operate successful programs, for enlisting dealers who will sponsor the students, and, often, for helping to recruit students who will be able to complete the course. Second, the company monitors the ASEP programs as they go along, ensuring that standards are met and that problems are solved as they arise. Third, the company provides the materials and equipment so that relevant training can take place. And fourth, the company is directly involved in continuous training of ASEP faculty to keep them up to date on current changes in the technology of GM products. Much of the work is performed by the network of thirty-one GM training centers whose fundamental purpose is to expand the technical excellence of those who service GM products.

Traditionally, except for a short period, these training centers have been responsible for providing training geared to the needs of GM dealers, and particularly to those of dealer service staff. At one time there was a charge for these services but, at present, training is provided at no cost to the dealer. Generally speaking, each of the centers services a wide geographical area, so individuals must often travel to the center to take advantage of the courses offered. To make it easier, the centers have begun in recent years to outstation their faculty in remote locations, sometimes using the physical facilities of community colleges for this purpose. Since the courses are designed primarily to upgrade auto technicians' skills and to keep them abreast of new developments in GM products, the courses are generally short, ranging from one- or two-day refreshers to an eight-day basic electronics course.

Dealers are not the only beneficiaries of the services of the training centers. They also train the mechanics of GM fleet owners. For example, in the Washington, D.C., area, the Fairfax center trains the mechanics employed by the federal government to keep its automotive vehicles in good repair. They also run summer workshops for high school vocational instructors. In the past few years, the activities of the training centers have grown enormously. In 1979, the training centers provided approximately 90,000 hours of training. By 1986, this figure increased more than three times to 285,000 hours.

The relation of the training centers to the ASEP program was described by Benjamin Wescott, manager of the training center in Fairfax, Virginia. Speaking to a group of dealers at the inauguration of ASEP at the Catonsville Community College in Maryland, Wescott said that his center would be responsible for providing vehicles, training aids, tools, and mock-ups; assisting the college in screening applicants; maintaining a list of interested dealers; visiting the students on the job and monitoring their progress; reviewing the curriculum annually; providing information for presentations to local high schools; and reporting to the corporate Product Services Training office on a regular basis. This same service, which his center is already providing to the ASEP program at Northern Virginia, supports ASEP around the country.

The liaison between the centers and ASEP seems to work smoothly, perhaps because both are administered under the same corporate umbrellas. At the corporate level, the Product Services Training office is headed by a vice-president responsible for customer and sales and service staff. In the Technical Services Group, headed by Grosse, there are five major divisions: Training Center Operations, National College Coordination,

Professional Development, Training Development Operations, and the Video Training Network. Responsibility for ASEP lies in the office of the national college coordinator, John Choulochas. Four regional coordinators, who report to him, work directly with the colleges. To provide additional support for ASEP, he can call not only on the GM training-center network, but also on other divisions in the group, which are responsible for the development of instructional programs, training guides, and statistical support.

Role of the Community Colleges

The community colleges—perhaps one of the most dynamic educational institutions of the present day—are constantly looking for new ways to serve their communities, and are showing increasing interest in working with business and industry in partnership arrangements. ASEP is, of course, just that. In fact, one expert calls General Motors "the single corporate leader making the best use of the community colleges."

More community colleges than can be accommodated apparently would like to be involved in ASEP. In selecting a participating college, GM looks for several things. First, the college must have demonstrated experience in operating automotive technicians' programs at the journeyman level. Second, GM requires, in the words of Burck Grosse, "an administrative group that is innovative, willing to try new things." Finally, the college must be willing to work closely with GM in the selection of students, in the "GM-izing" of the curriculum, and in the training of its faculty. In addition, in selecting a college, GM stresses that the course must emphasize basic liberal arts as well as the technical aspects, since it regards the ASEP students as "something special," a "cut above the regular automotive students," according to Grosse.

For the college, participation in ASEP brings definite benefits that go beyond the financial and technical support that is provided by the program itself. The faculty training is especially important and helps to get the new automotive technology into the regular automotive programs as well as into ASEP. It allows the college to develop for itself an important role in the transfer of technology and thus to find yet another way to serve its community. One example is Delta College in Michigan, which now sends some of its trained faculty to the GM training centers to provide instruction for dealer service staff there—a reversal of its original role. Delta has gone even further and at the present time has eighteen faculty members, located in GM training centers or other GM facilities, providing instruction to engineering and technical staff as well as to workers on the line.

Future Directions

Implementation of ASEP is not without its problems, some of which have already been mentioned. The dropout rate is one, of course, but for the most part it appears not to be serious. Retention of employees by the dealers after graduation could be a problem for individual dealers, but it would not affect GM unfavorably. Auto mechanics frequently switch after three or four years from one employer to another. However, they tend to stay in the field—so even if one dealer loses, another gains. Saturation of a particular area could become a problem, but apparently it has not happened yet. Some colleges that have had to lower their intake of students one year have been able to increase it again the next. Distance can deter dealers from participating in the program—although even here, ways have been found to accommodate students who live far away from the college. But with over 10,000 dealers in the country and only thirty-nine programs, it is clear that distance could be a deterrent and that not everybody will live within commuting distance of a participating college. Despite these problems, however, the program is succeeding. Certainly, all of those to whom this writer talked—students, instructors, dealers, college administrators, and the GM training center staff—were universally enthusiastic.

General Motors is continuing with its plan to increase the number of colleges participating in ASEP programs to fifty or more. In addition, the company has begun the development of an exciting new concept, the GM Faculty Development Institute.

The concept starts with the desire of the company to facilitate
the transfer of its new technology to the nation as a whole. This,
GM believes, requires that a place be established where the
technology can be more or less easily accessed by the public.
The plan is to establish four such schools around the country—at
Delta College in Michigan, serving the eastern and central states;
at the College of Southern Idaho, serving the western region; at
Glendale College in Phoenix, Arizona, serving the southwest; and
at Greenville Technical College in Greenville, South Carolina,
serving the southern region. Community college faculty would
be trained at the institutes, with the training not limited to ASEP
faculty but available to all college faculty. The plan also envisages
expansion of the program to provide training for secondary
school instructors at a later date, perhaps in summer programs.

In addition, plans are under way to set up some sort of
certification system so that GM can be assured that the faculty
involved in training technicians to work on GM equipment will
be fully competent. These are ambitious schemes, but so, indeed, was ASEP. With the record of success that has already
been achieved, GM can confidently count on further success.

"Will we be ready for the future?" This is the question
GM managers ask themselves. ASEP and its spin-off programs
are certainly helping to provide an affirmative answer.

Appendix

ASEP programs have been established at the following community colleges:

American River College
Sacramento, Calif.

Arapahoe Community
  College
Littleton, Colo.

Bessemer State Technical
  College
Bessemer, Ala.

Brookdale Community
  College
Lincroft, N.J.

Brookhaven College
Farmer's Branch, Tex.

Broward Community
  College
Hollywood, Fla.

Camden County College
Blackwood, N.J.

Catonsville Community
  College
Baltimore County, Md.

Central Piedmont Community
  College
Charlotte, N.C.

Cerritos College
Norwalk, Calif.

College of Southern Idaho
Twin Falls, Idaho

Community College of
  Allegheny County
Pittsburgh, Pa.

Dakota County AVT
  Institute
Rosemont, Minn.

De Anza College
Cupertino, Calif.

De Kalb Area Technical
  School
Clarkston, Ga.

Delta College
University Center, Mich.

Des Moines Area
  Community College
Ankeny, Iowa

Glendale Community
  College
Glendale, Ariz.

Greenville Technical College
Greenville, S.C.

Hudson Valley Community
  College
Troy, N.Y.

Longview Community
  College
Lee's Summit, Mo.

Macomb Community College
Warren, Mich.

Mass. Bay–Minuteman Tech
Lexington, Mass.

Monroe Community College
Rochester, N.Y.

Nashville State Area Vocational Technical School
Nashville, Tenn.

New Mexico Junior College
Hobbs, N. Mex.

Northern Virginia
  Community College
Alexandria, Va.

Oklahoma City Community
  College
Oklahoma City, Okla.

Owens Technical College
Toledo, Ohio

Portland Community
   College
Portland, Oreg.

St. Philip's College
San Antonio, Tex.

San Jacinto College Central
Pasadena, Tex.

Sinclair Community College
Dayton, Ohio

Southeast Community
   College
Milford, Nev.

Southern Illinois University
Carbondale, Ill.

Traviss-Polk Community
   ASEP College
Eaton Park, Fla.

Triton College
River Grove, Ill.

Waukesha County Technical
   Institute
Pewaukee, Wis.

Weber State College
Ogden, Utah

21

National Technological University: Learning by Satellite

Leslie Stackel

The era of the "electronic university" has arrived, and with it comes a new model for learning at the work site, namely the National Technological University (NTU).

NTU is a high-tech "campus without walls." It provides higher education to engineers and computer science professionals by satellite, linking corporate classrooms to a space-age system that can beam lectures from twenty-four universities to locations anywhere in the United States. Students take courses by merely tuning into instructional television, and they can carry on two-way conversations with instructors over 2,000 miles away, take exams, and earn credits toward a master's degree, without ever having set foot on a graduate school campus.

Education that is delivered directly to the work site is clearly the wave of the future, claims Lionel Baldwin, NTU's cofounder and president. In fact, it is happening today at over fifty-five companies, including such major corporations as IBM, Hewlett-Packard, and General Electric.

"Technical change has accelerated recently and promises to continue on a steep, upward curve," says Baldwin. "Clearly, the engineering profession needs continuing education alternatives that don't conflict with the demands of full-time employment. Media-based programs delivered directly to their offices and laboratories are the most effective, affordable means for meeting the need."

The National Technological
University Network: An Overview

National Technological University is a private, nonprofit educational corporation based in Fort Collins, Colorado. It acts as an umbrella organization for colleges across the country—more accurately, for certain of their curricula. It serves as a consortium of universities—using satellite technology to offer the best courses to be had around the country within the engineering discipline, in terms of both the technological information taught and the teaching expertise. NTU is truly revolutionary, particularly in view of its value to companies located in remote areas. It enables employees virtually anywhere to earn course credits from such prestigious institutions as Purdue University and Georgia Institute of Technology without ever leaving their home base.

NTU is an outgrowth of the Association for Media-based Continuing Education for Engineers (AMCEE), a nonprofit consortium of engineering universities that offers short, noncredit courses. NTU takes a giant step beyond the AMCEE, however, in both its program curriculum and its delivery system.

It got its start in January 1984 after AMCEE, created nearly ten years earlier, proved so successful. The potential benefit to engineers, who are perpetually battling the high rate of obsolescence in their field (now estimated to occur in five-year cycles—three-and-a-half-year cycles for software-related areas), was incontestable. So the AMCEE board of directors decided to expand its original short-course concept to include accredited master's degree programs.

The AMCEE directors organized a board of trustees to

govern NTU, similar to that of any private university, but composed mostly of industrial executives. The boards of AMCEE and NTU interlock, since Baldwin and AMCEE's director hold membership on both.

The schools within the NTU network are drawn from the AMCEE consortium of thirty-three colleges and universities. (The consortium began with twelve original member universities; new applicants are voted in by two-thirds of the current membership.) Any college opting for entry into the NTU system is evaluated by a membership committee set up by AMCEE. They qualify by meeting certain criteria, which include having an accredited engineering program, adequate facilities, and a history of offering off-campus instruction via television media. Course offerings are selected by a curriculum committee, also set up by NTU, which consists of faculty members from each participating university. NTU also welcomes input from companies using the system.

Just as the curriculum has grown in sophistication beyond that of its parent institution, so has its means of delivery. Unlike AMCEE, which operated much like a central clearinghouse by renting out educational videotapes to companies, this new "national university" broadcasts live over two channels via a new satellite. (Currently, AMCEE also uses a satellite delivery system, but continues to rent tapes as well.) The NTU broadcasts originate with universities equipped as *earth stations* or *uplinks,* meaning they transmit live classes to company sites, called the *downlinks,* which have receiving satellite dishes. Thus, instructors can simultaneously teach both on- and off-campus students. There are 15 uplink facilities and 140 downlink sites. Ninety of the downlink sites were enrolled during the fall 1987 semester. In addition, 9 "non-uplink" universities participating in the NTU network—those universities not equipped to broadcast—send videotapes of their lectures to a nearby university earth station with broadcast capability, and these are transmitted over the air. Or, if the industrial site fails to record the lecture, NTU can duplicate the videotape and send it to the company site, the normal procedure before NTU began airing live via satellite.

Baldwin predicts that by fall 1988, the university will

double its current course output by adding two television channels to its network, for a total of four. At the moment, NTU carries 452 courses in five separate master's degree programs: computer engineering, computer science, engineering management, electrical engineering, and manufacturing systems engineering.

The actual number of NTU students is expected, consequently, to increase, as well. A total of 956 off-campus students were enrolled in the 1987 spring semester; 266 were on the audit basis, 440 were nonmatriculated, and 250 were taking courses and had applied for admission to master's degree programs (at the time of this writing)—with the majority already having been accepted.

Annual student enrollment grew rapidly during the 1986–87 year to a total of approximately 3,200 students. With an average of only twenty off-campus students nationwide per class, the potential for growth is considerable. NTU projects that it will serve an average of about fifty-five off-campus students per class in the future. (Were it not for the administrative load added on for each student, the possibilities might be limitless.)

Despite these figures, NTU's marketing manager, Mark Bradley, asserts that NTU's admissions standards will not be lowered to accommodate a growing student body. To maintain its high level, a faculty group within the curriculum committee was elected to act as "watchdog," making sure these standards are met.

In August 1987, NTU was granted initial accreditation by the Commission on Institutes for Higher Education of the North Central Association of Colleges and Schools (NCA). In the same month, NTU graduated its second class of master's level students. Because NTU was the first national university to be accredited, NCA had to organize a special review committee, with representatives from the other regional accrediting associations.

NTU's national status has triggered other dilemmas not as easily resolved. One problem is the disparity in semester lengths of participating universities and the resulting complications in coordinating a student's program. The solution is, if not simple, then manageable, according to Bradley.

Claiming that "we're a slave to each university system," he reports that NTU runs each university course as it naturally occurs, without trying to fit it into a fixed, uniform time frame. Although NTU operates on a semester basis, various university courses may run on a trimester or quarterly basis. To deal with this, NTU prorates credit hours and tuition for each course, based on its length.

To aid site coordinators in managing this administrative matrix, NTU publishes the calendars of all twenty-four universities in its network and sends these to member companies. Since each NTU catalogue course identifies its sponsoring university, a coherent schedule can be arranged by checking the calendars against each other.

A more serious drawback of NTU—and the one most cited by member corporations—is that of communication between the instructor (who teaches on a television screen) and the pupil—or lack of it. NTU is attempting to address this issue by increasing contact between instructor and pupil through the use of new communication systems and by reducing some of the administrative difficulties that might contribute to the problem.

For instance, operational kinks involving time delays between submission of homework assignments and exams by students to instructors, and their return, are being cleared up. At present, exams and homework are mechanically sent by mail. But both electronic mail and an even newer approach—mail by satellite—is being tested by NTU. The latter is NTU's favored solution. According to Bradley, NTU will experiment this summer with a system "that permits us to transmit tests and homework through our satellite apparatus. We type the material at hand on a computer equipped with a special circuit board that allows digital information to be encoded onto videotape, and then we play it through our network to the company sites. They, in turn, will return messages by rented telephone lines, since the work sites do not have uplink capability."

If this experiment works, company sites would have to purchase the circuit boards (costing from $700 to $800 each), but these, he adds, "will greatly help communication."

Electronic mail presently has limitations, Bradley reports, mostly because of its "inability to handle graphics and complicated equations.'' When facsimile machines with graphic capability are improved, this may open new options for NTU and other media-based educational formats, he notes.

Moreover, NTU is applying for a grant to set up computer work stations throughout its university system. This would permit students and instructors to communicate directly with the aid of a computer telephone attachment, or modem, without the delays of computer log-ins and log-outs. Another plus: these more advanced machines have graphic capability.

Meanwhile, NTU is working closely with company site coordinators to develop ways of easing the burden of an admittedly complex administrative load. First, NTU publishes a 150-page *Site Operational Procedures Manual,* with guidelines on everything from whether or not to use a course facilitator to the recommended hardware for an NTU start-up. Second, Lionel Baldwin recently organized an advisory board consisting of representatives from various company sites. ''This is another way to keep standards up and to advise on operational issues that the board of trustees may not be familiar with,'' explains Bradley.

On an ongoing basis, NTU monitors the classes in session to see that professors also address the needs of off-campus students, who view lectures simultaneously with those seated in classrooms on campus. For example, NTU staff can identify the lecture about to begin and the course number, and they can note if blackboard markings are legible, if diagrams are suited for the TV screen, and so on. Essentially, the job of NTU is to see to it that the off-campus student gets as complete and high quality an education as students in the classroom—or even better, as described later in this chapter.

Of the companies using NTU, each has its own set of reasons for selecting this ''space-age university,'' as well as its own responses to the system. The three case studies that follow—Hewlett-Packard, Digital Equipment Corporation, and Eastman Kodak—illustrate the use of NTU by these companies.

Hewlett-Packard

Hewlett-Packard (HP), based in California's Silicon Valley and one of the nation's leaders in electronic equipment, has been a staunch supporter of NTU from its conceptual phase. The company partly underwrote an NTU feasibility study in 1984 and helped to fund the building of satellite earth stations. Today, HP promotes the use of the university throughout its manufacturing divisions coast to coast. (All eighty-two of HP's sales and manufacturing sites have downlink facilities; nineteen manufacturing sites are actually using NTU.)

HP's support of NTU stems from its strong corporate commitment to education. "In the preamble to our official policy statement, it says that the company must have a well-educated, highly skilled work force and must engage in a vital continuing education program to keep that work force updated. So there's no question where our policies come from," says Alfred Moye, manager of continuing education, corporate engineering. "They are built into our statement of corporate objectives." To prove the point, when HP selects sites for expansion, it intentionally locates near highly reputable universities and encourages branch divisions to establish a close rapport with the schools in its vicinity.

Currently HP uses media-based programs offered by Stanford University, the California State University at Chico, the University of California at Berkeley, AMCEE, and the Institute of Electrical and Electronics Engineers (IEEE), plus a series of in-house courses, workshops, and lectures whose structure, delivery, and time factors are designed to maximize the benefit of each. NTU is one more option in the potpourri of educational systems now open to HP employees. "We try to give people choices so they can pick and choose what is best for them— what they need and where they think instruction is best," says Moye. He adds, "We promote all programs equally . . . but it's quite likely that every HP manufacturing site will eventually adopt NTU by virtue of the diversity in offerings." Other NTU benefits that Moye cites are:

- *Flexibility in scheduling.* "If absent, you don't have to miss a class; you can tape it."
- *Top expertise and teaching ability.* "Knowledge in any field is not limited to a small number of select institutions; therefore, NTU draws upon the resources of many universities for

expertise. Also, unlike most major research universities, which choose professors primarily for their research credentials rather than for their teaching ability, NTU carefully selects only those faculty members who have excellent teaching reputations. Thus, the NTU network provides instructors who are not only good scholars, but good teachers as well.''

- *Extensive enrollment.* "With a faculty of some 3,400 instructors in twenty-four universities, no one university with a limited faculty resource has to bear the burden of administrative overload. When over 100 people took a course on Introduction to Artificial Intelligence one term, NTU hired more teaching assistants to help the instructor. There have been other popular courses originating in a number of schools, thus spreading the administrative responsibilities among many institutions.''

As for NTU's cost-effectiveness, Moye points out, "This is not our major concern. Opportunities are more important." He notes, "There is only one thing to compare NTU's cost to—the cost of ignorance." Described below are the experiences of two separate HP sites—Rockaway, New Jersey, and Andover, Massachusetts—with NTU.

Hewlett-Packard at Rockaway, New Jersey. Situated in an outlying New Jersey suburb, isolated from neighboring buildings, is HP's Rockaway plant for the design and manufacture of electronic instrumentation.

Located some distance from Rutgers University and the New Jersey Institute of Technology (NJIT) in Newark, the HP site has four educational programs open to its engineers and managerial personnel. These range from on-site engineering instruction by NJIT faculty members to tuition assistance programs applicable at any accredited college.

Each claims some percentage of the HP student enrollment: 16 percent of the work force is enrolled in an after-hours, in-house series of workshops for math and verbal skills; 13 percent, in an educational assistance program; and 3 percent, in

NTU. The relatively low NTU enrollment is due largely to its newness, says local NTU coordinator John Breault, and to the fact that only one-eighth of the employee population is eligible to enroll in the high-level technical courses offered by NTU. Nevertheless, the number of NTU students at the Rockaway plant climbed from three enrollees when NTU was introduced in fall 1984 to seventeen in the fall 1985 semester. Breault believes that once NTU catches on, it may outstrip the other programs in enrollments. The reasons, primarily, are its flexibility and convenience, but also the high level of instruction. "The benefits of having so much quality education at your fingertips outweigh the inconvenience of learning from a TV screen rather than directly from a teacher," he says. Breault also points to a Stanford University study that shows televised instruction—when aided by a tutor or facilitator—to be more effective than live classroom lectures. While it is too soon to say if HP's experience bears this out, Breault is confident of NTU's educational effectiveness, provided the company makes available such necessary resources as course facilitators or tutors when appropriate.

Richard Williams, a development engineer on the technical staff at Rockaway, cites NTU as his educational preference over other options at the plant. A transferee from HP's Cupertino, California, site, Williams has sampled the media-based Stanford program and finds NTU up to par. "NTU is deliberately not offering 'easy' courses, because it wants to establish a solid reputation—and not just give you a few easy credits," claims Williams. "You have to really work here. These courses are on the same level of difficulty as other college courses I have taken."

Having already taken four NTU classes, Williams anticipates four years of study before receiving his master's degree in computer science. However, the cutback in travel time to and from the NJIT Newark campus after working hours plus the various advantages of NTU will ease the pressure, he believes. He lists these pluses:

- HP allows NTU viewing time during work hours. Because Williams's course selection is broadcast live Friday evening from 6:00 P.M. to 9:00 P.M., he videotapes weekly for more convenient viewing. He tends to break up the three-hour program into shorter segments, watching between meetings, on lunch breaks, and during other free time.

- There is a potential for repeat viewing of instruction by playback. "When I don't understand a point, I play it back three or four times and listen again. This makes up for a lot—it's even better than a live classroom." He adds, "In a classroom, there are small points you wouldn't stop a teacher for, but I don't hesitate to stop the videotape."
- The lack of facilitator and/or classroom interaction is balanced by the presence of classmates on the premises.

With the increased number of course participants enrolled since the program's inception, Breault found that the administrative load required the aid of added personnel. A full-time assistant from the personnel department has since taken on the task of daily communication with NTU headquarters and oversees the television room, videotapes scheduled courses, and generally aids Breault as a consultant for employees seeking registration information on NTU.

The division's financial investment in the installation of NTU's receiving equipment was minimal. A satellite dish was already in place, and on-site classrooms were available. Meanwhile, the potential for return to the company is tremendous. In Williams's case, for instance, the investment to date has already paid off. He points out: "One of the first NTU courses—software engineering—presented an interesting viewpoint on how to test software. Since you can't test anything 100 percent (because there are too many variables), the advice was simply to test a product or software more intelligently. The course taught me how to do my engineering work a little better and a little smarter. Now I've applied what I learned to my daily work here at HP."

Hewlett-Packard at Andover, Massachusetts. In Andover, Massachusetts, not far from Boston, lies a sprawling HP site with three divisions, one geared to the design and marketing of cardiac ultrasound imaging systems. The employees of this division total 600—eighty of them engineers.

As technology advances, HP finds the emphasis shifting from hardware to software equipment, demanding a whole new orientation on the part of its engineering staff.

"We have to keep our engineers up to date, or the Japanese will kill us," says Lawrence Banks, section manager for R&D in engineering. "In industrial electronics, we're still ahead of Japan, but with technology changing so fast, what we did three years ago is obsolete. Our engineers need formal schooling constantly—and, right now, the push is on for software education."

To encourage its engineers to meet the forty-hour-per-year company minimum of continuing education, HP at Andover is offering a wide spectrum of courses to appeal to its staff. And one of those options is NTU.

Compared to the media-based program from Stanford University and individual programs from the Massachusetts Institute of Technology (MIT) used by the Andover plant for many years, NTU is "not as tough—the MIT and Stanford courses are definitely harder," according to Banks. But the bias toward challenge here is tempered by the need for practical, accessible course work. And, as Banks puts it, "NTU provides a product that is a very good offering. It has the right things in it and, so far, has good quality." This combination makes NTU especially useful to industry veterans of ten years or longer who lack the training in computer science of the younger generation. Retraining, Banks points out, "has to be done on a piecemeal basis, over time. NTU fits this need nicely."

At present, the total engineering population at Andover signs up for about four courses per term, distributed among the different media-based programs. These might originate from Stanford or from HP's own broadcast network. One course per term might be from NTU. In addition, one-day seminars from AMCEE and IEEE are often offered.

"We may have only fifty-five professional engineers in the lab at a given time. Maybe 20 percent will want a course during the term. But we try not to run any class with less than four or five people; we like to create a classroom environment whenever possible," explains Banks.

Although this limits opportunities for individuals willing to monitor a class independently, Banks believes that some form of interaction is a must. He contends that the one-to-one interaction in a classroom environment "allows you to learn practically through osmosis.

"If we really want someone to get up to top speed, we'll send that person perhaps to MIT or the Wang Institute for maximum education. But practically speaking, we can't afford to send everyone back to school. So, although we have found satellite and in-house programs to be much less effective, they are also essential. They are vastly superior to what we used to have—which was nothing."

In regard to media-based programs, NTU "offers a better variety of quality courses than is available anywhere," according to Banks, "but in terms of administration, they need improvement."

"NTU is prepackaged—the schools, the catalogues—all ready to go. The program is structured well, but it's very complex. The coordinator has to juggle possibly twelve courses from twelve schools, each on its own schedule—and there's a lot of overlapping. If someone is trying to put together a degree program, with some schools on quarterly systems, others on a semester basis, it's a logistical nightmare." Still, in the final analysis, Banks and HP believe that, for the most part, NTU will be successful. He concludes: "What they're doing is essential to forward-thinking companies."

Digital Equipment Corporation

Its interest in providing growth and learning opportunities for its engineers, coupled with the industrywide need to match galloping technological growth with engineering know-how, has propelled Digital Equipment Corporation headlong into a series of educational programs, the latest of which is NTU. At its Marlboro, Massachusetts, site, Digital's design and manufacturing facility for high-performance computer systems now has two satellite dishes—one recently added to receive NTU's broadcasts. "As a high-tech company, we have to worry about education. We're vested in seeing that people go on for course work and degrees," says Christine Rudomin, Digital's education specialist at Marlboro. Rudomin believes that in education, a company has to "strike a balance between method, timing, and type of delivery, and have as many options as possible."

NTU is expected to draw an increasingly large percentage of the 650-member worker population in the High-Performance Systems Group, of which 60 percent are engineers. The convenience factor will be key, she says. "It's not just a question of getting engineers enrolled in courses, but actually getting them to attend," claims Rudomin. "In this respect, the media-based nature of NTU's design is a plus." From the start, Digital made a strong commitment to NTU, both monetarily and in terms of the time invested. Five separate sites have had downlinks installed (Marlboro, Maynard, Shrewsbury, Colorado Springs, and Tewksbury). Each site must also pay the salary for a site coordinator to administer the program. It's a slow process to get a site on line. An engineering plan is needed for the installation in addition to a cabling plan, and to do both requires an interface between purchasing, plant engineering, security, and corporate telecommunications. "It's a highly complex process," says Rudomin.

At present, the Marlboro facility has a dedicated classroom, split in half, soundproofed, and equipped with two sets of televisions and video cassette recorders. Classes are aired only from 8:00 A.M. to 8:00 P.M. (although the system broadcasts twenty-four hours a day). Rudomin doesn't have the staff to videotape the sessions yet, so all are viewed live, generally by groups of three to five students per class. Ten NTU courses to date have aired at Digital. NTU's pluses, from Digital's perspective, far outweigh its minor disadvantages, which Rudomin generally relegates to the category of mechanical foul-ups.

On the positive side, Rudomin describes NTU as "a highly flexible, on-site delivery, cross-credit transfer system," which is very responsive to industry needs. "It's rare to be able to influence the skill set that engineers come away with, but with NTU it is possible to influence curriculum," says Rudomin. "NTU enforces a certain ecumenicalism in engineering and computing, with all its input from different companies."

In daily contact with NTU headquarters, Rudomin finds

that the organization responds speedily to feedback from its site coordinators and, moreover, invites suggestions on curriculum. "I'm impressed with NTU," she says. "The instructors know their subject matter and handle the medium well. But when there's a bad apple, NTU hears about it and doesn't wait for a semester to end before acting. . . . One term, there was a course in the catalogue that was poor. I'd had experience with it, so I called them and suggested that they pull it out of the program— and they did." Rudomin also sees the potential here for "two-way technology transfer" between member corporations and the university. "Research goes on at Digital, too, and I can envision a time when our experts are shipped off to an uplink facility and put on the air as lecturers. In this sense, NTU can act as a conduit for new and different ideas within the industry."

Digital finds that the quality of instruction offered is well worth the cost. Its ability to draw from twenty-four universities is, in Rudomin's view, a strong selling point: "No school has a monopoly on the best instruction," and with NTU, "only the best courses from each college are selected. There is a natural culling process." The down side of NTU, in Rudomin's opinion, involves mostly start-up problems. Technical difficulties related to the satellite installation and generally "getting the system debugged" were the main targets of early complaints about NTU.

However, one irksome point for Digital remains, and that involves courses that are videotapes rather than live classes. "These, in general, are less interactive," says Rudomin. "And sometimes they will even be broadcast out of sequence—the students then come to me and complain." For faculty members who contribute to these problems, she says, there should be some policing action. Moreover, Rudomin believes that "we should demand that universities adhere to standards on the transmission quality of broadcast videotapes as they do with live delivery." Sometimes the tapes themselves are inferior, thus aggravating the problems of maintaining high quality in broadcast transmissions. Placed in perspective, though, these flaws are minimal when compared with NTU's overall contribution to engineering education, claims Rudomin.

Eastman Kodak Company

At Eastman Kodak headquarters in Rochester, New York, some changes are occurring as the company moves into more high-tech production than ever before. "As our product mix has changed over the past few years, the need for graduate-level technology has grown," says Charles Miller, manager of video instruction. While two area schools, Rochester Institute of Technology and the University of Rochester, have graduate programs for engineers leading to master's degrees, their course offerings at the graduate level are not sufficient to meet the needs of Kodak's diversified engineering population.

When NTU began offering courses leading to master's degrees in electrical engineering, computer engineering, and engineering management, starting in the fall of 1984, Kodak was very interested in the NTU concept. The company conducted pilot programs with a few enrollees for the fall 1984 and spring 1985 terms. "The results were exciting," claims Miller. Approximately 130 engineers took part in the two-term pilot, and 60 percent reported that the technological information drawn from the NTU graduate courses was immediately applicable to their jobs. "The engineers found the NTU courses to be extremely rigorous and advanced, meeting the expectations of 'graduate' technical education," says Miller.

Kodak proceeded with the NTU program and now has facilities available to receive satellite-transmitted courses. The classes at Kodak's headquarters are not held during working hours. They are taped for viewing after work at the employee's convenience. Some courses have leaders, or facilitators, and officially meet at specific times after working hours. For example, courses with five or more employees enrolled use facilitators and meet twice a week. The facilitators are experts in a given field, and their responsibilities include previewing the videotaped lectures and enhancing lectures with practical applications where possible.

"The key ingredient is to mix the practicality of work applications with the theory from the university lecture," explains Miller. To manage classes with fewer than five students, Kodak

has created a ''counselor umbrella.'' A counselor, like a facilitator, will be an expert from Kodak, or perhaps a graduate (doctoral) student from one of the local universities, and will generally
be assigned to four courses. There will be one or two students
per course. The counselor is available to assist students with
homework problems, advise on projects, or help with other
significant assignments that are difficult to work out with professors over the telephone or through electronic mail. Most of
the more than 300 employees taking NTU courses are enrolled
as credit students; less than 10 percent audit courses.

Kodak appreciates NTU's role as that of a serious educational mainstay in the university system. Nevertheless, there
is room for improvement, Miller points out. Assignments need
to be graded and returned to students more quickly. Off-campus
students are miles away from the campus classroom and require
recognition from instructors on a continued basis.

Despite these shortcomings, Miller emphasizes the convenience and flexibility of NTU, combined with its high-quality
instruction. ''The fact that top faculty members are drawn from
several of the nation's leading engineering universities is a big
plus for our employees,'' says Miller.

PART FIVE

COMBINING CONTINUOUS LEARNING AND EMPLOYMENT SECURITY

Continuous learning—described in the introduction to Part Two as a concept "in which everyone in the organization is involved in an ongoing process of learning new skills"—is a dynamic and cost-effective corporate response, not only to changing technology, but also to the continual shift in products, services, processes, markets, and competition. In this part, several companies are described that have attempted to incorporate this new mode of learning into their corporate cultures in combination with employment security. Together, these two practices complement and strengthen each other and provide a more powerful response to the changing nature of the economy and the workplace. Employers that invest most heavily in employee learning also make the strongest commitments to employment security in order to protect their investment. Employees are regarded as permanent assets of the firm, whose skills must be continuously upgraded. Thus, employee turnover tends to be very low.

When implemented together, continuous learning and employment security serve both individual and corporate goals: Companies committed to the continuous upgrading and training of their employees improve their competitiveness and thus their ability to provide employment security. At the same time, employment security policies encourage acceptance by employees of the continuous learning that competitiveness demands and motivates them to learn new skills—not only for their personal growth and career advancement but also for the long-term success of the organization.

Although some employers have equated employment security with job security, the concept discussed here refers to programs and practices that offer employees some degree of protection against the loss of employment rather than the guarantee of a specific job. In companies that are committed to employment security, layoffs are the last resort—to be used only after all other practical alternatives have failed. These employers place greater emphasis on training redundant employees to fill new positions and, when dismissals are unavoidable, to assist them, through training or other means, to find jobs outside the firm.

While employment security is often regarded as an impractical policy that restricts the corporation's flexibility to manage its resources, employers who have actually practiced it report just the opposite effect. *Employment Security in a Free Economy,* the report of an earlier Work in America Institute policy study (Pergamon Press, 1984), clearly demonstrated that employment security offers competitive advantages not available to companies operating in a more traditional mode.

The cases presented here are further evidence that employment security practices, in combination with continuous learning, represent a viable, cost-effective strategy for strengthening the competitiveness and long-term prosperity of the firm. The examples cited focus attention on three aspects of the continuous learning–employment security connection: retraining current employees whose skills have become obsolete, as opposed to firing them and hiring skilled employees from the outside; managing the redeployment of employees from old to new jobs; and familiarizing retrainees with their new work environments as early as possible.

Retraining Versus Fire-and-Hire

Employers generally prefer to fire-and-hire rather than retrain workers because they judge the former to be less costly and easier to manage than the latter. Xerox Corporation's Critical Skills Training Program proves otherwise. This Xerox program, in the company's Business Products and Systems Group, is especially significant because it involved retraining chemists, engineers, and other types of professional specialists to fill altogether different professional slots in such high-demand fields as computer science and computer engineering. That kind of retraining is usually considered to be impractical. Xerox, however, has found the retraining option to be cost-effective and reports that the adjustment for the trainees and their work units has been a smooth one.

Managing Redeployment

The redeployment or reassignment of surplus employees to other jobs, either within or outside of the firm, is essential for the cost-effective management of employment security. To ensure that the process occurs in an orderly fashion, there must be ample lead time to anticipate job declines and openings, assess training needs, carry out training, and have employees ready to fill the new jobs as they become available. The full cooperation of supervisors and employees from both the originating and hiring organizations is needed to implement a smooth transfer from an old job to a new one.

The retraining experience can be an important step in the redeployment process and is often crucial to fulfilling the goals of employment security, as demonstrated by two cases. The first is General Motors' Packard Electric Division, which supplies wiring components to U.S. and foreign auto and truck markets. The division is undergoing a major transition as it gradually moves all its high-labor, low-tech assembly work out of its Warren, Ohio, facility, while simultaneously introducing high-tech, low-labor component manufacturing to the Ohio operation. Nevertheless, massive job losses have not taken place because a jointly negotiated agreement between the division and Local 717 of the International Union of Electrical Workers provides a cooperative framework for extending employment and income security to the 9,000-member work force. Management and labor monitor all volume changes that may affect hiring, redeployment, and training and then jointly develop and implement the needed training programs.

The second example describes the turnaround that occurred at General Electric's Fort Wayne, Indiana, facility, which had been in serious decline due to decreased demand for its products, electric motors and transformers. Half the factory was mothballed, and thousands of employees were on layoff, with many more layoffs expected in the future. The company's decision to transfer its prosperous, high-tech aircraft engine electronics facility and "graft" it onto the Fort Wayne operations was based on several factors, including the availability of retrainable, laid-off workers. Despite the vast technological differences between the two operations, the retraining required—although critical to the successful transfer of jobs—was not extensive.

Finally, Pacific Northwest Bell's efforts to redeploy managers is described. It has done this through a computerized system, known as the Job Skills Bank, which helps management employees apply and train for high-opportunity jobs in the firm. The project is still being refined. Despite some "pockets of resistance" in engineering and technical areas, the system is working well, not only in matching managers with available job opportunities, but also in identifying employees for special projects or promotion and in estimating skill deficiencies and surpluses. Company officials also predict that the skills bank will be a useful tool in planning new business ventures.

Familiarization with the Work Environment

Increasingly, employers are realizing that successful retraining experiences depend not only on the trainee's mastery of specific skills and knowledge related to the new job, but also on that individual's familiarity with the work environment: how the work unit operates, its specific objectives and the kind of problems that can arise, supervisory expectations, and how the work unit interacts with other parts of the firm. A Hewlett-Packard program, which retrains surplus production employees to fill high-demand office positions, demonstrates that the earlier such understanding of the work environment occurs, the more successful is the retraining and the transition to a new job. Several procedures were built into the program to familiarize trainees with their new work units: the provision of "career mentors," who provide trainees with relevant on-the-job training experiences; the involvement of supervisors from both the hiring and originating departments, to ensure a smooth transition to the new job; panel discussions, in which people from the major career tracks describe their jobs and answer questions; and specially arranged tours of departments with job openings.

22

Xerox's Critical Skills Training Program: A Commitment to Retraining Pays Off

Richard Morano
Jeanne Leonardi

Xerox Corporation's Critical Skills Training Program (CST), now in its third year, is a successful cost-effective effort to match potentially surplus professional personnel with the company's unfilled staff requirements in the high-growth fields of computer engineering and computer science. Originating with the company's commitment to employment stability, CST represents an alternative to laying off or relocating staff whose particular talents might no longer be in demand while openings exist in other areas. As it has developed, CST is a full-year reeducation and career-change program, carried out by Xerox in cooperation with the Rochester Institute of Technology (RIT) in

Note: The authors wish to thank Jocelyn F. Gutchess for her valuable assistance in preparing this chapter.

Rochester, New York. In the first two years, thirty-three individuals successfully completed the program and are now employed by Xerox in new jobs. Another eight people completed the program in March 1987. The program is not inexpensive but has proved cost-effective. Nor has it been a static program. As the company and RIT have learned from experience, evolutionary changes and improvements have been made.

Beginnings

The revolutionary nature and fast pace of technological change that have characterized the last decade have presented difficult challenges to human resource managers throughout U.S. industry. To stay on top in an increasingly competitive world, line managers have had to develop and deliver new products, while human resource staffs have struggled to provide the technical and professional personnel to make that possible. Nowhere have the impact of technological change and the effort to remain competitive been more dramatic than among professional staff, whose formal education and hard-won work experience can become inadequate, and even obsolete, in a few short years. Like other U.S. companies, Xerox has had to cope with these problems.

The Critical Skills Training Program got its start at Xerox's Reprographic Business Group (RBG), now part of the Business Products and Systems Group, with worldwide operations. This group is responsible for Xerox copier business—where managers had been wrestling with a mismatch problem for some time. On the one hand were competent, loyal, experienced people with skills that, either now or at some point in the future, could become less relevant to Xerox. It was possible that these employees might, therefore, have to be let go or relocated. In this group were mechanical engineers, chemists, physicists, and other analytical specialists. On the other hand, there was a real need for specialized staff, particularly in the field of computer engineering, electronic engineering, and computer science. The company, which as always supported a broad-based program for updating and upgrading the skills of its employees, was finding it difficult in this case to fill openings in these fields. Underlying all of this was the company's commitment to the concept of employment stability for its employees. Although there is no specific job guarantee at Xerox, the company is deeply concerned about employment stability, giving high priority to its human resource management policy.

As the problem was discussed over a period of time, the choices were clear. To solve the problem of surplus skills, experienced workers could be laid off, relocated, or retrained. To solve the problem of skill shortages, new staff could be recruited and hired or existing staff could be retrained. Not surprisingly, and despite the risks involved, the choice was made for retraining. It was not certain, of course, that such professional retraining was even possible, and there were those who said it could not be done. Further, there were no guides to use, no model to follow, no courses tested, and no standards established for any part of the retraining process. However, an analysis of estimated cost savings, plus adherence to the basic policy objective of conservation of valuable human resources, proved conclusive. With the support and encouragement of top management, it was decided to initiate a nine-month, intensive program of full-time study to prepare employees for new high-tech careers.

As a first step in the development of the new program, a task force was established with responsibility both for the design of the program and for monitoring and oversight as the program progressed. In addition to the human resource staff, headed by Norman Deets, the task force included managers from several divisions of Xerox—the Electronics Division, Xerox Systems Group, and Reprographic Business Group, which have been reorganized into the Business Products and Systems Group—as well as representatives from the Rochester Institute of Technology. In effect, the task force included the program's customers.

It is useful here to describe the close relationship that exists between the Rochester Institute of Technology and Xerox. RIT is a topflight private technical and engineering school offering undergraduate and graduate degrees as well as some nondegree programs. RIT, with 16,000 students, maintains close connections with the Rochester community and derives considerable support from Rochester business and industry. About five or six years ago, RIT established a subsidiary organization, the RIT Research Corporation, to develop and carry out professional and technical training programs to meet the needs of the community. Over the past few years, several such programs have been implemented for Xerox, with RIT staff working directly with—and indeed sometimes physically located at—Xerox, providing liaison between the two organizations and developing and administering the program.

As it started its work, therefore, the task force had the advantage of well-established relationships between the company and the educational institution at which training would take place. RIT knew Xerox and Xerox knew RIT. Nevertheless, the group was breaking new ground, with the outcome not by any means assured. Although some mistakes may have been made in the initial round, the continuing involvement of the task force has made it possible to correct and improve the program as it has progressed.

Program funding was still another problem that had to be overcome. This was resolved by allocating funds to the training department that might normally be used to redeploy or lay off (with severance pay and benefits) employees in surplus skills categories. These funds were used to cover the costs of administration, equipment, course development, and the full-time salaries of employees during the training period. No budgetary costs were charged either to the organizations from which the trainees were drawn or to those to which they reported after training.

The Program in Operation

The first step for the task force was identification and analysis of Xerox skill needs. Engineering management spelled out the range of skills and knowledge that they expected the trainees to possess after completing the CST program. These included:

- understanding of computer and microprocessor concepts and technology
- possession of specialized knowledge of software operating

systems and languages and knowledge of hardware, such as digital design and hardware interfacing
- experience programming in at least two different languages
- ability to learn and apply various software languages to the development of microprocessor-controlled products and capabilities, and to contribute to the design, debugging, and documentation of microprocessor-based solutions to engineering problems

In addition, it was deemed very important that the program provide the basic background and understanding for the trainee to continue to take additional educational courses in the electronic/computer engineering area. This program was to be only the first step in preparing for a new career—the base on which further career development could be built.

Having determined skill needs, the group set out to design a curriculum that would meet those needs. A course of study was developed that included seventeen courses, with class loads of sixteen hours each quarter for the enrollees for the year. (RIT operates on a full-year, quarterly system.) Of the seventeen courses, twelve were customized to meet the special needs of the company. The courses were all held at the RIT campus, and although there was some duplication of other courses being offered, the CST courses were run separately. Only CST enrollees attended CST classes.

Trainees not only received full pay and benefits for the period of training, but Xerox also provided each person with a computer terminal in his or her home to help with computer programming assignments and to reduce travel time and expense to RIT's computer center. Xerox also paid for the telephone charges to link the terminals with the school's mainframe unit.

Selection of trainees proved to be something of a challenge. With no previous experience to assist in determining individual potential for success in the program, the task force had to rely on their judgment and intuition in selecting the first group of trainees. The program was announced through regular company communication channels, resulting in application by approximately 100 people. No specific effort was made to identify individuals who might at some future date be faced with relocation or layoff. Rather, the approach was positive, offering interested individuals a chance to shift career direction and to prepare themselves for opportunities in new high-tech growth fields. However, generally speaking, the individuals who applied were those who for one reason or another believed or saw that the opportunities for career advancement in their current occupations were limited. It was not so much a question of "If I don't do this, I'm going to be laid off," but "Here is an opportunity I don't want to miss." Neither managers nor supervisors saw the program as a means of dumping unwanted personnel. Instead, the opposite occurred—very able, highly motivated people applied, sometimes to the dismay of their supervisors and managers.

Application required completion of a simple form, along with submission of other personnel data, followed by a series of interviews with management members of the task force. Since the program involved such an intensive course of study, requiring hours of work at home as well as in the classroom—a difficult adjustment at best for most adult workers accustomed to a regularly scheduled workday and workweek—motivation was deemed to be extremely important. The interviews were the principal method for determining this aspect.

Twenty-nine individuals were finally selected for the first round of training. They started classes in the fall of 1983. Eighteen (62 percent) completed the program in the spring. Regarding previous education, a number had bachelor of science (B.S.) degrees in mechanical engineering, but the class included chemists, physicists, and others who had B.S. degrees in mathematics.

The course was not easy and, as implied by the completion rate, a significant number found the pressure too great and were forced to drop out. Xerox and RIT realized that changes would have to be made, and they were. First, the program was lengthened to a full twelve months, thereby easing the academic burden on the trainees; the nine-month program was simply too intensive. Second, various measures were taken to strengthen the support given the trainees. From the beginning, tutors were provided to help trainees, if necessary. In addition, before the training began, participants were selected by the department to which they would report at the completion of training, thus ensuring a smooth reentry. Individuals from these departments were assigned to each trainee to serve as mentors—to be aware of the enrollee's progress in the training program and to keep the trainee informed of developments in the organization to which he or she would be reporting. More important, the selection process was refined and improved.

As the program administrators looked for reliable predictors of success, research conducted after the completion of the first-year program showed a high correlation between mathematics test scores and program grade-point average, and between programming grades and the program grade-point average. Obviously, math and programming abilities were extremely important. To ensure that the trainees had these skills, the selection process was revised, and subsequent programs have included math and programming aptitude tests as part of the candidate's preliminary self-selection process. Further strengthening the process, the program was expanded to provide a three-week, fourteen-hour math refresher course open to all employees and given in the fall, before the math test is administered and before the applicants are interviewed by management for acceptance in the program. Once a person is accepted into the program, he or she is required to attend an additional preliminary, four-week, twenty-four-hour course, Introduction to Computing, which is designed to ease the transition into the RIT computer curriculum for those students who are not familiar with computers. The course is taught in-house by instructors who have worked closely with RIT in developing its content.

Other characteristics that the research identified as being necessary for success included:

- *Personal and family commitment.* Not only did the individual's motivation and commitment have to be high, but the sixty to seventy hours weekly required by the trainees meant that their spouses and children also had to understand and accept the trainees' commitment. To help resolve this problem, the program now includes a special orientation program to which families are invited, and also occasional social events for trainees and their families so that the families will feel a part of the process.

- *Personal flexibility.* Someone who has settled into a comfortable schedule of work, play, outside interests, and television, for example, is not as likely to succeed as someone whose life-style is more malleable. Participants needed the ability to adjust to a radically different work schedule of class, homework assignments, and constant time demands. Counseling is available to help trainees meet these demands.

All of these changes have paid off. All but one of the nineteen trainees in the second group, which started in December 1984, completed the program a year later. Four trainees in the third group, which started in March 1986, had to drop out for preexisting health reasons, but eight finished the program successfully.

Some Results

Throughout its development, the program has been carefully monitored and evaluated. The same task force that was involved in beginning the program is still engaged in fulfilling its overview responsibilities, meeting once a quarter to provide guidance and support for the program. Some of the results are evident.

1. Reentry has not been a problem, either for the individual trainees or for the organizations to which they have moved after completion of training. Follow-up evaluations are made at intervals of six months, one year, and two years—with both the former trainee and the appropriate manager being asked to respond to similar evaluation questionnaires. Responses have been good, with managers giving the trainees excellent ratings. Interestingly, the former trainees tend to rate themselves slightly lower than their managers do, but they still express satisfaction with their jobs, the relevance of the training, and their decision to change to a new career. Former trainees are given a two-year protected period during which they cannot be demoted or laid off. They can, however, be promoted, and many have been.

2. The group dynamic that the program engenders has also been an important element in its success. The way the program is structured requires this relatively small group of people from diverse backgrounds to spend an entire year together— sitting together in the same classrooms, working on the same problems, coping with the same assignments, deadlines, and tests. As a result, there is a high degree of camaraderie among the participants. The program has a reputation for being tough, so co-workers regard the trainees as special, as do the trainees themselves. They put great value on the program, and feelings of accomplishment are high. The obvious interest and pride of the company in its success further enhance this feeling.

3. The program has proved to be a cost-effective solution to the mismatch problem of surplus skills in some fields and un-filled openings in others. Unit costs of the training itself vary with the size of the training group. These costs can be measured against the alternative of relocating or laying off surplus employ-ees, plus the cost of recruiting and training new employees to fill the company's high-tech skill needs. Relocation, which at Xerox can entail a move from Rochester to, say, the company's operations in California, is very costly for the company. Layoff is also expensive, particularly since company policy allows an individual six months at full pay to find another job. In addi-tion, severance pay and benefits for those professional employees the company would be forced to let go are also a heavy expense. To these costs must be added the cost of recruiting, training, and supporting new employees for the approximately six months it takes for them to become fully productive.

4. The program has produced some valuable spinoffs. One is the development of the Technician's Opportunity Pro-gram for nonexempt skilled employees. It guarantees partici-pants an exempt, professional position with the company after completion of a bachelor's degree in electrical or mechanical engineering. This program was developed on the basis of ex-perience gained in the CST program, which, although designed for professionals, has also allowed highly qualified nonexempt, nondegreed employees to participate. In fact, one such partici-pant, who had previously had only three years of college, did

so well in the CST program that he was accepted directly into a master's degree program at RIT—the first such person ever accepted into an advanced-degree program.

5. Perhaps the most important result of the CST program has been the recognition by the company and particularly the human resource management staff that there is and will continue to be a need for an established process to enable employees to change direction, change careers. Some people will always be caught in the whirlpool because of the constant technological change. The organization, therefore, has to be aware that things are changing and must have something in place to help people adjust to the change. The CST program is only one effort to meet that need. It is not and will not be the only one. These are the problems that Xerox managers are currently addressing.

Factors for Success

Can the CST program be replicated by other employers faced with similar problems in human resource management? Before trying to answer that question, it is useful to examine some of the factors that appear to have contributed to the success of the Xerox program.

Commitment to Employment Stability. Foremost among the conditions contributing to the successful outcome of CST is the commitment of the company to the concept of employment stability—a basic belief that the company's employees represent valuable assets that should not be lightly discarded. At Xerox, all operating groups are charged with responsibility for implementing this employment stability policy. Of course, business conditions must be taken into consideration, but the overriding policy thrust is to conserve human resources—to find a way to retain and productively utilize all employees. Retraining is an important element of the company's employment stability policy. It is easy, of course, to adhere to such a policy in good times, when a company is growing. The problem is always whether an employer facing the need to downsize, retrench, or restructure in order to remain competitive can afford such a practice. A good argument can be made that the presence of capable, experienced people within the company can contribute to growth; in fact, it is a necessary commitment for growth. Certainly this is true in the intensively competitive high-tech industries. Xerox's CST program provides a good example of how an employment stability policy can be implemented. The company did not—and does not—want to lose its good people, and CST provided the means of retaining them. Wayland Hicks was president of the Reprographic Business Group (RBG) when the CST program was launched. Now he is president of the Business Products and Systems Group (BP & SG), with worldwide operations, of which RBG is now a part. In discussing the problem Hicks comments, "There are two main reasons why we're proud of this effort. First, it has allowed the graduates to realize their professional goals—to begin a new career that is consistent with their interests and offers a long-term growth potential. Second, it has given Xerox a strong source of expertise that we need to keep our business strong and competitive."

Relationship with the Educational Institution. The close relationship that exists between the educational institution and the company—RIT and Xerox in this case—has certainly been a major factor in the success of the retraining program. Without such a relationship, it would be very difficult, if not impossible, for an employer wishing to embark on a sophisticated retraining program to develop and successfully carry it out. Professional retraining requires that the courses be specifically designed, custom tailored to meet the exact pre-identified skills needed by the employer. Further, the educational institution must be both knowledgeable about company operations and sensitive to its needs, and vice versa. Many companies already have or are in the process of developing close working relationships with post-secondary educational institutions—colleges (particularly community colleges) and universities. Similarly, many educational establishments are reaching out, trying to find new ways of serving local business and industry in their communities. However, there is still a long way to go. In the case of the CST program, Xerox was fortunate that it already had a close working relationship with RIT—a relationship that could easily be built on to launch the new program.

Selection of Candidates. When the CST program was inaugurated, selection of candidates for participation in the program was a venture into the unknown. Experience (and a flexible approach on the part of both program administrators and educators) has led, however, to the development of reliable predictors of individual success. Any employer wishing to launch this kind of retraining program must be willing to experiment with the selection process and to take some risks. The indicators developed by Xerox and RIT might well be useful to employers retraining for similar occupations but, of course, they do not have universal applicability. It should be noted that for the first round of training of the CST program, the selection process was almost entirely carried out by the company; for the second and third rounds, RIT was brought more directly into the process. It has been evident that the longer the period of time the trainee has been away from a formal school situation, the harder he or she has to work. Previous occupation does not seem to make training any easier, although in the CST program, math skills and an aptitude for programming were clearly very important.

Attention to Reentry. Probably the most frequently voiced criticism of retraining schemes is that they are carried out in a vacuum—in other words, "retraining for what?" This criticism has been leveled particularly at retraining programs designed for workers who have lost jobs as a result of the introduction of new technology. In contrast to many retraining programs, the CST program begins with clearly identified specific job needs, for which training is then specifically designed. Equally important has been the attention paid to the reentry of trainees into full-time work at jobs within the company. Not only are the trainees placed in the jobs before they start the training program, but continuity is assured through the mentor system, under which each trainee is regularly kept in touch with his or her future work situation. Career change, therefore, becomes not a blind jump into unknown territory, but a guided landing on at least a somewhat familiar field.

The Labor Market. All of the success-contributing factors mentioned so far are potentially controllable by an employer wishing to retrain professional personnel. We believe that other factors contributing to the success of the CST program are the special characteristics of the labor force in the Rochester, New York, area. Rochester is a high-tech town, where there is stiff competition among employers for highly skilled workers, both technical and professional. Retraining, reeducation, and skill upgrading are broadly promoted and supported by local employers and expected by employees. The CST program operates, therefore, against a background of community familiarity with the problems of continuous skill development and retraining. Not only is there a general acceptance of the necessity for retraining, but there are high expectations for the utility of undertaking such programs. Community attitudes can be an important element in success—and seem to have been in Rochester.

Costs. Finally, it is necessary to say a few words about the costs of professional retraining. While it is clear that the Xerox program has been a cost-effective alternative to layoff or relocation, such might not always be the case in other companies. Each employer will have to make its own determination. One reason that the Xerox cost-benefit analysis is so positive is that the cost to the company of layoffs and/or relocations is relatively high. A less generous employer might show quite different results. On the other hand, layoff and relocation are expensive for the company precisely because of its commitment to employment stability. And this commitment, in turn, has payoffs that do not show up in the cost-benefit analysis of the retraining program. These benefits include, among others, higher productivity, increased loyalty to the company, and a climate that encourages creativity—all ultimately enhancing the company's ability to grow and compete.

Conclusions

Can the CST program be replicated? The answer must be yes, but with the important caveat that certain essential steps must be taken to help ensure its success. Retraining of this nature would likely be problematic without considering these steps.

Xerox plans to continue some kind of retraining program, now that the current group finished its training in March 1987—even though the immediate problem that led to the development of the program in 1983 has eased. The company can, however, envision similar conditions on the horizon. Experience with the program has convincingly demonstrated the continuing need for retraining and for helping employees move into new careers as they find their present skills outmoded and no longer in demand. If employment stability is to be given real meaning, then, not only must employers embrace the concept of retraining, but employees must also be given the opportunity to make career choices and then helped to realize those choices.

In discussing the future direction of any retraining effort, it should be stressed that a system must be in place—an ongoing process to help individuals who want and need retraining and career change. Such a process is a necessity for any organization that hopes to prosper in areas of rapidly changing technology. Thus, Xerox is currently instituting a career center, where personal assessment, career counseling, and guidance can be provided.

For Xerox the retraining as incorporated in the CST program has proved to be worthwhile. Although initially a gamble, the program has paid off. Money that would have been used to pay layoff or relocation expenses has been used by the company for more positive results. Experienced, competent employees have been retained and have become more valuable to the company. And valuable lessons have been learned that will enable the company to mount more efficient, more effective retraining programs when the need arises, as it surely will.

23

Linking Retraining with Job and Income Security: The Packard Electric Experience

Kathleen C. Hemmens

Packard Electric Division of General Motors Corporation (GM), headquartered in Warren, Ohio, is an international supplier of wiring components for the U.S. and foreign auto and truck markets. With over 30,000 employees in six countries, Packard Electric currently manufactures and ships over 7,000 parts to 3,630 different points on the globe every month. The company's Warren Operations, the subject of this chapter, is made up of nineteen separate plant facilities and presently employs approximately 9,000 hourly workers, who are represented by Local 717 of the International Union of Electrical Workers (IUE).

Packard Electric is currently engaged in a long-term transition that will eventually move the majority of its traditional high-labor, low-technology assembly-line work out of Warren to plants in Mexico. At the same time, the company is moving into high-technology, low-labor wiring component manufacture, which entails the introduction of new equipment and machinery into its former assembly facilities. In 1984, Packard Electric and Local 717 negotiated a local agreement that provided lifetime job and income security for approximately 9,000 hourly workers whose assembly jobs were threatened by foreign and domestic competition. This landmark agreement, which goes well beyond the national GM-IUE contract in its job and income security provisions, has both practical and symbolic significance for Packard Electric management and workers. It provides a cooperative structure for the training and quality assurance activities that Packard Electric must undertake to remain competitive in a rapidly changing automobile manufacturing environment. It also constitutes a promise to the division's hourly workers in Warren that they will be participants in the major transitions that are occurring as the division responds to new customer requirements and standards.

Although it is too early to make a definitive assessment of what is becoming a unique industrial partnership, the early results hold valuable lessons for observers who are concerned to find ways in which industrial competitiveness *and* industrial jobs can be retained in the United States.

"A Unique Industrial Partnership"

Retraining for new technology at Packard Electric's Warren Operations has grown out of a ten-year history of labor-management struggle and accommodation, which resulted in 1984 in a trailblazing local collective bargaining agreement that provides lifetime income and job security for the Warren Operations' hourly workers.

In the mid 1970s, Packard Electric began moving its final assembly operations to Mississippi and later to Mexico in an effort to improve its competitive position in the industry by reducing labor costs. This shift signaled what appeared to be a permanent reduction in work for the 10,000 or so assembly-line employees in Warren whose jobs were being moved south.

At the same time, union feelings were volatile all up and down Ohio's Steel Valley, where steel mills and factories were closing down or moving out—victims of foreign competition, bad management, and a slowing economy. As Packard Electric's Ron Noble puts it, "Everyone was watching as new 'tombstones' appeared in the valley"—abandoned plants that symbolized the transformation of Steel Valley into an industrial graveyard.

As tension increased over the feared loss of jobs in the Warren Operations, a small group of union and management representatives began to meet informally to discuss ways to both improve the negative labor-management environment and reverse the movement of jobs out of Warren. Members of the group included IUE Local 717's current chairman, Harold Nichols, and Packard Electric's director of industrial relations, Larry L. Haid, both of whom continue in major leadership roles today in the implementation of joint programs to keep jobs in Warren by improving the company's competitive profile.

Taking steps toward mutual understanding was not easy or without risk to the participants. Robert Holden, now one of two division-level Quality of Worklife (QWL) Program coordinators appointed by the unions, says of those days, "For a union member, being seen drinking coffee with a management guy was as good as drinking poison come election time." But despite opposition and skepticism from both sides, the group continued to meet and to undertake noncontroversial joint projects like blood drives and the "toys for tots" collections before the holidays.

After these first tentative efforts proved successful, the goup was formally recognized by both union and management in 1978 and established as the Warren Operations Jobs Committee. The focus of its work and discussions was to be: "Get jobs back in Warren!" In 1981, after several years of joint discussions and activities that later would be subsumed under a formal QWL Program, the committee announced a jointly conceived Plan to Compete, which had two main thrusts: (1) it spelled out a variety of methods to reduce the Warren work force by offering such inducements as voluntary early retirement, job buyouts, or part-time work, and (2) it proposed a simultaneous expansion of component preparation work to replace the assembly work that was moving south. The Plan to Compete assumed the continued movement of labor-intensive, low-technology electrical harness assembly work to other locations but, at the same time, it looked toward an expansion of other high-technology, low-labor work, generically termed *remote lead preparation,* by which the electrical components of the harness are prepared for final assembly.

These hopeful signs were somewhat obscured in 1981 when two events occurred that intensified the already high feeling evoked by the job security issue. On June 1, 1981, Packard Electric's director of personnel and public relations announced that no employees would lose their jobs through shifts of business to other operations. But then, as the 1981 recession bit down on demand for Packard Electric products, the Packard management laid off 2,500 hourly employees—approximately 800 of whom were not called back even after all of their benefits were exhausted. Local 717 Jobs Committee representative Nichols felt that Packard had reneged on its earlier commitment to the hourly work force, and most of the local's members apparently agreed, because Nichols was elected chairman of the Local 717 shop committee in the union's November 1983 election.

National and local contract negotiations between GM, Packard Electric, and the IUE were scheduled to take place in 1984, shortly after Nichols took office. During the year leading to those negotiations, an ad hoc group made up of Packard Electric's top management group and the union's bargaining committee met regularly to address job security and other local contract issues. Formally termed the Resource Group, this team was to brainstorm possible solutions to the conflict between the economic demands of the marketplace and the employees' demands for employment and income security.

It is a testament to this group's imagination and perseverance that it managed to work out the concepts of a local contract that now forms the basis for a comprehensive management-labor partnership to improve productivity and quality within the context of employee job security. This historic agreement, entitled "Lifetime Job & Income Security Agreement," was developed through the use of problem solving rather than traditional collective bargaining techniques and was ratified in December 1984 by 77 percent of the local's membership—the largest plurality ever recorded in favor of a contract.

The Commitment to the Warren Operations

The contractual agreement negotiated in 1984 between Packard Electric and IUE Local 717 represented a fresh start in union-management relations and commitment to cooperation; it also articulated the philosophy and structure that undergird all current joint union-management activities at Packard Electric, including training. The job and income guarantees spelled out in the agreement significantly reduced the employees' fear that technological change and the introduction of high-technology machinery and equipment into Packard Electric plants would inevitably lead to loss of employment. The contract created a context for a positive psychological change that could enable Packard's hourly employees to experience technological innovation as a challenge in which they could participate rather than as a threat they needed to resist. Specifically, the agreement states its purpose as follows:

A. To provide Job and Income Security until normal retirement of an employe who acquired seniority prior to January 1, 1982, and who is capable of performing a job in accordance with the applicable provisions of the GM-IUE National Agreement and the Local Agreements between Packard Electric and Local 717.*

B. To provide Quality of Worklife Programs and jointly encourage participation of supervisory and bargaining unit with employes.

C. To provide a workplace environment that will improve operational effectiveness and stimu-

*It is the custom in the automobile industry to spell the word *employee* with a single *e*. Thus, quotations from company documents use the word *employe,* while the general text conforms to the more conventional spelling.

late efforts to understand and meet the com-
petitive needs of business.
D.   To provide a Hiring Plan for Progressive Hire
Employes and Temporary Part-Time Employes.

The agreement stipulates that "no [protected] employe
will lose his/her job due to a shift in work from Warren Operations to other locations or because of technological change"
and that no permanent layoffs of protected employees will occur.
Section II.C lays the groundwork for retraining of employees
to meet the requirements of the new technology: "Opportunities
to maximize employment for employes will be provided by
training employes and reassigning employes and/or work within
the Warren Operations and pursuing new business so that income security will be provided."

The job and income security provisions, it should be noted,
apply *only* to those employees who attained seniority prior to
January 1, 1982; they apply, in other words, to the generation
that came of age and went to work in the era of high inflation
and high wages and was most hard hit by the abrupt deflation
of employment security expectations that occurred with the industrial crisis of the 1970s and 1980s. The 400 or so employees
hired after the cut-off date—as well as temporary part-time
employees—are covered under a separate multitiered compensation structure. They do not enjoy the protection of the job
and income security provisions of the contract, although they
are eligible to participate in all training and QWL Program
activities. The contract also stipulates that the job and income
security provisions will not apply in the following cases: a strike
that interrupts production at the Warren facilities, natural disaster or national emergency, a situation in which Packard Electric
suffers a permanent loss of business to a nonallied competitor,
or the selling or termination of the division by GM.

Although consistent in all points with the IUE's national
contract with GM, the "Lifetime Job & Income Security Agreement" between Packard Electric and IUE Local 717 goes well
beyond the national agreement in its job and income security
provisions and in its emphasis on retraining as well as on other

joint ventures. Management and union spokespersons at Packard Electric agree that this contract has already resulted in:

improved union-management relations
improved plant flexibility
a system for increasing operational effectiveness, improving productivity, and providing job security

How the Training Program Works

With the contract framework in place, management and union officials moved quickly to create a new cooperative training and QWL structure in the nineteen Warren facilities. Packard Electric's hourly training activities constitute one component of the comprehensive QWL Program, which includes employee participation groups, quality teams, QWL committees, plant newspaper staffs, and statistical process control projects, to name just a few. According to Packard Electric organization development (OD) consultant Noble, who is responsible, with two union-appointed counterparts, for overseeing the QWL Program, "All the activities, including training, are conceived, implemented, monitored, and evaluated by joint union-management committees."

Structure. At the top of this joint QWL administrative pyramid is the Packard Electric–IUE Local 717 Jobs Board, composed of Packard's operations directors and labor relations director and the chairman and president of Local 717. This group, inaugurated in December 1984 immediately following ratification of the Warren agreement, is responsible for providing overall direction to the QWL activities in Packard Electric's nineteen Warren facilities and for determining, through joint review of the annual and long-term business plans, what the hiring and training needs of the various plants will be.

"Two major factors are driving training decisions at Packard Electric," explains Noble. "The first is the long-term plan to move all high-labor, low-tech assembly jobs out of Warren plants to locations in Mexico while simultaneously introducing high-tech, low-labor component manufacturing into the Warren Operations. The second factor is the customer. If the customer specifies new or more stringent quality requirements for the products we are producing, as General Motors is now doing with its recently introduced GM-10 Program, we must train our people quickly to meet the new standards and demands—or else lose our competitive edge." The GM-10 Program introduces quality standards and procedures for the production of the new GM-10 vehicles.

The Jobs Board administers all aspects of the lifetime job and income security agreement and monitors volume changes that may affect hiring and training plans. Finally, the board communicates the results of its deliberations—and these include projected training needs in each plant—to the Plant Units, which are its lower-level counterparts in each of the division's nineteen Warren plants.

The Plant Units are joint union-management committees accountable to the Jobs Board and composed of plant managers, superintendents, and labor relations representatives and, from the union side, subchairpeople and zone committee members. It is the responsibility of these groups to determine specific training needs for their plants in accordance with the business plan and to establish joint design teams and task forces to plan, develop, and implement the needed training programs. The Plant Units are also charged with initiating, developing, and implementing proposals to improve the operational effectiveness of the plant and to resolve operational or personnel problems. In short, it is the task of these joint committees, according to Noble, "to manage the business and the work force for Packard's Warren Operations."

To support the committee process in the plants, Packard Electric has two full-time Warren Operations QWL coordinators appointed by Local 717, Holden and Robert Robinson, and one organizational consultant, Noble, in division headquarters. These three function as a team and are responsible for overseeing all company QWL activities. "We function," says Noble, "as links between the Jobs Board and the shop floor." The team works with a resource network of forty-two people—among them, thirteen full-time hourly employee involvement coordinators appointed by the union, nine full-time salaried employee involvement consultants, and eight full-time statistical process control consultants. Additional support for QWL activities and training is provided by the Divisional Employee Development Group, which consists of a manager, three OD consultants, and a training coordinator. This group serves as a resource for the joint committees at the divisional and plant level as they plan training programs or other QWL activities.

This complex joint structure (see Figure 1) is one that mandates cooperation and communication from the top of the administrative hierarchy to the plant floor and back up again. The initiation, design, and implementation of training programs occur at all levels. A program or activity can be initiated at the top by the Jobs Board or at the bottom by hourly employees who discuss a perceived training need with a QWL coordinator. Wherever the initial idea comes from, it must go to the appropriate joint committee at the plant or divisional level for discussion and approval. If the idea is accepted, a design team is created to develop the curriculum and to stipulate the methods and technology necessary to meet the training need. If the new training program is to be divisionwide, serving employees in all plants, the design-team members will be drawn from all of Packard Electric's Warren units; if it is to be plant-specific, members will come only from within that plant. A typical technical training design team will be composed of a manufacturing supervisor, an engineering supervisor, an hourly operator, a Local 717 committee member, an industrial engineer, and the senior administrator of the Skills Development Training Center. In addition, the QWL staff, a union appointee, and an OD consultant will attend all design-team meetings and facilitate the development process. Instructors are also identified in the course of designing the program, and an instructional team is selected, with representatives from the union and management.

Technical Training. The Skills Development Training Center, located in Plant 12, administers a major portion of the divisionwide technical training programs, which prepare

Figure 1. Functional Structure of the Quality of Worklife Program.

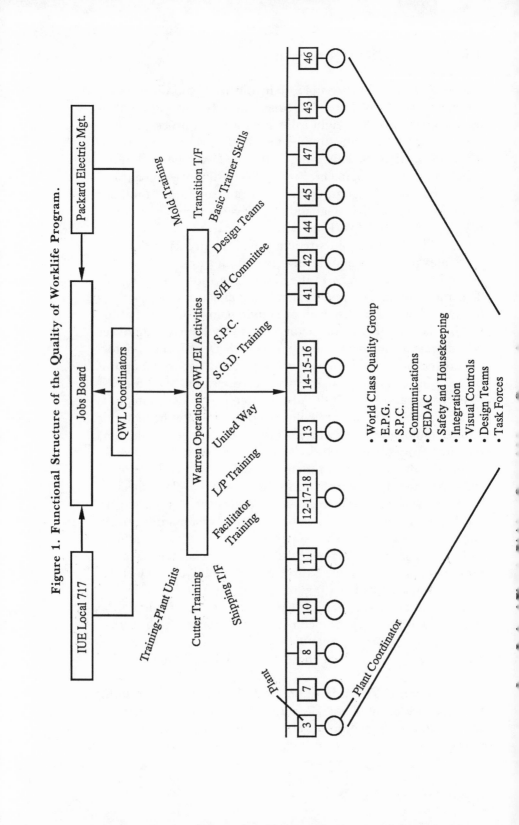

employees to operate the new high-tech machinery being introduced throughout the Warren Operations. Here, hourly and
supervisory employees are trained in the operation of Artos cut-
ters and plastic injection insert molding machines—two major
types of new machinery being introduced in the transition from
final harness assembly to component manufacture. Doug Welker,
senior administrator of the center, sees his role as "working with
engineering, manufacturing, and the union to provide the employee skill development needed to run this highly technical
equipment."

The April 24, 1986, edition of Packard Electric's newspaper, *Direct Connection,* describes how the Plastic Injection Insert
Molding Program was designed and what it is intended to do:

> Packard Electric and IUE Local 717 through a task
> force have jointly developed a new training program
> for the Rubber/Plastic Molding classification—Job
> Code 080. . . .
>
> "As Packard continues to concentrate on lead
> preparation in the Warren Operations, there will
> be a need for additional employes in this classifica-
> tion," said Doug Welker, training administrator,
> Skills Development Center. "The main thrust of
> the mold training program is to achieve uniform
> knowledge and skills among mold operators. This
> will support world-class quality efforts and competi-
> tiveness through productivity improvements.
>
> "Although those new to the 080 job code will
> be required to take this program, task force mem-
> bers also agreed that the Warren Operations would
> stand to gain the most if trainees included those
> already working within the 080 job code classifica-
> tion. Supervisors, technicians, and engineers will
> also have the opportunity to attend."

In addition to providing ongoing technical training at the
center, Welker's instructor teams travel to other plant sites to
do what he calls "modular training" in response to specific

requests initiated by Plant Units in those sites. In 1986, Welker trained approximately 1,100 employees overall in cutter operation and injection molding, either in the Skills Center's regular classes or through on-site specialty training. As indicated above, employees new to a job classification are required to take the technical training courses. Employees bid into these job classifications as they learn about openings "through the employee grapevine" and are selected on the basis of seniority.

In 1987, the Skills Center acquired the additional responsibility of training cutter operators in the new systems of monitoring component quality required under the GM-10 Program. The training program, developed by a divisional-level design team, is conducted in a newly purchased modern factory/office complex, where all divisionwide training activities now take place.

Quality Assurance. In addition to the job-specific technical training described above, joint teams have also developed a series of short courses and workshops to train employees to understand and use high-technology methods to improve quality control and solve production problems. One such course covers statistical process control technology, a new method for monitoring component quality at the point of production that places the responsibility for quality control with the machine operator. A more advanced course teaches problem solving with statistical tools to identify and solve manufacturing problems. It is known at Packard Electric as "fish-bone analysis," after the conceptual diagram that illustrates the analytical process of breaking down a problem into smaller and smaller units to isolate the source or cause of the difficulty. A variant of fish-bone analysis—taught in a separate workshop—is called CEDAC: Cause and Effect Diagram with the Addition of Cards. (CEDAC is a registered trademark of Productivity Incorporated, Boston, Mass.) This analytical tool enables employees to take the problem out onto the shop floor. A fish-bone diagram illustrating the production problem is set up on an easel on the factory floor, and employees participate in solving the problem by affixing pink cards with their suggestions as to its cause and/or solution to the appropriate place on the diagram (see Figure 2).

Figure 2. A Sample Cause-and-Effect Diagram.

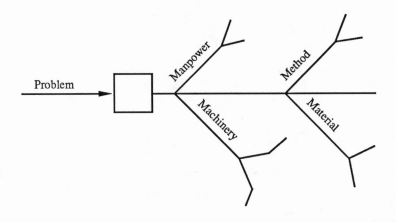

Source: Packard Electric Division, General Motors Corporation.

In addition to courses such as these, which enable an employee to take an active role in improving product quality and plant operational effectiveness, courses specific to each QWL activity have been developed through the joint union-management design process, and employees are required to take them prior to participation in any QWL activity. Thus, an employee who wants to write for the plant newspaper must first take a course in journalism.

Social Skills. Training in social skills is considered a necessary prerequisite for participation in any joint activities available through the QWL Program, including training for new technology. "There is no point in bringing people together to solve a production problem," says Noble, "if they don't understand group dynamics and how to work together in this kind of context. Social skills training introduces employees to the concepts of individual and group problem solving and conflict resolution. It enables them to have more awareness of the variety of skills and problem-solving styles that different people bring to a situation."

Figure 3 illustrates how essential both social and technical training at Packard Electric is to its employee involvement

Figure 3. How Social and Technical Training Support Employee Involvement.

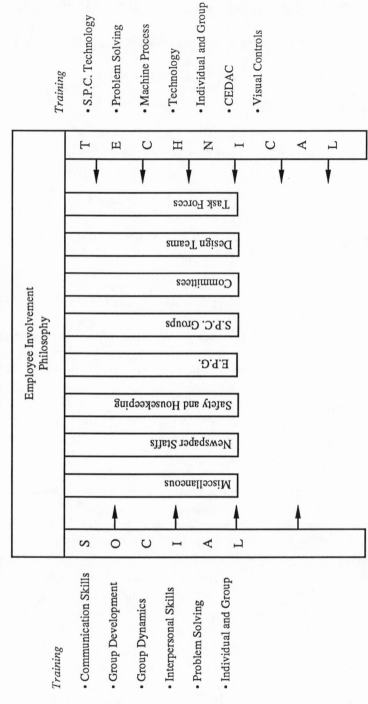

Source: Ron Noble, organization development consultant, Packard Electric.

philosophy; the two types of training support a structure of activities that are intended to produce an involved, quality-conscious work force and an innovative, customer-responsive organization.

The concept guiding all of these involvement and education activities is excellence, and this, in General Manager Elmer Reese's words, is "a concept broader than product. We wanted a concept that would involve all our people. We wanted a concept that would apply to everyone and everything we did. My vision is to fashion an organization second to none . . . the most innovative customer-responsive organization in the industry. Excellence is the way to make this vision a reality. That will be our true job security."

Reese's commitment to excellence through training is represented by his recent creation of the Excellence Training Center, where training and consulting services will be offered to employees at all Warren Operations facilities, and where meetings and training events can be held. According to Reese, as reported in *Cablegram,* a Packard Electric publication: "Our purpose [in establishing the center] is to provide training that is essential to a broad spectrum of our people as well as training which is specific to a particular job. We must provide our people with the tools, the skills, and the knowledge they need to understand their roles in creating excellence as a way of life at Packard Electric."

Results to Date

Packard Electric's "commitment to excellence," combined with its contractually binding commitment to the Warren work force, has significantly altered the division's culture in the nineteen plants that make up the Warren Operations. At least at the upper levels, management and union officials share a common understanding that true job security—especially for the generation of workers not protected by the lifetime security clauses of the contract—will only come from success in the marketplace. Some union members, though not completely trusting of management's stated commitment, have been relieved of their worst fears by the 1984 local agreement and by the visible evidence that Packard Electric is investing in its Warren plants and in its employees. "The psychological effect of job security is positive," says union member Holden. "When you know you can't lose your job, you are willing to innovate and get more involved." Although both Noble and Holden acknowledge that many hourly employees are still reluctant to get involved in QWL activities, they assert that employees who do are finding these activities and the prerequisite training a positive and rewarding experience.

One major change in the working environment at Packard Electric is the alteration of communication patterns between union members and management officials and between different levels of the company. Within the very comprehensive context of cooperative activities, managerial employees must work on an equal basis with union members who may also be subordinates out on the plant floor. This erosion of traditional managerial prerogative has not been accepted easily by some middle management and supervisory personnel, according to Noble. Another change that goes against the grain of traditional labor-management patterns is the continuing migration of responsibility for quality control and productivity down to the plant level and the machine operator. In a reversal of Taylorism, Packard Electric hourly workers are now being asked to think about their jobs. Welker points out that it has become obvious in the joint training design activities just how many smart people are employed at Packard Electric and how much they have to offer, once asked to participate.

Packard Electric has taken a look at some costs and benefits of this new way of doing business, and more cost-benefit studies are planned for the future. Early figures do show, however, that employee morale has improved, absenteeism has fallen, and productivity has improved. These results, according to union and management officials, are in conjunction with, if not in direct response to, the Warren agreement and the new manufacturing environment that is being created at Packard Electric by union-management cooperation at all levels.

By linking a competitive strategy for industrial survival

with a commitment to their community and work force, Packard Electric and IUE Local 717 have provided job security to over 8,500 people in the Warren facilities. Both union and management leaders realize that true job security can only be achieved by being competitive in the marketplace. At Packard Electric, the lifetime job security agreement sets in place an innovative, cooperative approach to job retention, retraining, and improving operational effectiveness. It is an approach that deserves wide attention.

24

General Electric, Fort Wayne, Indiana: High Tech Comes to the Rust Belt

Peter S. Smith

In 1983, General Electric (GE) undertook a bold plan to reverse the technology drain that characterizes U.S. industry today. The company moved a high-tech electronics facility from Evendale, Ohio, to the Rust Belt city of Fort Wayne, Indiana, and "grafted" it onto a traditional manufacturing operation. By all accounts, the operation is a success:

- The erosion of jobs, which had plagued GE's Fort Wayne operations for a decade, has been stemmed. Further, the job base has been enlarged, since more employees were hired for the new facility than were laid off due to reduction in existing divisions. Moreover, the nature of the jobs was changed relatively easily through specially designed worker retraining programs.
- Worker morale and satisfaction in the new facility are very

high, and at least some of that has spilled over to GE's other operations in Fort Wayne, simply because there appears to be good reason to believe that something has been done to halt the depressing tailspin in manufacturing employment.

- Union-management relations, which were good prior to the introduction of the new facility, have improved even further, as the union has responded to GE's investment in the retraining of its workers.

Briefly, the company shifted its aircraft engine electronic controls manufacturing and assembly operations into the empty half of a small electric-motor factory, creating in the process a state-of-the-art manufacturing facility that sits within the structure of the early 1940s Taylor Street plant. The other half of the plant is used for motor manufacturing. The contrast is striking: one moves from a noisy heavy industrial environment, where the floor is concrete and woodblock, to a quiet, postindustrial, carpeted milieu. There is, thus, a physical and environmental difference between the two facilities; although they share a building, they are as different as night and day. Air circulation systems are completely separate, and temperature and humidity in the high-tech facility are strictly controlled, in contrast to the traditional industrial area. They are, moreover, sealed off from one another by a wall; standing in one, it is hard to imagine that the other exists a few feet away.

Training of workers began almost immediately after GE announced on November 1, 1983, its decision to create the new facility. Workers were drawn from those in the motor manufacturing plant who had been given notice of layoff or who had already been laid off.

That this experiment took place at all in Fort Wayne is a tribute to all the elements involved: GE management, Local 901 of the International Union of Electrical Workers (IUE), the workers themselves, the City of Fort Wayne, the State of Indiana, and the area's elected federal representatives. All had to work hard—and cooperate—to make this unusual venture happen.

Setting the Stage

The story begins in the "good old days," or, rather, as
the good old days were coming to an end, in the early 1970s.
The company's principal products in Fort Wayne were electric
motors, transformers, and magnet wire. At that time (1973),
the total GE labor force in the city approached 8,000, and the
company was prospering. The decline that set in thereafter—
which coincided with the general downturn in the U.S. economy
after the first OPEC oil-price hike—took its toll on the GE work
force; it declined to some 5,200 in 1980 and continued to fall,
sinking to 3,100 in 1983. By then, only 100 employees were
under thirty years of age, and the average length of service with
GE was nearly twenty years. Many of the reductions had been
accomplished through retirement and other forms of attrition.
The principal products were still electric motors, transformers,
and magnet wire—but some models had been transferred to GE
facilities in other U.S. cities or to border-zone plants in Mexico.

General Electric had established itself as an integral part
of Fort Wayne late in the nineteenth century and, in the process
of becoming an institution in the ensuing decades, gained a reputation as a company that paid its employees well and provided
good benefits. There are a lot of "GE families" in Fort Wayne
who are proud of their long association with the company.

The principal union representing workers in the four GE
buildings in Fort Wayne is IUE. There is also a local of the
International Association of Machinists (IAM) certified within
GE's facilities in Fort Wayne. IAM Lodge 70 currently represents about 100 hourly tool and die makers, and its members
were not directly affected by the introduction of the electronics
facility. Local 901 of the IUE, on the other hand, represents
1,900 hourly production and maintenance workers in all GE
facilities (Taylor Street, Winter Street, East Broadway, West
Broadway) and was directly involved in and affected by the move
to Fort Wayne. The 1970s were characterized by work stoppages and confrontation tactics. In 1978, for example, 92,000
worker-hours were lost through work stoppages.

In 1979, however, John Carpenter, who had been elected

president of IUE Local 901 in 1978, and James Daughtry, who had been business agent of the local since 1974, decided to try a different approach to the situation. They went to Marvin Hamilton, who was then manager of union relations for GE in Fort Wayne, and struck an agreement to call a meeting within twenty-four hours of a potential work stoppage issue. As Daughtry notes, "Strikes had kind of gotten out of hand," but no one had been willing to resolve disputes.

Both sides complied with the new procedure, although Daughtry emphasizes that the transition was difficult. "It was much easier," he says, "to let a strike happen." The primary motivation, says Daughtry, was economic: jobs were disappearing, and there seemed to be no end in sight to the cycle of attrition.

Proof that the policy worked appears in the work-stoppage figures for subsequent years: In 1982, 150 worker-hours were lost in only one strike; in 1983, there were no stoppages; in 1984, there were two strikes for a total of 70 hours; and in 1985, there was one stoppage costing 100 hours. Daughtry emphasizes that this was not an overnight transformation but the product of slow, hard work on both sides. While, as Daughtry says, "differences of opinion still existed," by 1983 the atmosphere surrounding union-management relations had changed from "heavily adversarial" to what Charles Welch, who was at that time manager of employee communications, called "constructively adversarial."

The Critical Mass

In mid 1983, a number of factors came together to create the conditions necessary for the transfer of GE's Aircraft Engine Electronic Controls Department (AEECD) to Fort Wayne. The first of these factors was the by-then solidly established "constructively adversarial" relationship between Local 901 of the IUE and GE Fort Wayne management. William McShain, who succeeded Hamilton as manager of union relations, points out that had that climate not existed, Fort Wayne would not have been considered as a possible site for the high-tech facility.

A second factor was relations with the community. These were also good, based on the well-established institutional stature of GE within Fort Wayne. Confirmation had come in response to the hardship caused by the 1982 flood of the three rivers that snake through downtown Fort Wayne. Local churches started a food bank to help those hit by the disaster, and GE employees, led by Local 901, responded well to the appeal. Every year since, the union and the company have conducted a drive for the food bank that continues to serve those in need throughout the community.

A third factor was available manufacturing space. As a result of the prolonged downturn and serious overcapacity, GE had plenty of space in Fort Wayne. In that city, GE paid up to 30 percent more for wages and benefits compared to motor competitors in low-cost areas, and production costs had to be reduced. Motor production capacity in Fort Wayne was to be cut significantly: operations at two plants were to be discontinued, and a product line at another plant was to be transferred out of the area. Five hundred and fifty jobs would be lost as a result. Further, part of the small-motor manufacturing facility on Taylor Street had been mothballed in 1982 as a result of depressed market conditions, and that part of the Taylor Street building appeared to be suitable for the projected needs of AEECD production.

The final factor in the Fort Wayne area was the availability of retrainable, laid-off GE employees. In 1983, 1,000 GE employees were on layoff, most of them with at least ten years of service to the company. Moreover, hundreds were targeted for layoff in the very near future as GE reduced its Fort Wayne motor manufacturing capacity.

The introduction of AEECD into Fort Wayne would create 800 jobs (500 hourly and 300 salaried) in the next three years, which would more than offset the 550 that would be lost as a result of the consolidation under way in the motor business. At the time the move was announced to GE workers, McShain said that the company expected to be able to reduce the recall list of laid-off workers by 400 to 500 people over the subsequent three years, taking into account anticipated retirements as well as the production changes. Those facts alone made the move of compelling interest to all parties involved—local management, union, city, and state.

AEECD Moves to Fort Wayne

At that time (1983), AEECD's manufacturing facility was located with its present Aircraft Engine Business Group in Evendale, Ohio. Production of the electronic controls was inefficiently scattered over nine separate areas of the giant Evendale plant. Moreover, the successful aircraft-engine manufacturing group needed space to expand its engine-assembly operations. It made sense to remove the controls manufacturing function and locate it in one place.

GE management had been looking for a suitable site and had reached a tentative decision to locate the controls operations in an empty building available in Florida. The operation would thus be self-contained, or "freestanding," in a nonunion facility. A corporate facilities review had, however, indicated Fort Wayne as an alternative, particularly since a further reduction in the work force was imminent. According to Welch and McShain, corporate headquarters executives approached Fort Wayne motor management about the possibility of "trying something different" in Fort Wayne, given the size and nature of the space available, the work force, and the union-management climate. William Fenoglio, then vice-president of the Component Motor Division and GE's top Fort Wayne executive, carefully considered the current skills and potential trainability of the workers (the new facility would involve a wholly different product, working environment, and production style), the economics, and the space availability—and said it could be done.

Having made the decision to try Fort Wayne, GE had to nail down several necessary parts of the equation quickly and more or less simultaneously: The willingness of Local 901 to negotiate on work-force selection and placement procedures had to be explored, as did the extent to which the city and state might be willing to assist in the relocation.

Because the Fort Wayne facility was competing with a

freestanding alternate site in Florida, it would have to provide
work practices that were as comparable as possible. That meant
that the AEECD plant would have to operate as independently
of the rest of the GE Fort Wayne facilities as was possible within
the framework of the national GE-IUE contract: a separate local
supplement to the contract would have to be agreed to for
AEECD. In specific terms, the union would have to agree to
isolate the AEECD workers from the ''bumping'' procedure
followed at other GE operations in Fort Wayne, in which layoffs
took place on a seniority basis; staff, moreover, would have to
be selected first from personnel in the motor and transformer
businesses who were ''on the move'' (those slated for layoff)
and then from people on the recall list (those already laid off),
subject to seniority. These practices were necessary to minimize
disruptions to the work force in the motor, transformer, and
wire operations—and to ensure that AEECD would not lose its
retrained workers because of the ups and downs in the other
GE Fort Wayne businesses. Workers could not volunteer to
transfer to AEECD but had to be on the move so as not to
decimate the existing work force and make a shambles of current production needs in other facilities. AEECD, further, would
be an option, not a required transfer, and refusal would not
jeopardize an employee's seniority for recall to other facilities.
By the same token, a worker who agreed to transfer to AEECD
could not opt to return to motors or transformers but would
have to be on the move (again, management felt that this was
less disruptive for GE Fort Wayne management as a whole).

McShain says that he met with Local 901 business agent
Daughtry in late October 1983 ''on a Sunday morning in the
union hall'' and told him of the possibility of the AEECD move
and the special conditions that had to be addressed in local
negotiations. A week of ''hard bargaining'' in closed sessions
ensued, says Daughtry, and then the two sides reached agreement on November 1, 1983. Both Daughtry and McShain agree
that there was an immediate appreciation of the fact that the
company was bringing new business into an old manufacturing plant, that management was willing to buck the trend of
moving production away from the Rust Belt, and that for such

a promise of jobs some sacrifices were necessary on the part of Local 901.

In keeping with the sense of AEECD being freestanding, Local 901 leadership and GE agreed to several departures from work practices followed in the motor and transformer businesses:

- Promotion would be from within AEECD, and promoted workers would be replaced from the on-the-move pool of motor or transformer jobs.
- Streamlined lack-of-work procedures would operate for AEECD—in brief, workers would have only one option rather than several when lack of work was declared. Conversely, jobs would not be posted if work became available, but qualified people would be offered the positions, based on seniority.
- Compensation would be based on measured day work rather than on an incentive basis—that is, workers would be paid a straight hourly rate, and a standard of output would be established for job categories.
- There would be no bumping between AEECD and the remainder of GE facilities in Fort Wayne (this is still something of a sore point with the union leadership, but as Daughtry admits, ''You don't have any place to go if you don't have the jobs'').
- A broad job classification approach would be in effect within AEECD: a worker there would be expected to carry out a broad range of tasks, rather than performing a specialty. Training would, therefore, include cross-training to equip workers for the variety of tasks expected of them, and there would be very few job classifications.

It fell to GE's Fenoglio to negotiate with the local community, and he was able to come up with considerable support from state and civic leaders, again reacting to the promise of a bold experiment, a reversal of a trend, and some hope for the depressing employment picture. On November 1, he announced that an economic support package had been secured from the city and state:

- The Northeast Indiana Private Industry Council (PIC), through the Fort Wayne Area Job Training Partnership Act Consortium (JTPA), would provide on-the-job-training cost reimbursement for retraining up to 630 production employees. The local PIC approved a program that offset 50 percent of GE's retraining costs (the maximum training period was seventeen weeks), and which amounted to a total reimbursement of $2.2 million through 1986. The Indiana Office of Occupational Development pledged that funds would be available through JTPA and the Indiana Training for Profit program. The City of Fort Wayne guaranteed the availability of PIC and state funds for the worker retraining program.
- GE also acquired inventory tax credits as a result of its location in one of Indiana's six urban enterprise zones.
- City Council granted property tax abatements for new facilities and new equipment, to a total of $1.9 million.

Training

AEECD is primarily an assembly and test operation, assembling electronic circuit boards from components purchased elsewhere, assembling the completed boards into modules, and then assembling them further into finished units. Parts are small and color-coded, which means that dexterity and excellent color vision are required of production employees. All units are tested over temperature extremes and vibration to simulate operating conditions; much of the test equipment is built in the plant.

Training started in an off-site training center a few months after the decision had been made to bring AEECD to Fort Wayne. Training began long before the facility was ready for production. The half of the Taylor Street building that had been mothballed was turned over to AEECD; it was necessary to gut it completely, bulldoze the floor, and rebuild it from top to bottom—a process that took fifteen months. Workers were trained in a variety of tasks because they would work in groups as components were soldered and assembled rather than in a traditional assembly line, with each worker carrying out one small operation as part of the entire process.

Management approached IVY Tech, a state vocational and technical college, which agreed to help develop training courses in cooperation with AEECD personnel from the Evendale facility. Preparatory courses began in early 1984, outside the GE complex, eleven months before the new plant would be ready to begin production. Then the worker selection process began. (Many of the management and professional employees came from Evendale or other GE locations; all production and maintenance personnel were hired from other Fort Wayne GE businesses.)

It has been policy from the outset that potential candidates are identified by the GE Central Employment Office in Fort Wayne. Although qualifications are a determining factor for a few classifications, the vast majority of the hourly jobs are filled in order of seniority. Those who express an interest in being considered for AEECD employment are placed on a waiting list until a job opening occurs. In the interim, candidates for some jobs are counseled to complete additional electronics courses at such local technical schools as IVY Tech. All candidates who seek assembler or assembler/solderer positions are sent to the state employment service for manual dexterity and term-recognition tests (they must score medium to high for further consideration), as well as tests for visual acuity and color blindness (glasses may be prescribed for acuity, but failing the color-blindness test will remove the candidate from consideration unless the defect is of a correctable nature). When openings are actually available, candidates are interviewed one-on-one by members of the shop supervision and employee relations functions, during which the prospective employee is shown examples of products to be worked on and told what is expected of employees. If the interviewee still expresses interest after being informed that several weeks of classroom and on-the-job training, followed by a test, will be required, then formal training is initiated.

There are two basic programs—one for assemblers and a more difficult one for assembler-solderers. The latter course is taken over a period of twelve days in four-hour sessions in both the morning and afternoon of each day. All training is during working hours, at full pay. On the first day, candidates are introduced to AEECD, its parent group, and the AEECD business philosophy and are given an overview of methods and planning and shop operations. Key managers are introduced, and "active listening" is demonstrated. In the afternoon, candidates are introduced to technical training and safety, receive a tool kit and a description of its contents, tour the plant, and complete the day with questions and answers.

On the second day, hands-on training begins. Candidates learn how to read a measuring scale and are shown parts and wire colors. Then, after a sound/slide presentation on materials handling, they spend the rest of the day assembling and taking apart a printed circuit board.

Days three through six are used to cover nine lessons, during which trainees are taught the full range of soldering skills. Each lesson is preceded by a videotape presentation, which is then discussed. Some of them involve practice, and textbook study is sometimes required.

The next two days are taken up with practice sessions: wrapping and soldering standard electronic components, vacuum desoldering, lowering components onto pin, and "torquing." Then the certification test is explained to candidates, and they are given a final written examination.

The balance of the course is spent on certification. If the candidate passes the test on the first attempt, he or she can begin on-the-job training after the ninth day. If the candidate fails the test, the balance of the course is spent practicing and retaking the certification test.

The course for assemblers is set for eleven days, most of which is on-the-job training. Day one is much the same as for assembler-solderers, with a general and specific welcome and an introduction to the specific techniques assembling requires. The tool kit is explained, as are tooling and cut-and-form techniques, and there is some board assembly practice.

On day two, candidates continue with assembly techniques and begin practicing the assembly of printed circuit boards, using operations sheets. After that, their training is on the job until day eleven. At that point, they are tested, which involves assembling a board with a time limit. If the first board is not completed within the time limit or if its quality is unacceptable, a second board may be attempted. Failure at the second board results in disqualification and a return to layoff.

If a prospective assembler-solderer fails the test, he or she is then a candidate for an assembler position. If unsuccessful in the course, the candidate may also elect to go back on layoff, with full benefits, as if he or she had just been laid off, regardless of how long the layoff had actually been prior to training. Successful completion of either course qualifies the candidate for immediate assignment to open jobs in AEECD and a period of on-the-job training. (Assembler-solderers must pass periodic solder certification tests to demonstrate that the quality of their solder techniques meets military and Federal Aviation Administration standards for flight hardware.)

In addition, after successfully completing either of these courses, or completing qualification for a tester position, workers participate in a two-day course on team building. Topics covered include active listening skills, assertive communication, awareness, communication role play, team formation, team dynamics, team problem solving, and communication/team problems and feedback.

On-the-job training involves a variety of people: the other production workers in the cluster into which the new worker is placed; salaried supervisors, much of whose job is to facilitate on-the-job training and support requirements; salaried quality and production methods personnel; and the actual instructors (salaried employees at GE), who are available to workers when they are not teaching.

Courses were originally taught off-site. Later, a prototype production facility was built, and newly qualified workers were fed into positions in the prototype area. By the end of 1984, over 100 employees were working in the uncompleted AEECD plant. (Roger Clarke, manager of AEECD employee and community relations, commented on the "pioneer spirit" in those early days: workers participated in much of the setting-up process, in the design of operations, the choice of work-surface materials, and the design of the chair that would be used in the assembly area.) In very short order, permanent training facilities were built within the new facility, and courses have been taught there ever since. (IVY Tech also offers a range of additional electronics courses, and GE encourages workers to take them by offering tuition refunds. Such courses are offered after hours, in contrast to the actual training.)

Another example of personal commitment toward achieving qualification for higher-rated AEECD positions is the effort put forth by employees to pass the eleven-week electrical fundamentals course and the subsequent fourteen-week testers' course. Both courses are taught on an after-hours basis.

Initially, Local 901 officials had some concerns about the training required of the prospective AEECD workers. They were also concerned that it was a long time since some workers had been in any kind of school—twenty-five years, in several cases— and that it might be difficult to adjust to the classroom environment. Yet, as Daughtry and Carpenter are quick to point out, many of those who had been out of school for that length of time passed with flying colors. Additionally, although there was concern with the administrative process for JTPA, the value of having a training subsidy to help bring well-paying manufacturing jobs into the community is unquestioned.

"The result of all the training," asserts Clarke, "is a highly motivated work force which is committed to meeting our customer requirements for highly reliable, cost-effective products. When you consider that many of our employees had been laid off for years, it's really great to see how they responded to the opportunity to learn a new occupation. There is much joy in watching people successfully qualify for a good job opportunity. The smiles on their faces are worth all the hard work that was required by the start-up team to put this plant together."

Focus Teams

Production in the AEECD facility is done through a team approach. Clarke emphasizes that employees are very involved in quality control and take full ownership for the product they build in this inspectorless facility. People have responded well to working in teams.

While there is an assembly area, work is done by groups of people working adjacent to one another in ergonomically designed cubicles containing four work areas. The area in which each set of work surfaces is located is partially partitioned off from its neighbor and yet gives a sense of openness. A transporter system carries components to each work area on request, and the entire inventory system is computerized. The atmosphere is cooperative, pleasant, and cheerful; employees are busy but not driven; and the emphasis is clearly on quality. Each employee is expected to have cross-functional capability—no one specializes in one narrow capability. This cross-functional approach provides manufacturing flexibility and facilitates problem solving, because people understand one another's roles and how products are built.

Bridging the training and work areas are regular communication meetings, which are held on a weekly basis to update employees on product status, manufacturing techniques, and business results. These meetings are supplemented by focus-team meetings, which zero in on specific manufacturing problems. The focus teams, made up of employees who can best solve identified problems, include both hourly production and salaried support employees who have the resources to resolve problems that inhibit productive output.

By contrast, in the adjoining small-motor plant, employees work alone at specialized tasks. The whole operation is much more akin to a traditional assembly line, even though robots have been introduced for some functions. Some of the state-of-the-art production techniques from AEECD have, however, been introduced on a very limited scale in the motor and transformer operations. For example, participatory management is appearing as part of a move toward a more self-directed work force. What this means, in essence, is less paternalistic and authoritarian management, with workers taking more responsibility for quality as well as for their own work areas.

The Union's Reaction

''We're elated with what we've got. At times we (management and union) still have problems, but we're working on them.'' This, from IUE business agent Daughtry, seems to summarize the feeling of GE employees about what the AEECD facility means to them. Daughtry adds, ''If we can make a success of it, maybe we can prove to the doubters that we have common interests.''

It bears repeating that this is a radical departure from the norm that characterizes management-union relationships. True, as Daughtry is careful to emphasize, differences of opinion still arise, ''and we could be out on the street tomorrow,'' but Local 901's leaders are clearly excited about what GE's trend-bucking move may represent—nothing less than a possible blueprint for the reindustrialization of America.

The reaction of the IUE national hierarchy is more guarded. Says Daughtry, ''They are still surprised at the novelty, particularly that it has happened with GE.'' The national union is watching events in Fort Wayne very carefully and is willing to be convinced that it could happen elsewhere.

25

Pacific Northwest Bell: A Job Skills Bank

Claudia Feurey

Before divestiture, a job with a telephone company—anywhere in this country—was as close as most American workers would come to "employment for life." Now, the newly formed local and regional companies are finding that they must operate in increasingly competitive markets for the services they offer. In addition, technological change means that companies will need fewer but more highly skilled workers in the years ahead.

The approach to employment security taken by one of these companies—Pacific Northwest Bell (a subsidiary of U S WEST)—illustrates that a commitment to employees can be compatible with fast-paced technological change and the development of new markets and services. The Job Skills Bank, which matches management employees with available jobs in the company, has given employees greater control over career decisions and has proven to be a useful tool in identifying skill deficiencies and surpluses.

The Start-Up

Until quite recently, Pacific Northwest Bell (PNB) had a formal but fairly low-key means of routinely notifying current management employees of job openings in the company, through a weekly printed bulletin. However, following divestiture, PNB (which serves the states of Washington, Oregon, and Idaho) made a strategic decision to foster greater awareness of management opportunities within the company and to alert managers that they could indeed have a future in the company outside their traditional career path.

In 1985, therefore, PNB began to compile skills and occupational preference profiles on all its management employees. Now, through this newly created Job Skills Bank, employees are notified directly whenever there is a job vacancy that matches their personal profile of skills, work and education background, and relocation preferences. Employees are encouraged to discuss these job matches with their supervisor and to apply through that supervisor for any jobs that interest them, whether within their own division or outside of it.

According to Louise Scalzo, staff manager of human resources data for PNB, this new, more aggressive approach to management mobility will be critical to keeping talented managers in an environment that may offer fewer jobs overall in the future. "The most important attribute of this system," Scalzo observes, "is that it now gives employees much more control over their career development and is a very positive way to broaden our managers' horizons."

First, a Test Run

The Job Skills Bank began in part with PNB's Finance and Comptrollers Department. As a result of some extended departmental meetings and discussions with its management employees, this department found that career development was a major concern among its managers and that many managers felt they were not fully informed of the range of available career paths. Many management employees also told their managers they had skills and work preferences that could benefit the company but that were not being fully used.

When the Finance and Comptrollers Department managers came to the Human Resources Department for help, they were pleased to learn that human resources had been working on developing a means of matching employee preference with job openings—the Job Skills Bank. In an agreement worked out with finance and comptrollers, human resources tested its program on that department in 1984. In 1985, it opened the skills bank to the more than 4,000 managers throughout Pacific Northwest Bell.

The job-matching process works like this:

- Each PNB management employee is asked to prepare a detailed profile of skills, experience, and work preferences, which is then encoded into the Job Skills Bank computer system.
- When management jobs become available at PNB, supervisors are required to submit a Management Job Vacancy Form, using the same codes for the skills needed to fill the position.
- The Job Skills Bank computer program searches the skills bank for employees to fill the job and notifies the employees and their supervisors that a job exists for which they appear to be qualified.

The number of potential candidates identified varies widely, generally from a handful to several dozen.

- If an employee is interested, he or she must first discuss the opportunity with the direct supervisor. The supervisor must be the one to nominate the employee for the vacant position; the employee does not go directly to the manager with the opening.
- As a courtesy, personnel administrators in departments with job openings are notified of the employees who have been matched to vacancies.

According to Scalzo, managers with job openings and personnel administrators generally respect this protocol, and there have been very few instances of applicants or managers trying to bypass the supervisor-must-nominate system. Also, since all management job openings must flow through management staffing, employees participating in the Job Skills Bank have the opportunity to be matched to all available management jobs at PNB.

The managers with job openings decide on which employees to interview and, based upon the interview, make the final selection.

According to Judy Sandberg, manager of PNB's corporate management staffing, in order for the matching process to work properly, both the employees seeking jobs and the managers with job openings must use the most precise codings possible. It is particularly important for managers with job openings to be specific about the skills required. In general, the personnel administrators in each department screen the Management Job Vacancy Forms and, in some departments, work directly with the managers in their preparation.

While the supervisor-must-nominate procedure is intact for the present, Scalzo predicted that as PNB's experience with the skills bank increases, it may eventually switch over to some form of direct contact between an interested employee and a manager with a job opening.

Employee Reception: Generally Enthusiastic

Participation in the Job Skills Bank is voluntary for employees. According to Scalzo, the response has been very enthusiastic, with a number of employees finding that they are qualified for jobs they might never have thought of pursuing.

Scalzo cites the case of one woman with line experience in writing PNB procedures who was matched, because of her background, to a supervisory job she probably would not have considered previously. Although the skills bank has been fully operational only since April 1986, several other employees have had similar experiences, and employee participation is high. As many as 80 percent of the employees in some departments have their profiles in the system.

However, there are some pockets of resistance, Scalzo points out, particularly in engineering and technical areas. In some of these departments, only 11 percent of the employees have completed personal skills inventories for use by the skills bank. One engineering manager has expressed concern that the personal profile forms used by the skills bank are not finely tuned enough for the highly technical skills represented in the engineering department. Too broad an interpretation in coding for one particular job vacancy has already led to an instance in which 199 potential candidates were matched to an engineering opening, causing a flurry of burdensome paperwork. There is also some concern that the program could raise false expectations about employment possibilities in a time of constricting employment at PNB.

Scalzo acknowledges that there are a few managers who have actively discouraged their employees from participating, possibly out of fear of losing valued and skilled employees to other divisions. But she says that PNB is working with these supervisors to make sure that no employee is discouraged from using the skills bank for his or her own career development and that the supervisor-must-nominate procedure is not used to block any employee who wishes to advance.

"We want to be sure that supervisors realize the company will gain by the proper placement and increased job knowledge of all employees through development of their managerial abilities. We encourage all of our employees to work for excellence throughout their careers," Scalzo affirms.

PNB is currently conducting an evaluation of the first few months of the program's operation.

A Complete Dossier

When employees are asked to prepare their current profile, PNB stresses the usefulness of this document in planning their future with the company. Using a comprehensive handbook that explains the detailed computer coding of a wide variety of skills and experiences, employees provide human resources with detailed information on the following topics:

- skills, work experience, and preferences both at PNB and elsewhere (hundreds of specific skills are listed in such areas as business, management, and scientific skills and specific technical telecommunications skills)

- academic and technical education
- professional licenses, certificates, and memberships
- foreign languages, indicating level of proficiency
- significant achievements (that is, a free-form section for highly personalized information that would not normally appear on the employee's job description form, such as civic participation, academic honors, patent awards, or books or articles written)
- willingness to relocate, whether it is within the same city or to any location within the U S WEST region

Employees are asked to update their profiles at least once a year and are encouraged to make changes any time they deem them necessary.

A Resource for the Future

According to Sandberg, one problem with the Job Skills Bank, mentioned earlier, is that even the seemingly detailed breakdown of skill codes may not be specific enough to meet future demands placed on the system. PNB is now working to refine its coding, with special attention to properly indicating proficiency levels.

While the Job Skills Bank was set up to match current employees with available jobs in the company, PNB has already looked to the skills bank to seek out employees with needed backgrounds for special projects, to identify high-potential and promotable employees, and to estimate skill deficiencies or surpluses in certain areas.

Planning new business directions is a high priority at PNB. As decisions are made on new ventures, Scalzo predicts, the skills bank will prove an important tool in this process.

Sandberg notes that two other U S WEST companies, Mountain Bell and Northwest Bell, also have job skills banks. PNB is currently working with these two companies to integrate the three skills banks so that employees can be matched to jobs across the fourteen states represented by the three companies.

26

Hewlett-Packard: Partnerships for New Careers

Jill Casner-Lotto

Hewlett-Packard's recently launched retraining program, Partnerships for New Careers, is an ambitious effort to move employees from surplus production jobs into administrative and computer fields. The program reflects the company's drive to maintain its record of product excellence in an increasingly complex, competitive global market, as well as its long-standing objective of providing employment security. Partnerships for New Careers is unique at Hewlett-Packard (HP) because it has been fashioned as a model for future retraining programs, representing the best practices of existing retraining programs at HP sites across the country. The purpose of the model is to coordinate retraining efforts on a regional basis and thus avoid duplication in implementing local division programs, encourage the sharing of resources and ideas, and promote consistency in the philosophy of designing retraining programs on a national and, potentially, worldwide basis.

The program was piloted in June 1986 in the San Francisco Bay Area, the most populous HP region, where about

397

twenty-five company facilities are located, including the corporate headquarters. Enrollees are offered training in six major career tracks, from general administrative support to more specialized computer and telemarketing fields. So far, thirty-five HP employees have completed the retraining program, most of which takes place off-site on the campus of Mission College, a community college in Santa Clara. Recognition ceremonies were held in September to honor this first graduating class, and among those participating was HP executive vice-president and chief operating officer Dean Morton, whose presence reinforced the top-level corporate support the Partnerships program is receiving.

The majority of trainees have been placed in their new positions, and the feedback from the hiring supervisors and department managers is "wonderful," according to Peggy Campbell, retraining program manager for the Bay Area. "In fact," she adds, "we're getting requests for enrollment from some divisions whose employees were reassigned, but who didn't have the opportunity to go through this program."

The program is characterized by an extraordinary degree of organization and planning. *Partnerships for New Careers,* a seventy-page manual, which has been distributed to HP personnel managers across the country, covers every aspect of the program, including a communication plan, selection criteria, course outlines, job placement, and evaluation and tracking. A condensed version of these program guidelines will soon be distributed worldwide. Another characteristic of the Partnerships program is the level of involvement of various individuals in the retraining process: the participants, their current supervisors, hiring supervisors, career mentors, and program coordinators from both the current and hiring divisions. All have clearly designated roles and responsibilities, which are outlined in an agreement form signed by each individual before the training process begins.

None of this should suggest, however, that the program operates on a rigid basis. Evaluation of the Bay Area pilot has been ongoing, and HP human resource officials are incorporating what they have learned from this first effort into the Partnerships model. The challenge, notes human resource planning manager Jennifer Konecny, is to take the philosophy embodied in the retraining model and apply it to regional needs.

Retraining: A Link to Security and Competitiveness

Global competition in the computer field, coupled with the accelerating rate of technological change, has triggered HP's retraining efforts. Specifically, several factors are affecting the work force: The general slump in the computer and electronics industry has brought out excess manufacturing capacity. Some products that were formerly assembled in the company are now purchased from the outside. There is increased pressure to produce at the lowest cost and highest volume possible while simultaneously maintaining quality control. And increased automation is changing both manufacturing procedures and product design.

Simply put, fewer people and less time are required to assemble products and, at the same time, increasingly sophisticated technological skills are needed to perform both new and existing jobs in the office, as well as on the production line. While the easy solution to cope with these changing conditions would be to lay off employees whose skills are no longer needed by the company and recruit from the outside, such a move would be inconsistent with the corporate culture HP has established. Its impressive record of providing employment security to its 83,000-member work force has been achieved over the years through the planned use of a variety of business strategies. In recent years, an array of "human resource rebalancing" measures—retraining, redeployment, hiring freezes, voluntary severance, and enhanced early retirement—have all been implemented to stabilize the level of the work force and meet the needs of the business.

The retraining option is viewed both as an essential link to employment security at HP and as an especially effective tool for adapting to constantly changing technology—points which are clearly emphasized to employees interested in the Partnerships retraining program. In one of the presentations describing the program, employees are told that "some form of learning and retraining will become a way of life for everyone at Hewlett-Packard."

All retraining at HP is voluntary and is considered to be the employee's responsibility. The company makes it clear that it will provide the guidance and the resources needed to gain new skills, but it's up to the employee to take the appropriate action. Judging from some of the trainees' comments, as reported in *Footprints,* an in-house publication of the HP Personal Computer Division, the Partnerships program represented the ideal opportunity to move out of the production area—where they could plainly see more and more tasks being phased out—into high-growth office and computer fields. In addition, it meant a chance for some to continue their education and even push ahead for a degree.

Planning and Design of the Partnerships Program

Planning for the Partnerships pilot program began in February 1986. A task force was formed, composed of corporate human resource staff members, plus representatives of ten San Francisco Bay Area divisions, divided equally among those anticipating declines in manufacturing jobs and those expecting to hire in the office and computer fields. It was the first time local divisions were coming together to model a retraining program on a regional basis. "It made the most sense, since the issues of matching supply and demand and distribution of the work force are regional in nature. And it increased our leverage in working with the community college," explains Teresa Roche, who was the project and task-force leader. Another critical task was the design of a process that could be repeated easily by other regions, made possible by the manual, which Roche was instrumental in developing. As noted earlier, this manual is a detailed blueprint for the planning, implementation, and evaluation of the retraining process.

The Bay Area pilot program was designed by task-force members in cooperation with instructors at Mission College. Based upon analysis of past and current job trends and one-year projections, the task-force members selected the six job categories that were in the greatest demand in the Bay Area, assessed the skills needed to fill these jobs, and then met with community college officials to develop a course curriculum. A core set of skills was designed to support six major career tracks: electronic data processing support, computer operator, administrative support, telemarketing operator, secretary, and coordinator (field and factory processing order support). Core-skills training includes math, English, typing, office procedures, time management, and introduction to computers. The program lasts three months, with participants spending all day Monday and four afternoons a week in classes at the Mission College campus. They also attend classes at HP's Office Learning Center, which offers both introductory and advanced computer courses. Those going into telemarketing and computer operations are required to take additional specialized computer courses that run beyond the initial three-month training period.

The program emphasizes the combination of academic and on-the-job training. Although placement in the new job may occur at any time during the retraining program, each trainee is immediately assigned a career mentor in his or her chosen field who provides career information and relevant on-the-job training experiences. In addition, those who are not placed in their new jobs during the training period are usually placed in temporary assignments related to their career fields. Besides preparing employees for new careers, an important goal of the program is to support the notion of lifelong learning, Konecny notes. By the time they graduate, trainees have earned fourteen units of college credit, which may be applied toward a degree-level program. And, in several cases in the Bay Area, trainees were doing just that.

All training is paid for by the company and offered on company time. The approximate training cost per participant (not including salary) is $2,200 for the three-month period, which includes books. Additional costs include mileage reimbursement and other related course materials. Training costs are billed to the trainee's current organization.

Selecting the Candidates for Training

Almost two weeks before the selection process of candidates got under way in the Bay Area, there was an extensive campaign to familiarize the prospective candidates with the program's objectives, the types of retraining offered, and the nature of the jobs to be filled. After posting notices of the program, personnel managers in divisions with excess production jobs presented an overview of the program to interested employees, including a discussion of the long-term market changes affecting the work force and the urgent need for retraining. Employees were also invited to participate in panel discussions led by individuals representing the major career tracks, who talked about their jobs and answered any questions. Special tours of the community college and of the divisions with job openings were organized. And, finally, prospective candidates had access to generic job profiles describing the qualifications and principal responsibilities for each of the six career tracks. This information is generally available in personnel departments and, in some HP regions, can also be accessed by computer from the employee's job site.

In general, three groups of employees are eligible to apply to the Partnerships program. First priority is given to those identified as "excess" employees within their division—in other words, employees whose jobs are no longer needed due to market or production changes, the relocation or closing of their units, or the introduction of new technology. The next targeted group includes "projected excess" employees, meaning employees whose jobs are being phased out within the next year. Finally, after employees from both groups have had the opportunity to apply, the program is open to any interested employees. Because of the acute skill shortage and high demand for jobs in the Bay Area, the pilot program could not accommodate this last group.

Prospective candidates fill out an application form that asks mostly open-ended questions concerning the reasons for applying, prior work experience, educational qualification, and any concerns they may have about retraining. The form is deliberately structured like a resume in order to draw out information that could eventually be used in the preparation of the actual resume if the candidate is selected for the program.

The application forms are sent to the personnel department in each candidate's current division, where they are screened for accuracy, neatness, and demonstrated interest. After passing the initial screening test, applicants are interviewed by a committee of representatives from the applicant's current division: a designated program coordinator, personnel liaisons, supervisors who would normally hire for these career fields, and the employee's current supervisor.

A selection criteria form is filled out, which rates employees according to four major criteria: expressed interest in career change; willingness to participate in a retraining program; demonstrated dependability, initiative, flexibility, and teamwork skills (as documented by the employee's last two performance evaluations); and ability to communicate well in oral and written form. The selection criteria form also includes a development plan, in which committee members note the employee's career objectives and list specific actions the employee can take to increase his or her effectiveness. Employees can see the completed criteria form (whether or not they are accepted into the program), so this development plan can serve as an important tool in future career discussions.

In the Bay Area pilot program, after the interviewing process, the program coordinators in each of the divisions with applicants sent a list of potential candidates, noting a first or second choice for each career field, to Campbell, the Bay Area retraining program manager, who then made the final selection. Out of a total of seventy applicants, thirty-five were chosen to participate—a number determined by the demand for specific fields within the region and optimal class size.

The Agreement Form

One of the first steps in the retraining process is the signing of the agreement form, a three-page document outlining the objectives of the program and the roles and responsibilities of the various individuals involved. According to Campbell, having such a tool ensures greater coordination and helps create realistic expectations of each individual's function in the overall process and his or her relationship to others. For example, participants are expected to regularly complete on-the-job training requirements assigned by the career mentor and to keep their supervisors and the program coordinators informed of their progress in the retraining program. The trainee's current supervisor agrees to adjust work schedules and responsibilities to accommodate participation in the retraining program and to assist the employee in job-placement activities.

If the transfer to a new job occurs during the training period, the current supervisor is expected to work closely with the hiring supervisor to ensure a smooth transition. The hiring supervisor agrees to provide a position plan for employees that includes a description of the job expectations. This is completed while the employee is in the retraining program. The hiring supervisor also works with the employee's career mentor to make sure on-the-job training occurs. The program coordinators— from both the current division and the hiring division—agree to oversee and monitor the program, working closely with the supervisors and career mentors on their responsibilities and meeting with the participants to discuss their progress in the retraining program. These coordinators also serve as contacts for their divisions, providing feedback to the Bay Area program manager and tracking requested information on the program and the participants.

Combining Academic and On-the-Job Training

An important element of the Partnerships program is the mix of academic and on-the-job training—a balance that is achieved through several means. But, even before the regular curriculum begins, the first course—since many individuals have not been in a classroom for years—is "Introduction to College," a comprehensive overview, which familiarizes participants with effective learning and study techniques, test-taking skills, career information, and interpersonal relations. Special tours of the community college and group meetings with instructors and other college officials are also scheduled.

Provisions of support services for trainees—that is, counseling, career advice, help with course work—is a shared responsibility of the community college and the company. For example, the Bay Area program manager and other divisional program coordinators are on the campus certain days each week so they can meet with the participants to discuss any problems. And the college will provide tutors if the trainees need extra help with class assignments.

Although the ideal way to combine academic and on-the-job experience, in the view of HP officials, is by assigning the trainee to the new position at the beginning of training, it is not always possible to make that match right away. If that is the case, divisions are urged to remove the trainees from their production jobs during the retraining program and to place them in a position similar to the one they will be going to—or at least to temporarily assign job responsibilities resembling the ones they will eventually be carrying out. In either situation, however, a career mentor is immediately assigned to work with the trainee, and this person can play a key role in linking classroom knowledge to on-the-job experiences.

Career mentors are individuals who usually work in the trainee's chosen career field, although, in some cases, the trainee's supervisor or the divisional program coordinator may serve as the mentor. Career mentors are expected to familiarize themselves with the course curriculum and, whenever possible, provide on-the-job training oportunities that apply to the material being covered in class. To help them in this role, they are given detailed outlines with specific examples of on-the-job tasks and assignments related to the courses. For example, the computer operations overview suggests that mentors help trainees "operate all system-line printers" and "understand various distribution methods." The outline on the office procedures course lists over twenty activities, such as "recognizing microcomputer functions" and "building an information-processing vocabulary," or more general assignments, such as "applying problem-solving techniques in work situations and dealing with office support staff."

Depending on when the actual job placement occurs, the career mentor may be from either the trainee's current division or the hiring division. If the trainee is placed in the new job when the training starts, a career mentor from the hiring division is assigned immediately. If not, someone from the current division acts as mentor, generally spending time each week with the trainee, until the trainee is hired into the new job, at which point a mentor from the hiring division takes over.

"The use of career mentors turned out to be very successful," notes Campbell. "Those departments that were unable to find someone in the trainee's career and instead had to rely on the program coordinator were not as pleased, since a person working in the same field could be more empathetic and understanding of the trainee's needs."

Making the Transition

As noted above, the ideal scenario for reentry into the work force is job placement at the beginning of training. But if a full-time position is still not available by the end of the retraining program, employees are placed in temporary assignments in their chosen career fields until a permanent job match occurs. In the case of the Bay Area pilot program, an in-house "temporary pool" turned out to be an effective mechanism for providing a kind of introductory work experience before employees started in their regular jobs.

Job placement is a multistage process, not unlike the normal job placement process that occurs at Hewlett-Packard, says Konecny. "It's just that there is greater identification of and more support given to these candidates. There are people keeping track of these individuals—both in the current and hiring organizations—at each step along the way." Job-search assistance, including interviewing and resume-writing techniques, is provided by the employee's current supervisor and by the personnel department during and after the retraining program.

The trainees' resumes and completed transfer request forms are distributed to divisions that have current openings, where they are screened by the hiring supervisor. The supervisor and program coordinator in the hiring division interview their top two choices for each job category before making the final selection.

By the time the Bay Area pilot program had ended, only four individuals had not been assigned to new full-time positions. Five had been placed when the training started; the others were placed at some point during the program. As Campbell notes, the training experiences of those who were placed at the earlier stages of the training turned out to be the most successful. While it is generally understood that the training is directed toward specific positions, working out the placement arrangements at the start of the training period not only instills a more positive outlook on the part of the participant, it enhances the training process itself.

"By addressing all the requirements for placement before the training begins, you get the support and involvement of the trainee's supervisors and the program coordinators from the hiring organizations right away," Campbell points out. Since these individuals play such a key role in familiarizing trainees with the new work environment, their participation early in the training process ensures a smooth transition to the office setting.

Evaluating the Program and Making Changes

Although it is too early to assess the full value of the program to the company, its success so far demonstrates its potential and has convinced HP officials they are headed in the right direction. Plans are under way for more rounds of training in the Bay Area, and several other HP divisions are adopting the Partnerships retraining model. "The biggest ambassadors of this program have turned out to be the employees themselves. As the trainees have moved into the new office environment, their enthusiasm—conveyed through informal people-to-people contacts—has spread to other divisions," observes Jennifer Konecny. While initially some managers were reluctant to participate in the program because of difficulty in defining jobs for trainees as opposed to outside recruits, the success of the trainees in the pilot program has encouraged several other managers to take part.

After the pilot program concluded, the task-force members met to evaluate the program and discuss any changes to be made. And, in order to gain insights from the trainee's point of view, they planned to reconvene the first group of students to see how they have done in their new jobs and to assess the relevance of the training experience to the work they are now performing.

There are already a number of changes on the drawing board. HP officials may make another program available to employees currently working in office positions who want to advance in secretarial fields. Campbell explains why: "We found that in three months we couldn't adequately train a production employee to fill a senior secretarial spot—only two out of the thirty-five candidates were qualified to fill those positions. So, in the administrative support career track, we may offer two types of training—one for production employees that is geared to entry-level administrative jobs, and one for office workers that is directed toward more advanced secretarial positions."

Another major change in the program may be a greater emphasis on job placement before the training begins. As mentioned earlier, the assignment to the new position in the early stages of the program had a beneficial effect on both the training experience and the transition from the production line to the office. "Our goal for next time," says Campbell, "will be to place at least half of the trainees in their new jobs before the actual training gets under way." In the other cases, when the transfer to the new job occurs at a later point, the program coordinators and supervisors from the current and hiring divisions will be encouraged to make contact and work together as soon as possible in order to assure a good fit between the trainee's qualifications and the specific job needs and to ease the transition process.

The process of selecting training candidates has also been modified and somewhat expanded. Potential candidates, after being interviewed and recommended by a team of representatives from their division, will then be tested for English and math skills prior to acceptance in the program. HP officials found that, in some cases, one obstacle to prompt job placement was the trainee's difficulty in mastering certain English and math requirements. Therefore, they believe a basic level of proficiency in these skills may help determine success in the program and in job placement. After being tested, the candidates will be interviewed by a regional team, consisting of a task-force member, a potential hiring supervisor, and a potential hiring personnel manager. The final selection of candidates will be determined as a result of this interview. "We feel that this step should help facilitate job placement," notes Campbell. "If an opening exists, it will be easier to make the match after this interview has been conducted."

Campbell also plans to meet with the program coordinators in each division on a regularly scheduled basis. "It turned out to be kind of hit and miss this last time," she notes. "Scheduling meetings every two weeks and requiring some sort of progress report will increase communication and provide a better basis for evaluation of the program and the participants."

In looking back at the pilot program, Campbell emphasizes the importance of communication and coordination. "When you have so many different entities and individuals involved in the training process, there is a strong need for an overall coordinator to make sure things happen. The various divisions within the company need one place where they can go for information and help, and so does the community college. If industry and education are to successfully cooperate on something like this, it's important that the college has that contact point," states Campbell.

Konecny concludes that the program demonstrated its cost-effectiveness "very quickly." Though a detailed cost-benefit analysis was conducted, "cost was never a major issue for us," she notes. "The cost of retraining each student—approximately $2,200—is less than each individual's salary for two months. In our view, having employees sit idle in jobs is a much greater cost to the company."

References

Crosby, Philip B. *Quality Is Free: The Art of Making Quality Free.* New York: McGraw-Hill, 1979.

Gutchess, J. F. *Employment Security in Action: Strategies That Work.* Pergamon Press/Work in America Institute Series. Elmsford, N.Y.: Pergamon Press, 1984.

Scalpone, R. W. "The Effects of Stimulus Complexity, Arousal, and Frequency of Stimulus Exposure upon Attitude Change." Unpublished doctoral dissertation, Claremont Graduate School, 1974.

Scalpone, R. W. "Education Process Is Vital to Realization of CIM Benefits, Handling of Pitfalls." *Industrial Engineering,* Oct. 1984, *15,* 110–116.

Thompson, H., and Scalpone, R. W. "Managing the Human Resource in the Factory of the Future." *Human Systems Management,* 1985, *5,* 221–230.

Strassman, P. A. *Information Payoff: The Transformation of Work in the Electronic Age.* New York: Free Press, 1985.

Weinstein, H. "White Collar Retraining: New Options." *Los Angeles Times,* June 21, 1985.

Index